Service Science

Design for Scaling and Transformation

T0324646

Service Science

Design for Scaling and Transformation

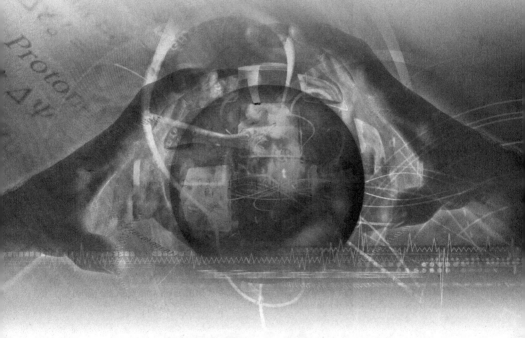

Cheng Hsu

Rensselaer Polytechnic Institute, USA

 **World Scientific**

NEW JERSEY · LONDON · SINGAPORE · BEIJING · SHANGHAI · HONG KONG · TAIPEI · CHENNAI

Published by

World Scientific Publishing Co. Pte. Ltd.

5 Toh Tuck Link, Singapore 596224

USA office: 27 Warren Street, Suite 401-402, Hackensack, NJ 07601

UK office: 57 Shelton Street, Covent Garden, London WC2H 9HE

British Library Cataloguing-in-Publication Data
A catalogue record for this book is available from the British Library.

ISBN-13 978-981-283-676-2
ISBN-10 981-283-676-4

Typeset by Stallion Press
Email: enquiries@stallionpress.com

Printed in Singapore.

Dedicated to My Family

Preface

My original intent was only to write a different kind of a scientific book about service: not one about marketing service *per se*, or service operations, or consulting; but one offering an interdisciplinary explanation to why service matters and how we can help. But in the end, writing the book has become a journey of its own. Like an actor getting carried away by his role, I got convinced by my investigation that service matters a whole lot more. I started to try to explain that we are already in a service-led revolution which is not just post-industrial revolution, but also post knowledge economy for further fundamental transformation. I put the explanation in a new *theory of service scaling and transformation: digital connections scaling* (*DCS*). This is the book.

In this book, I attempt to ask, and then answer: What is the big story about service? What are the grand research problems in service? What does "a connected world" mean? Does service require a different kind of design science? What will be the next waves of the Web? How to make enterprise information systems adequate for service scaling? How to unite cyberspace with physical space? Is it feasible to massively connect independent information resources everywhere? Is a service-led revolution reality or gimmick? Each question and answer becomes a chapter of the book, which, hopefully, adds to a new service science.

I must admit that the notion of a new service science itself can be controversial (discussed in Chapter 1). However, I am a believer. I base my work largely on the visions of the Cambridge Papers 2008, but with my own particular convictions. I believe the scientific field has major holes awaiting a new service science to bridge them. The situation is not unlike what management science faced in the 1950s and computer science in the 1960s. A counter-example is information technology of the 1990s, which is a would-be field that failed to materialize scientifically. If a new service science is to be realized, it has to be interdisciplinary and integrative, as opposed to merely being multi-disciplinary. It has to possess certain defining properties that not only distinguish the field but more importantly unify past results for new expansions powered by its own new paradigms.

For example, I believe a new population orientation paradigm has arisen in scientific research for the digitally connected world. The emerging networks science and Web science, and their applications in traditional fields such as information systems, are all evidence. Such a paradigm studies directly the population knowledge (laws and probabilities) rather than the inference of them through samples (laboratory prototypes and statistics). It promises to cure the "theory-rich but data-poor" dilemma observed of new service research. The reason for pursuing the population is simple: we are now able to do it. Is it not always the population that matters? The situation is not unlike what astronomy had experienced before the advent of massive continuous observation data from arrays of space-borne probes, radio telescopes, and other large-scale observatories.

In this regard, I am actually a latecomer: someone who has just been converted. I used to rely on none other than laboratory prototyping to prove my concepts throughout my academic career. However, now I see why William W. Cooper and other pioneers insisted on building comprehensive empirical data sets about company practices for economic sciences. Service science may be in even more peculiar need of this population orientation since service is one of a kind *cocreation* between the customer and the provider of value. The provider wants to scale up, down, or transform the customer pools to gain benefits of scale (e.g., marginal cost, productivity, and complementary value propositions) and reduce the learning curve to do "mass customization". The customer wants to scale up, down, or transform the provider pools to gain benefits of scale (e.g., competition, choices, and quality) and reduce transaction costs and cycle times for their life cycle tasks. The society wants to scale up, down, or transform both pools for all persons and organizations to gain benefits of scale (e.g., unity of interests, synergism of resources, and ease of change) and enhance sustainability, advancement, and control. Only the population (of value propositions, systems, resources, as well as persons and organizations) can represent all the pools. Only the population can define and provide sufficient scientific knowledge for such cocreation. And, now *the population can be reached with digital connections scaling*. Indeed, *population-oriented cocreation* is the mantra of this book.

Clearly, I need to be broad in my perspective while striving to be concrete and specific in developing an answer to the questions I raised above. The writing journey has proven to be both challenging and rewarding. I have established a *design* theme for the new theory: the DCS model is substantiated with design methods for macro- to micro-innovation, industrial applications (e.g., smart highways and information supply chains), and a new class of microeconomic production functions to explain the paths of transformation. To help anchor its relevancy, this book has also embarked on analyses of new business designs emerging on the Web since the advent of e-commerce/e-business, and projected the findings onto their next waves. These interdisciplinary results have invoked microeconomics and the science of networks as their conceptual foundations, and encompassed systems planning and design at the level of business strategy, enterprise engineering, and information and database systems. Empirical examples as well as scientific literature are employed to justify the concepts developed.

I wish to share that I was surprised by some of the results from my investigation: Certain visions can be logically inferred for a future knowledge economy (Chapter 1). A cohesive set of "grand research problems" falls into place rather naturally when following an interdisciplinary interpretation of a new service science (Chapter 2). The DCS model seems to suggest a new small world phenomenon if role-based hyper-networks are recognized (Chapter 3). A modelbase may help reduce learning curves for service system designers (Chapter 4).

Next waves of new business designs may arise from synthesizing social networks and business in a pursuit of life cycle tasks integration (Chapter 5). New classes of service cocreation enterprise information systems may be designed from embedding them into societal cyber-infrastructure (Chapter 6). The environment — especially the infrastructure — may be instrumented and unified with cyberspace in a thought model similar to databases (Chapter 7). A market design may help massively distributed independent information resources collaborate for massive value cocreation (Chapter 8). And, finally, a new mode of production based on cocreation may permeate both service and non-service activities characterized by new classes of production functions (Chapter 9).

My work reflects a working definition of what I envision as inter-disciplinary research for a new service science. The first three chapters constitute the basis of the book. The remaining chapters deepen the theory of service scaling and transformation in technical aspects. For readers who are particularly interested in information systems and database theory, Chapters 6 and 8 respectively may be of some imme-diate value since they extend certain proven results in these fields. In a similar way, management science and industrial/systems engineer-ing students may find Chapter 4 immediately relevant; business strat-egy students, Chapter 5; intelligent transportation and global logistics students, Chapter 7; and microeconomics students, Chapter 9. I would be extremely flattered if the readers would care to scrutinize and verify these claims.

As is true for every scientific endeavor, I have benefited tremen-dously from previous results contributed by numerous colleagues in the field. I only have a limited capacity to cite them in this book. On a personal level, I have received indispensable support from many col-leagues, without which my work would be impossible. I wish to rec-ognize foremost Dr. James C. Spohrer, Director of Service Research at IBM Almaden Center. I had intensive discussions with Jim during my investigation for the book, and have benefited from his generous comments. He inspired, in particular, my work on formulating the research problems of Chapter 2, and advised me on the DCS model of Chapter 3. In fact, the phrase: digital connections scaling, is attributable to Jim to whom I owe my sincere gratitude. I am also indebted to Dr. John E. Kelly, III, Senior Vice-President for Research at IBM, for his encouragement of my research on service. Closer to home, I wish to express my deep admiration as well as appreciation of a long-time colleague, Dr. Daniel Berg, Institute Professor at Rensselaer. Dan is one of the pioneering researchers and educators in the field who have been advocating service science long before I came to realize its profound scientific meaning and promises. Dan continues relentlessly to champion the field and to provide inspiration and support to many, including myself. Many other colleagues at Rensselaer and elsewhere have also inspired me, especially Dr. James M. Tien, another long-time colleague who has developed seminal analyses on service systems engineering. Finally, I wish to thank wholeheartedly my colleagues, Drs. Gilbert Babin, Christopher D. Carothers, W. K. Victor Chan, Ananth Krishnamurthy, David M. Levermore, William A. Wallace and Thomas R. Willemain, who have provided invaluable comments on some of my earlier works leading to this book. It has always been an honor to work with them.

Cheng K. Hsu

Contents

Chapter 1

Service, Knowledge Economy, and the Transformation of the Digitally Connected World

What is the big story about service? Of course, the service sector is huge and can make or break a nation's economic competitiveness. Of course, e-commerce and other digital services propel the growth of knowledge-based economies. And of course, the knowledge services of innovation breed new economic activities and enterprises, and spawn further innovation. But, is that all? What is new here — that we do not already know — that requires a new service science? The field of service studies is indeed very old. However, the newness may be the realization that what we already know is just the beginning of an emerging story. The unknown then, is, *how the story will continue to unfold and what will result, all through service.* For example, if computing is being made a service (as the industry says so), then should manufacturing, energy, and agriculture also incorporate the service paradigm as a means to improve and even reinvent themselves? How does service characterize the ongoing transformation of knowledge-based economies? We observe that the scientific nature of the transformation is the pervasive connection of the world through digitization, and the transforming power of scaling through such digital connections. *Service makes digitization, scaling, and transformation happen.* We submit that in the best case of humankind where reason prevails, the story should progress to new genres of service transforming manufacturing, agriculture, energy, healthcare, and all other sectors of the economy, as well as the traditional "service sector". The transformation should have the promises to make the economy more *sustainable* and *equitable*, as well as *efficient* and *advancing*; so a new service-led revolution will result, reminiscent of the industrial revolution. A new science will consolidate results in the field and support the change. This book focuses on a *service scaling and transformation theory* for enterprise *design*, and asks how the big story will continue.

1.1 We Need a New Service Science

Service is a well-defined concept, but service science is not. In fact, the notion that the world needs a new service science could be perplexing. To many, the science of service already exists, in the form of knowledge accumulated over thousands of years from the continuing practices of service activities. The knowledge, in the eyes of the beholder, could refer to the scientific studies of service operations, systems, technologies, enterprises, and industries, in the literature of management (e.g., retailing, marketing, and finance), engineering (especially industrial and systems engineering), and science (mathematics and computing), as the substance of the service science. In this view, service science is an umbrella name for all these results — i.e., a horizontal encompassing of vertical scientific disciplines according to certain common characteristics such as an orientation towards service practices. As such, the service science has a natural-born research paradigm to accompany it — the application-dominated theory building and proof, to meet the requirements of a philosophy of science. This view renders any call for a new service science, based on the sheer size of service alone, to be scientifically ambivalent or even outright frivolous. This argument is well-supported in the field.

In fact, people can also question the value of a new service science from purely perceptive angles. For example, is service progressive? The notion of developed versus developing countries is historically tied to the level of industrialization. In this context, the developing world often equates a huge service sector in its economy to the lacking of industrialization: a sign of backwardness with some class stigma.

In fact, service practices in these two worlds do differ a lot even for the same genre (e.g., in terms of professional identity), not to mention the differences in the types of service industries that each features. Therefore, the dominance of service in GDP (70–80 percent in the US, EU, Japan, and Singapore; 50–70+ percent in most other, populous countries including China, India, Russia, and Brazil) *per se* is not a scientifically precise indicator of an advanced economy, let alone a proof of service being the driver of progress. Advocates of service in the developed world need to work harder to establish their case: Whether service holds the key to global competition and the future progress of humankind; or it just follows the lead of break-throughs elsewhere, such as technology and industrialization? Is service the locomotive of the economy, or the load on the loco-motive? (Read: does service deserve a new science?) In any case, people could suggest that, what can be done on service has already been done, and what will come for the economy may not come from service.

Then, why are many serious people, in the industry and acade-mia alike, urgently calling for a new service science, as evidenced in the Cambridge Paper by a service coalition (Cambridge 2008)? Why has there been a never ending parade of many other compelling calls under various popular banners in recent years, that consis-tently suggest the need for new basic scientific knowledge similar to the call of a new service science? They are unequivocal evidence affirming the existence of major basic gaps in the accumulated body of knowledge. One could recall the popular outcries of the challenges of the productivity paradoxes (e.g., the investment on information technology versus the lack of gains on productivity in the service sector), of the information revolution, and of the digital economy. The tenacious boon of the Web that society continues to enjoy in the aftermath of the bursting of the IT Bubble of the 2000s also offers a strong case. It clearly suggests that the widely perceived change due to the Internet is real, fundamental, and sus-tainable notwithstanding the proclaims that e-business is full of hype. The field has not provided sufficient scientific explanation to account for the discrepancies.

On the technical front, one could mention the emerging Web science (e.g., due to Tim Berbers-Lee) and networks science (e.g., attributable to Duncan Watts) as proof of the need for new scientific knowledge. They intertwine with service systems although they each pursue their own causes. Corroborating this also is the well-known large-scale challenges to the fields of management, engineering, and science which are direct results of new service practices on the Internet and other cyber-infrastructures. For instance, the basic concept of firms, which underlie virtually all management theories and models, is struggling to accommodate the changes. A firm, according to economics, is an (optimal) embodiment of transaction costs for economic activities, and offers definitive divisions, controls, and ownership of resources, production factors, and outcomes. However, an array of significant new activities ranging from social networking to e-business and global supply chains goes beyond the rigid boundaries of firms. The practices of virtual, complementary, and globally extended enterprises have become commonplace of late. They alter the traditional academic landscapes of business strategy, marketing, and organization, to name just a few within management.

Similarly fundamental challenges also abound in engineering, especially industrial and systems engineering. Traditional results in these areas tend to assume some steady states for their solutions; e.g., the production systems and service operations studied will reach a prolonged "normal and stable" regime for a period of days, weeks, months, or even years, during which some generalized solution algorithms and decision rules can apply without constant adaptation. Systems and operations are optimized according to these states. However, new service systems and operations in, e.g., e-commerce and consulting, tend to defy the premise of steady states and feature a whole different set of conditions, since they target individual user needs and real-time usage patterns. These conditions include constantly evolving and even customized parameters (individual client information and demand), real-time and comprehensive engagement of concurrent operations (e.g., massive Web-based ordering and production), and time-delayed or prolonged asynchronous interactions between system elements (e.g., distance learning). The resultant regimes, therefore, have to accommodate perpetually transient states (i.e., there is no steady state to optimize or analyze) and multi-modal real-time data streams (i.e., system inputs are convoluted from distributed online sources). Operations research, statistics, and some other disciplines of engineering have to re-examine some of their founding premises in the face of these new regimes. New robust results are in order.

Science, especially computational science, faces perhaps even more pronounced challenges. The field is increasingly exposed by the lack of theory to design, prove, and predict the performance of complex computing applications. As the complexity continues to explode, many fear the previous theory could implode. For example, concerning applications in natural sciences, how to fuse astronomical amounts of data from numerous sources using vastly differing measures, models, and technologies, to collaborate on the studies of the human being, the earth, and the universe? These studies are, by definition, multi-disciplinary and far exceed any one group's ability to comprehensively investigate them. In the realm of service, how to reliably collaborate amongst proprietary members of virtual global enterprises that involves thousands or perhaps even millions of databases, business processes, and individuals to swap files, retrieve data, and inter-operate algorithms, on demand? A root cause to the computing problems is simply the fact that computer science is built on the basis of single-machine models of the von Neuman machine and Turing machine. Controlling massively distributed computation on the Internet is beyond the charge of these models. In addition to this scaling up problem, service is utterly personal and hence requires scaling down, too. This personal dimension can tease technology and make researchers' eyes twinkle: just consider the enormity of the reward, and challenge, of really personalizing Internet search engines account for the user's context and perform with pinpoint accuracy. This example articulates simply that service requires personable intelligence to cocreate value.

All these technical challenges are not limited to service applications, nor caused exclusively by service. However, the innovations in service, foremost among them being Internet-based enterprises, have singularly heightened the issues and constantly been pushing the envelope. It is these new economic activities that have brought to the fore virtual firms, real-time and transient regimes, and large-scale collaborative computing. On balance, they all reflect the scientific challenges of the changes in knowledge-based economies, and hence resonate on the same need for a new service science. Therefore, a reasonable argument seems to be that the "traditional service science" is not sufficient for the new, knowledge-based practices of service. It follows that a new service science will address these new basic results; and an accurate approach to developing it is to focus expressly on the *common scientific characteristics of new service practices*. With this, the remaining question is the value of (new) service.

The answer starts with our experience in our Web-centric society. Given the support of the Internet in our lives, one has to wonder, is it not true that knowledge-based economies are based on (new genres of) service and led by innovations in service? Is it not true, then, that the value of a new service science is its pivotal contributions to the understanding and promotion of service's leading role for a knowledge-based economy?

To contemplate further, we recognize that service is not necessarily a homogeneous concept. The perplexity of service may be rooted in its double nature: *There is service; and there is digitally connected service*. Service may include many pre-industrial revolutionary activities, such as hair-cutting, cooking, and theatric performance. Digitally connected services, on the other hand, as exemplified by social networking, e-business, and digitization of systems, are definitely post-industrial revolutionary. If an economy is dominated by service, then the society may either be enjoying the leisure created by mature industrialization, as in the First World; or, be lagging behind industrialization as in the Third World. However, if an economy is dominated by digitally connected services, then the society is unequivocally signaling its transformation of industry, agriculture, energy, healthcare, education, government, defense, and all other sectors, as well as service *per se*, into a new, knowledge-based mode of production for a better future. Digitally connected services are philosophically a class of service, but this class is new and progressive, worthy of a new science to guide its transforming power toward sustainably prosperous knowledge-based new economies. The new service science will explain the transformation and growth where the linear extrapolation of the previous knowledge for service does not.

A small part of the overall effort by the field towards such a new service science is reported in this book: the *theory of service scaling and transformation*. We provide an overview of its basic concepts in the next section.

1.2 Service Scaling and Transformation: A Conceptual Overview

The book is about service scaling and transformation. It originated from the author's intellectual curiosity in a scholarly commotion: An industry-academia coalition led by IBM started an initiative of promoting a new service science in around 2005 (see the IBM Service Science, Management, and Engineering [SSME] Conference 2006 — Murphy *et al.*, 2006; where the call now includes design [SSMED]). A number of scholarly conferences, special issues of academic archival journals, and individual scholarly papers have since responded to the call to address the gaps in scientific knowledge about service research and innovation (e.g., Anderson *et al.*, 2006; Bitner and Brown, 2006; Cherbakov *et al.*, 2005; Chesbrough and Spohrer, 2006; Davenport, 2005; Dietrich and Harrison, 2006; Gautschi and Ravichandran, 2006; Hsu, 2007a; Hsu and Spohrere, 2008; Lovelock, 2007; Lusch and Vargo, 2006; Maglio *et al.*, 2006; and Tien and Berg, 2006; Spohrer and Riecken, 2006; Spohrer *et al.*, 2008; Spohrer and Maglio, 2008; and Zhao *et al.*, 2008). The recent Cambridge Papers (2008) represents an effort by some members of the coalition to provide a common reference point for the emerging field. We adopt the basic definitions of service provided there. Specifically, *service* is defined as the *cocreation* of value between *service systems* (customers, providers, etc.), and *service systems resources* (the dynamic configurations of people, technology, organizations, and shared information) connected internally and externally by *value propositions*.

As such, *service innovation is realized in the design of service systems to implement new value propositions.*

A fundamental question remains in these documents: What is the definitive intellectual nature of today's service — who cares and why care? The answer will directly determine, scientifically, why the previous results can or cannot sufficiently address the need of service science, and prescribe how to prove it. It may be that a service science is mainly an integration, synthesis, and formalization of the accumulated results in the service-related fields to date. Or, it may also be that the new science is a distinct new discipline that requires a new fundamental scientific field characterized by new research paradigms and education programs to advance its knowledge. Both views enjoy significant support in the coalition.

A moderate view, which avoids an outright judgment of the dichotomy, is provided in Hsu and Spohrer (2008) as follows: When practitioners are calling for a new science to guide their efforts to systematically innovate and improve service quality and productivity, they see existing academic disciplines as knowledge silos, each with something important to contribute, but nonetheless with only a piece of the puzzle. The most successful sciences (physics, chemistry, and biology) all provide models at the appropriate level of abstraction to deal with the phenomena (entities, interactions, and outcomes) relevant to their emergent layer of the complex systems that exist in the world. Economics and anthropology come closest. However, judgment of value from a customer-perspective involves psychology and marketing. Measurement of value from a provider-perspective involves computer science, management of information systems, industrial and systems engineering, operations disciplines, and more. The new service science is envisioned to integrate these knowledge silos and fill in gaps with new basic results.

This book goes one step further from the above view to attempt formulating a continuum of knowledge for a new service science (*the pyramid view* — see Chapter 2). We start our contemplation on the intellectual nature of service with some empirical, and pragmatic questions: Why do practitioners need a new service science? Where have the previous results come short? What is the economic mission of the new science?

We submit that a fundamental limitation of the previous scientific knowledge of service is its failure to explain *how service scales up, down, and transforms; and how this scaling yields benefits (economies of scale) to persons, organizations, and society.* In contrast, scaling of manufacturing is a well-established science. For example, the field of engineering provides standardization of parts, rationalization of processes, and optimization of systems to scale the production. The field of management develops strategies, organizations, and resources to guide the scaling of production. Economics explains the institutions required of the scaling. All these results have made economies of scale of manufacturing common knowledge in the field. In manufacturing, why auto makers and steel mills must strive to become global conglomerates to gain sustained and dominating competitive edge is considered self-evident. However, this is not the case with service. For service, there is little proven knowledge for similar standardization, rationalization, and optimization of resources, processes, and systems that involve, in particular, knowledge workers. Since the ensuing chapters will elaborate on this basic observation with specific topics ofss service science, we provide here only an overview about service scaling and transformation.

Scaling was first made a science by the industrial revolution. The story of the industrial revolution is the story of establishing an investment roadmap for solving the scaling problem for manufactured products, factory supply, and wholesale and retail distribution. Improving quality and productivity through standardization, specialization, and economies of scale have continued to this day, and have resulted in increased material wealth in a growing number of regions of the world. This product-dominant mode of production continues to dominate manufacturing and is manifested in such modern manufacturing techniques as computer-aided design, computer-aided manufacturing, computer-aided process planning, computer-integrated manufacturing, concurrent engineering, product data management, and product life cycle management. While craft production still exists, there is little doubt that scaling the production of any physical product is largely a solved problem.

Service, on the other hand, presents some more fundamental challenges when it comes to scaling. A root cause is the simple fact that cocreation is ultimately one of a kind; and hence service, by its very definition, is philosophically inconsistent with the model of manufacturing scaling. On the customer side, each customer is complex and unique, and service activities that aim to transform the customer (education, healthcare, business outsourcing) start with each of their own initial conditions and settings (or, a unique "as is" state of the world). On the provider side, each employee is complex and unique, and service activities that require an ongoing transformation of the knowledge and expertise state of an employee (professors keeping up with advances in the field, doctors keeping up with latest techniques, business consultants keeping up with the latest technology advances) start with each unique "as is" state of the world, too. Simply put, there are no standard sets of knowledge, knowledge worker, and knowledge process to develop standard bills of materials for knowledge cocreation. The productivity of 10 knowledge workers working together cannot be definitively proven as being superior to them working individually. Adding one more knowledge worker cannot be definitively predicted to yield lower average productivity, either.

Of course, in spite of the complexity and unique challenges, many service operations (geographically distributed franchises in retail, banking, travel, entertainment, etc.; on-line services, etc.) have indeed used standardization, specialization, and economies of scale to their advantage. To a large extent, this rather direct application of proven principles from the manufacturing-originated science of scaling constitutes much of the traditional service science about service operations. Nevertheless, more and more new service operations are falling outside of the earlier conventional boundaries. In general, the more complex and innovative the service systems are, the more challenging the cocreation of value between provider and customer will become, as shown in consulting and Internet-based enterprises. For providers, the challenge of scaling profits along with revenue (i.e., diminishing the marginal cost of scaling) is largely an unsolved problem, as compared to manufacturing. The propensity in the industry is towards its inability to enjoy any economies of scale.

A convincing illustration may come from none other than the originator of the present call for a new science of service, IBM. The company, which has been evolving from being primarily a manufacturer of computers and information technology (IT) to becoming a provider of IT and business services that exemplifies the globally integrated enterprise (Palmisano, 2006), helped the formation of computer science in the 1960s and promoted a manufacturing science in the 1980s. The new call reflects, without a doubt, on its own needs to resolve its productivity problems, open new markets, and advance the field that determines its fate. What concerns does IBM have?

One could ask what advantages does a company of 100,000 knowledge workers have over a collection of 10,000 companies with 10 knowledge workers each? The former has fixed configurations (the organization) to minimize its organizational transaction costs and accumulate resources and knowledge. However, the latter may arguably be more agile as well as being lean and mean when it comes to forming flexible task-based *virtual configurations*. Obviously, the critical success factors for large companies include how they can *share and reuse the accumulated resources and knowledge*, in *flexible task configurations*, to *reduce the learning curve* and *increase productivity* (diminish marginal cost). For smaller companies, success hinges on their ability and capacity to *collaborate, on demand*. In fact, the IT and business consulting service industry is highly fragmented with a large number of small players. This situation may be far from having reached an economic equilibrium; instead, it may be fragile and susceptible to rapid changes with a random chance of being tipped in any direction. The deciding factors seem to be which set of critical success factors will be developed faster and better. We submit that these pertain to service scaling and transformation which require new and more profound understanding of the *advantages of scale in cocreation*.

To animate the notion of a science of service scaling and transformation, we may use astronomy as a metaphor. That is, we envision service to be a recursive artificial universe whose basic laws are metaphorically comparable to the natural universe in which we live. As such, the whole (economic) world is a universal service system, and the universe of service devolves all the way to individual persons and resources. We wish to know the physics that pulls the dust particles of service activities into rocks, planets, stars, and galaxies of interrelated, inter-dependent, and yet mutually dispersed service systems and enter-prises, and make them revolving, evolving and expanding in the universal field of gravity of service values. The ***gravitational field of value*** dictates the feasibility and the economies of both the standing operation of the service universe and its continuous evolution with the coalescence reflecting the gains on value — the benefits of scaling. Unfortunately, we do not seem to know a whole lot about the coalescence and the gravitational field to scale service up, down, or transform it to gain unprecedented benefits, let alone the possible dark matter and dark energy in human society that keep people and civilizations apart. All paradoxes about service quality, productivity, and innovation seem to be related to this limitation of knowledge. To provide a technical rendition of the basic concept, in the spirit of the universe, we refer to the ***intellectual nature of service scaling and transformation*** as, succinctly, ***population-oriented cocreation***. Its technical implications are reviewed below.

   Scaling cocreation is the technical problem. If there is no science on the gaining of economies of scale for service cocreation, then there can be no science on the scaling of service, service systems, and service-based economy. That is, the field needs to be able to provide scientific guidance, substantiated with predictable results, on how to improve quality, productivity, and competitiveness ***from scale***, in order for it to provide reliable guidance on how a large service enterprise may com-pete better than any small enterprise; or how a collection of small enterprises may compete better than any large enterprise. We formal-ize the above discussion into this definition: ***population-oriented cocreation seeks scaling cocreation with a scope up to the population of its elements (customers, providers, systems, and resources).***

   Only on this basis can there be any theory, with verifiable confi-dence, to tell how a large service-based economy may continue to perform better than any upcoming economies in the global market. The case of IBM reflects this moral: size and experience may not necessarily give rise to any inherent advantages over smaller but numerous competitors; and while size may not yield productivity, it could be destined to incur prohibiting overheads. To generalize, do the USA, EU, and Japan possess any competitive edge due to the accumulated knowledge vested in their enormously mature service sector versus the emerging economies such as Brazil, Russia, India, and China, despite the lower labor costs that the latter possess? Conversely, how should the upcoming economies chart their courses in global competition and collaboration? How should any knowledge-based economy excel on the expansion of free trade agreements and the transformation towards global sustainability? These questions await a new service science for answers.

This book provides a reference point for the new service science: **Service Scaling and Transformation Theory**.

The theory of service scaling and transformation is concerned with advancing values to persons, organizations, and society through new business designs and service systems by digital connections scaling. Its technical heart is population-oriented cocreation, and its technical basis of scaling to achieve the cocreation is the connection by digital means. A design science accompanies the theory to enable the service systems of population-oriented cocreation.

The design science attempted in this book strives towards a few particular goals: *reducing the learning curve, enabling task-based virtual configurations, and sharing information resources*, all with a population orientation in the context of cocreation. (They are the topics of Chapters 4, 6, and 8 respectively.) These goals are concerned mainly with enterprise level (or microeconomic level) service systems. Macro-level designs have to do with new genres of businesses. (This is the topic of Chapter 5, with a particularization in Chapter 7.) The theory addresses the macro-design topics as new concepts of transformation stemming from population-oriented cocreation. In doing so, the theory employs a basic premise: *The provision and utilization of digital connections scaling for persons, organizations, and society is a fundamental mode of service that builds and grows knowledge-based economies.* These activities constitute digitally connected services and transform economic activities in other sectors to advance knowledge-based economies.

For example, when all information resources in the world (e.g., personal documents and photos, films and TV series, and enterprise databases and real-time environmental data streams) are digitized, then they can be connected; and all industries can be connected through these resources too, as the customers and providers of these resources. These digital connections can be the basis for cocreation of new values for persons, organizations, and society. New industries may emerge and old ones merged.

In a broad sense, the above concepts have general significance beyond the particular service scaling and transformation theory *per se*. Digitization is service, as well as the provision of new values and systems for and by digital connections. In the latter case, traditional economic sectors such as agriculture and energy may be transformed since they may reach out to end users, as well as expand to previously infeasible domains of production, such as home-based agriculture and difficult-to-recover crude oil reserves. From this perspective, *a new service science shall be concerned with the conspicuous knowledge of digitization, connection, and transformation that progresses knowledge-based economies.* With digital connections, the naturally distributed resources, systems, customers, and providers in the economy promise to become accessible, as a whole, to both customers and providers for any value propositions and scientific studies. This wholeness promises to spawn new values, including quality and productivity, in the economy — and hence its growth and even sustainability (through better and greener designs, operations, and consumption made possible by digital connections scaling — as discussed in Section 1.4). It also promises to open up unprecedented studies of the entire application domain of services to gain new population-level knowledge, through comprehensive data streams on all activities. Therefore, *a new paradigm is accompanying the new science, characterized by a population orientation* — the pursuit and sharing of the wholeness in value propositions development and scientific research alike. This is a general observation beyond the theory, *per se*, too.

The new paradigm reaches, studies, and uses the population for knowledge and application. Astronomy, again, provides a metaphorical precedence for service science in this aspect. The field used to be characterized by scientists as *"theory-rich and data-poor"* — i.e., there had been numerous astrophysics models about the universe, but not much observations and measures to either prove or disprove them. It was not until the later part of the 20th century when technology started to support deep space exploration by radio, optical, mechanical, and chemical means to generate observations that astronomy started to show scientific rigor in its results at the level of physics. The progress was also unattainable until the field started to fuse data from all sources, both real-time and archived, to collaboratively study the population — i.e., connections of all modes of data resources pertaining to the universe. Service is also theory-rich, data-poor. The population orientation may open up new possibilities of study.

Formally, we recognize these two concepts from the above discussion as the philosophical core of the new service scaling and transformation theory of the book: *digital connections scaling* and *population orientation*. They substantiate population-oriented cocreation. Chapters 3 and 4 formally define and elaborate on them respectively. They are also significant to our general vision of a new service science beyond the theory *per se*, as Chapter 2 proves in postulating the nature of a new service science. Below, we delineate the theoretical foundations of the design theme of service scaling and transformation from a value perspective i.e., we ask what is the basic value of digital connections scaling; why the value can be designed; and how to design innovation and transformation with digital connections scaling.

1.3 Design Visions: Service-Led Transformation for Advancement, Sustainability, and Equitability

The theory of service scaling and transformation is about design: designing value (innovative value propositions and cocreation) via digital connections scaling. Therefore, we first establish the relationship between digital connections scaling and design. It helps to start by painting a picture for digital connections from the traditional concept of service, especially the notion of cocreation. Digital Connection is a paradigm by which the customer, provider, and supplier resources are configured to realize certain value propositions. The way it is designed and implemented can help classify and characterize the types of service systems that co-create and deliver the service. In the broadest sense, the customer of a service can be a person or an enterprise (service system), and different customers can join forces with each other on demand if the utility that they gain from the service justifies this. The provider of a service can also be a person or an enterprise (service system), and different providers can collaborate on demand as well. Moreover, the service offerings of the providers can be inherently associated or even integrated with manufactured goods at many levels (e.g., leasing a car, the operation/maintenance of a power plant, and the provision of computing services on a platform). Examples of traditional service offerings include person-to-person, location-based services such as hair cutting and gardening; warranties and after-sale services for automobiles and machinery; and services and operation contracts in heavy industry. More recent service industries include consulting, telecommunications, finance, transportation, etc.

The previously mentioned *digitally connected service is now formally defined to be services that employ the digital connections scaling (DCS) model for their own service systems or their customers' service systems.* Digitally connected service can scale more cost-effectively, while traditional services cannot. For example, a physical therapist performs the exercise service in isolation and a fixed grain-size of interaction, but connected knowledge workers could draw information resources of multiple grain-sizes from all over the world to assist the jobs at hand. In a similar way, hairdressing is not scalable, but the promotion and continuing education of hairdressers by distance learning is; personal one-to-one counseling most often has to be synchronous (i.e., both the customer and the provider must be connected at the same instance of time), but an **ASP** (application service provider) of enterprise processes can perform asynchronous processing; and new papers are not personalized, but in-car information services such as On-Star provide person-centered assistance. Therefore, digitally connected services are further characterized with digital sharing of resources, service scalability, asynchronous co-production, and personalized assistance, when compared to traditional services. The basic platform on which the scaling of digital connections is enabled is societal cyber-infrastructure.

Digitally connected service describes many new business designs in knowledge-based economies, as well as many service innovation models that seek to create new value propositions and transform previous service systems. However, scaling service systems with digital connections pose significant challenges in system design and engineering (e.g., the previously discussed large-scale challenges). If the DCS model only exacerbates the problem, then, regardless of the merit of its intuitive logic, digitally connected service can only be a pipe dream or mere fancy talk. Therefore, one needs to address a critical basic question before embracing digitally connected service: Is DCS practical? That is, does DCS promise to contribute to the new service science required, and hence be able to promise to drive new innovation and transformation with new genres of service for knowledge-based economies?

We condense the previous discussion of the scientific challenges into these two basic issues: the unique characteristics of service, such as the one of a kind cocreation of value; and the large-scale nature of digital connections scaling. We might add that the properties of service also include the heightened complexity of it being more difficult to predict demand than in, e.g., manufacturing. However, how much of the problem is logically intractable and how much of it can be facilitated by proper design via DCS? Recall that the large-scale challenges exist in the field with or without the DCS model (e.g., the needs of science and national defense), and the drive to resolve them is already a national priority. Thus, we may consider these challenges as enabling factors for the new digitally connected service, rather than the inherent fallacies of DCS. Ironically, as it turns out, the DCS model, with proper design can actually facilitate the unique problems due to the one of a kind cocreation nature of service.

As stated above, digitally connected service possesses a significant promise amenable to scientific design, viz., it is integrated with physical systems which implement the digital connections. That is, the practice of DCS is based on some (common or sharable) digital environments, such as the societal cyber-infrastructure, which is manageable. Therefore, its productivity is measurable and controllable at least in part by the efficiency and effectiveness of the digital connection systems. In other words, *the DCS approach promises to turn some of the traditional uncertainty in service to certainty, and integrates the mature science of scaling proven in manufacturing and elsewhere into the new service science in a logically consistent way*. This is not the case with previous results on the design of service systems.

It follows that, although value cocreation is one of a kind, and even intangible, the system of cocreation is not. This system focus provides a *design handler* for the otherwise difficult to handle problem. Needless to say, the design science here is consistent with the design science everywhere to the extent for which digital infrastructure accounts. The new service science can now inherit the previous results as well as new results (e.g., due to the new population orientation) for digital connections scaling, and focus new efforts on new service cocreations, such as value propositions for digital connections scaling and new models of digital connected service. Consequently, we expect digital connections scaling to provide an approach to developing a design science for the new service science that the field needs, with digitally connected service becoming a direct beneficiary of the studies.

Many existing efforts of service design, mostly due to proprietary industrial results, show limitations in scope, consistency, or analysis when it comes to service quality and productivity. In general, the service systems design worldview has three important stakeholder perspectives: customer (creation of value for the customer), provider (improvement of productivity for the provider), and authority or societal (renovation of interpersonal interaction for society, where the person is both the customer and the provider, and value is perceived as an aggregate for the whole population). The provider side (industrial models) has received a great deal of attention (such as the component business modeling [CBM] and key performance indicator [KPI] from IBM — see Nayak *et al.*, 2007 and Sanz *et al.*, 2007), which may also include demand chains and hence incorporate some aspects of the customer dimension. Although they are proven to be sound and effective, these leading results still show gaps in designing customer values and tend to come short on cocreation, especially when considering the population orientation. They may also show limits in driving high-level activities to low-level (software) assets, and back up again. With these gaps, the synthesis of these differing levels of development may be left to individual projects. A dual but more significant phenomenon is the limited ability to reuse their accumulated assets and to reduce the learning curve by tapping into past practices.

The combined effect is that these results do not provide detailed roadmaps with predictable performance to guide the improvement of service quality and productivity. Accomplishing such roadmaps requires deeper scientific understanding of the characteristics of service systems and generic design theories, methods, and techniques suitable for them. This observation leads to the population modeling effort reported in Chapter 4, which extends the previous results towards such a design science for reducing the learning curve in service system design. Chapter 6 continues the development and presents a design methodology for cocreation information systems, which enable task-based virtual configuration of service systems. Chapter 8 concludes the development with a particular market design to support population-wide on-demand collaboration of independent information resources. They constitute a new design science using DCS.

Now, we shift to *innovation*, i.e., how digital connections scaling may shed light on the transformation of the old economic activities and the creation of the new. This is the macro-level of innovation concerned with business designs. In contrast, the micro-foci address system designs as discussed above. *Innovation gives design a purpose, and is measurable by value propositions*. From this perspective, the DCS model is also recognized as a basic method of design for innovation to achieve transformation for knowledge-based economies.

We must admit that although the conceptual formulation of the DCS model as presented in the book is new, the practices of (some)

DCS in the field are not. In fact, the raw ideas of digital connection have been behind the transformation of many traditional services of late. For example, e-commerce transforms retailing from relying exclusively on direct personal contact for real-time transactions to opening up to remote, impersonal processing. Even such personal services as health care and education are proven to be amenable to digital connection. The transformation has even made it difficult to distinguish some service offerings from manufacturing. Examples include designer medicine and IC design foundry which cater to individual clients, as well as leasing and contractual operation of generators, aircraft, and other major industrial equipment by the maker for the user (Dausch and Hsu, 2006). These DCS practices have also created whole new genres of economic activities that characterize the so-called new economy which range from industrial exchange (e.g., Glushko *et al.*, 1999) and application service provider (ASP — see Tao, 2001) to business designs for globally integrated enterprises.

Clearly, the transformation has given rise to new types of (extended) firms, production functions, and mode of production for our economy, as a result of these new major economic activities. To enumerate more specifically, the connection of (person) customers and providers has resulted in B2C (retailing), transaction portals, on-demand business (demand chain integration), public exchanges, and digital government. The connection of providers has led to B2B (procurement), consortia, private exchanges, ASP, and supply chain integration. The connection of customers facilitated the connection of persons and thereby opened up the space for peer-to-peer social networking and information resource utilities. These well-known stories are now converging to create even more potent new stories of the synthesis of social networking with e-business, and beyond. Have we seen enough — i.e., is the parade of new business designs nearing its end, or is the march just beginning? What will come next? Is the DCS concept only another superfluous term with empty substance, or does it actually add value in facilitating our deep investigation? Chapter 5 analyzes this topic, and Chapter 7 provides an application in the domain of Smart highways.

To contemplate the unique, substantial value of the DCS concept, we review how it may help the field understand the popular notion of the new economy (referring loosely to all new economic designs in our society due to the Internet) by using the general concepts of connection (e.g., Kauffman, 1993; Carley, 1999; Watts, 2003; and Blass, 2004) and value proposition (e.g., Norman, 2001). Are the changes of the new economy, perhaps reflections of a constant expansion of personal reach to ever new contacts and sources of information, and the expansion of new genres of service and designs of business to utilize that reach? Also, is the reach, perhaps, a direct result of digitization, which makes heterogeneous objects compatible and thereby opens them up for all the unprecedented, large-scale connections of resources, organizations, and persons, both within and across them, at affordable cost and cycle time? Finally, can the density of value propositions in different economic activities perhaps, be explained by their differing propensities to digital connections scaling of individual production factors, processes, organizations, and systems? That is, does the gravitational field of value work on the embodiment of DCS which becomes the enterprises of population-oriented cocreation?

In conclusion, is the DCS model perhaps, capable of serving as a cornerstone to a scientific explanation of the intellectual nature of the new economy? Indeed, we recognize *digital connections scaling as a defining phenomenon* of the new economy, as described above. Since digital connections scaling is knowledge-based and its design knowledge-intensive, we embrace the term *knowledge economy*, first suggested by Robert M. Solow, to be the more descriptive equivalent of the new economy that we use as the context of the service scaling and transformation theory of the book. Chapter 9 justifies the notion with a class of production functions featuring DCS.

On this note, we may add that DCS is a more scientific concept than the popular statement that IT explains the knowledge economy. The DCS model leads to precise and theoretic propositions verifiable by scientific methods. Equally, one may assert that the DCS model is a concrete elaboration of the general statement that it pinpoints why and how IT explains the knowledge economy. The DCS propositions are fundamentally measurable in terms of interactions among customers, providers, and resources. Investigating population-oriented cocreation through them promises to be concrete, and may orchestrate particular new results around a particular theme, e.g., value cocreation. This ability, just like its being the common denominator of many new business designs, is not coincidental: *digitization makes objects connectable and hence connections scalable* (Hsu, 2007b). What can be studied via DCS may not be attainable in traditional research paradigms without it (e.g., the general notion of connection and enterprise).

We now suggest some visions of the theory of service scaling and transformation to illustrate why we care — i.e., to contemplate some value propositions for studying and promoting population-oriented cocreation. They represent some possibilities of DCS in a digitally connected world, focusing on the values of connections of persons and organizations in the society of the knowledge economy. Again, the provision and operation of DCS — or the transformation services — are themselves digitally connected services, as are the services being transformed or created. We discuss them in the next section.

1.4 Future Service: Transformation for the Knowledge Economy by DCS

Service Transformation

Design, as discussed above, is about transformation towards gaining new basic values. A natural path of transformation using DCS is *integration of previously separated (service) industries*, to thereby develop or promote their complementary values to customers and providers. The synergism between computing and entertainment, as shown in the success story of iPod integrating with iTune, is a prime example. This is clearly only the beginning. One will expect the eventual convergence of traditional industries, especially network television, telecommunications, Internet business, news media, and entertainment, *because their resources and systems are concerned with the same objects and subjects, and pertaining to the same life cycle tasks* (e.g., raising a family, employment, and retirement) and needs (e.g., living, education, and socialization) of the customer's whole person. These industries all employ the same Internet and telecommunications infrastructure, and all create and use the same types of texts, photos, videos, films, and all other information resources of the same persons (e.g., customers, providers, and avatars) and organizations for the same (types of) uses in society where the businesses realize themselves. For example, digital connections scaling performed on these resources and systems can bring search engines to bear on movies, news, and homepage contents for the same persons, products, and events; and similarly bring the same into education, shopping, and even production.

The general principles are that these businesses are highly complementary in their value propositions and have already been largely digitized. Therefore, their cocreation systems may be connected: digitization makes the connection of resources and other systems elements feasible, and thereby enables them to share and scale, and reap the benefits of scale and complementary values (services). Following these principles leads to their potential possibilities: These industries will form alliance with utility and other industries related to the same life cycles of persons and organizations that can be readily digitized. In this vision, the household computer and TV are but two different devices connected to the same monitor-set-up-box system receiving content from different providers on the common cyber-infrastructure such as the Internet. Other devices and equipment, ranging from phone and camera to appliances, bathrooms, and utility control boxes, could plug in, too. For example, with a digital electricity meter that can detect the use of particular light fixtures and appliances, and a digital system that controls house electricity usage, the house owner could remotely turn on and off the lighting and appliances via the Internet.

An intriguing aspect of this DCS is *conservation*: the connections may help house owners optimize household operations and save energy, and thereby enhance the sustainability of a way of life. For example, when customers can see the current hourly electricity usage on their appliances, this may shape their behaviors to economize and do certain chores and activities in off-peak demand periods. The awareness of population illuminates the scope and direction of new value propositions; while DCS shows the means. They make the above visions natural, and perhaps, even logically inevitable.

Finally, digital connections may liberate knowledge workers from their dependency on large firms. Combining personal infrastructural support with person-centered institutions such as pensions and home offices can prove to be formidable for empowering professionals. The fact that they can work from home may not be the biggest story; rather, the daunting prospect (for traditional firms) may be that they can work as independent enterprises which franchise with others on demand, with proper DCS support. Many consultants have already been working in this mode except that they do not generally enjoy the promises of collaboration. Further DCS may help. We refer to this possibility *home-based production*, which applies to all other economic sectors, too.

Manufacturing Transformation

A second natural path of transformation is found in *integration of service with manufacturing*, or even the visions of *manufacturing as service* and *manufacturing-based service*. From the perspective of service scaling and transformation, this path arises logically from cocreation: *integrating the utility of product with the making of product by connecting the customer with the provider at the level of the resources* that each possesses and the value that each demands. That is, expand the manufacturing life cycles to the life cycles of the customer's demand chain. The basic ideas are not new in the field: For example, the integrated products and services (IPAS) system at Rolls Royce Jet Engines incorporates their clients' jet engine operation and maintenance systems into their own jet engine production systems on a real-time basis. Similar practices have also been discussed before. They show a powerful new concept: the jet engine-centered view where information integration is conceived around the jet engine's *life cycle tasks*. This concept can be coupled with the notion of building real-time population data for optimal fleet management.

In fact, the *subject-centered view* (jet engines in this case) and the *subject population* are logically complementary; they are just two sides of the same coin for the service scaling and transformation theory.

These ideas can be combined and expanded to cover all aspects of the making and using of the products, from the user's (the demand chain) as well from the maker's (the supply chain) perspective. The integration naturally lends itself to cocreation of values for all. IBM could give away computers in exchange for the business of running and using the computer for the clients. Similarly, GE could lease power generators or sell them at deeply discounted prices in order to get the contract of operating and maintaining the machines through their life spans. Their control of the population data will give them competitive advantages (e.g., best fleet management) that few competitors in the operations service industries can match. Digitization of the control and measures, and all other aspects of the production and operation of the products, makes digital connections scaling on like-products, their users, and their producers possible; while their complementary values and benefits of scale make such scaling desirable.

As is the case of service, home-based production, or e-manufacturing, may prove to be both viable and a preferred mode of production for certain application domains. For example, craft production may be ready for transformation into independent small-scale workshops assisted by DCS. Other domains that feature small lots and self-contained production may be amenable, too. More broadly, *home-based manufacturing* may be a way to accomplish mass customization, as long as DCS can be designed without being hindered by the limits of public cyber-infrastructure (i.e., proprietary control).

Physical Environment Transformation

Digitization can also happen to natural environments — i.e., the *instrumentation of the environment*. Many scientific disciplines have already widely adopted sensors, including both wired and wireless, to monitor seismic movement, animal migration, and human traffic, just to name a few. When one considers satellites, on the one extreme, and radio-capable tags and chips mounted on moving subjects and the earth's surface, on the other, and everything in between in both civilian and military sectors, then one can argue that the world is already being instrumented to a significant degree. The instrumentation generates real-time data streams about the "population" of the subject matter, such as planet earth and the weather. When these real-time data streams are fused with the usual aggregate, archival data customarily stored in enterprise databases, then a more comprehensive informational cyberspace of the population is constructed. In other words, the DCS model along with population orientation can proactively suggest some value propositions for progressive building of an instrumented world. Real-time data streams, enterprises databases, and subjects on the move (e.g., vehicles, cargos, and even persons) are integrated in such a world, which may open new dimensions and frontiers for unprecedented value cocreation.

The problem with the current state of instrumentation lies mainly in the lack of integration among different modes of data, and the lack of comprehensive reach to the whole populations of the application domains, especially in non-military domains. Military applications have proven that comprehensive instrumentation of the subject populations can scale down (zoom-in) to supporting individual foot soldiers as well as scaling up (zoom-out) to a whole theater, including the planning and control of global logistics. However, civilian domains still see largely segregated instrumentation and applications. New fundamental value propositions may help change this situation and the DCS model and population orientation may help develop these value propositions. For example, one can expect *all environment-sensitive industries*, ranging from transportation to energy and agriculture, to benefit from *tapping into a literally digitally connected world* and transforming themselves. The move can propagate to the rest of the economy, too. As stated above, the transformation itself, from its provision to its operation, constitutes some (new) digitally connected service. Chapters 7 and 8 present some results for possible integration of multi-modal data to support the instrumentation envisioned, with Chapter 7 also presenting a particular design of instrumentation for infrastructure to enhance global logistics, highway operations, and tourism.

Energy Industry Transformation

The energy industry offers some compelling examples of digital connections in their core production systems, such as petroleum drilling. A recent presentation by BP (the IBM Almaden Institute 2008) shows that population data (both real-time data streams and enterprise databases) help the control and operation of individual rigs at sea bed petroleum wells so significantly that the technology actually *made some previously un-recoverable petroleum reserves* in North Sea now *recoverable*. One can expect similar stories to arise in exploration, logistics, and refining. However, we must point out that BP' practices, albeit so admirable, is still short of the population premise of service scaling and transformation. That is, the population knowledge that has benefited BP seabed rigs comes mainly from BP itself and the public domain. Notwithstanding BP's noticeable share of the earth's reserve, its scope of operation and exploration may still not be sufficient to give it comprehensive population knowledge. It can benefit BP even more significantly if its knowledge is joined with the private knowledge of other oil companies. By the same argument, all companies can benefit if the public domain knowledge is further expanded by the joint effort of industry, and indeed by the joining of all other industries that can benefit from the same earth population knowledge. Clearly, there is much room on both fronts for improvement of the knowledge.

The same logic extends to alternative energy, as well. One may even expect the population orientation to help in alternative energy even more than in the petroleum industry, since the established knowledge and experience are rarer and more scattered. To generalize, we suggest that service scaling and transformation can be applied to the *core production systems* of energy and some other traditional industries by focusing on *improving knowledge at all levels of real-time planning and control*. One methodology is to seek integration and/or inter-operation of the individual elements of the cocreation systems, including the individual production factors (and information resources) and the customers and providers (and their knowledge workers). On this note, *the population orientation guides the application of the DCS model*. This transformation covers individual grassroots production (e.g., solar panel batteries and windmill farms), fleet management (e.g., fields' coordination), and enterprise strategies (e.g., collaboration). The common value propositions, or goals, of the trans-. formation will continuously be uplifting the production functions of the energy industry.

We wish to point out that the service scaling and transformation theory may be most significant to *home-based energy production*. Household solar panels, thermal sources, and fuel cells are just some well known examples. There is little reason why energy production should not use a distributed regime when the technology allows for distribution, since the sources are by their nature distributed — wind, sunlight, petroleum, natural gas, and thermal. The DCS model, from this perspective, is a distributed, population-oriented regime supporting such a transformation.

Agriculture Transformation

The transformation applies to other sectors of the economy in a similar way, except each may face its own peculiar constraints. Consider agriculture, whose importance to human survival is now in a state of renewed and drastically heightened global awareness. The first level of application of the service scaling and transformation theory is obvious and rather mundane: The DCS model can help build communities for the entire agricultural population in the world, which may lead to formation of digital *grassroots markets* and *support networks* for buying/ selling, distribution, and other agricultural life cycle activities, as well as for the dissemination of agricultural education and cooperation information. This class of application does not push the envelope beyond the common practices of e-business and social networking; and their value may be marginal compared to the already established institutions in the sector.

However, the DCS model may reach farther and open new frontiers, such as increasing the supply of agriculture resources (e.g., "land" and labor) and thereby promoting sustainability, in the face of the rapidly increasing global demand versus limited supply. In particular, the DCS designs may facilitate the promotion of part-time farming based on individual households in the now non-agricultural regions. It may also support new agricultural technology and packaged systems that fit home farming practices, such as *aeroplantics* (above ground or hanging cultivation using LED and other efficient artificial lighting), in a similar way in which it supports utilities, appliances, and entertainment. New genres of distributors and other service providers may rise to the occasion.

Joining all these possibilities together, the above application of the DCS model for farmers *may increase the production of agriculture by expanding to individual households* at the grassroots, to facilitate the practices of *home-based agriculture* using the basement, balcony, and yard. Individual households — the part-time farmers — can become professionally knowledgeable in agriculture by drawing online support from digitally connected markets and communities, just like independent farmers do now. With this massive user base, it may be practical to develop new population resources for both part-time, home-based agriculture and traditional farming. These new, DCS-promoting resources may include real-time agriculture information and support services to improve the efficiency and effectiveness of the agriculture life cycle tasks. The support may expand to include, among other things, collaborative fleet management using collective experience and knowledge, and access to local, regional and world markets with all of them drawing from the pools built with a population orientation. The "agriculture information" may be delivered just like today's weather information on TV, computer, and any other devices which may be digitally connected together.

Home-based agriculture may not appeal much to countries rich in land and other natural resources, especially North America; but it may make good sense to many other parts of the world where agriculture faces crises due to depleting land and labor supply. As the global population continues to explode and urbanization continues to swallow arable lands, a way to facilitate the *coexistence of agriculture and urban living* will definitely contribute to the sustainability of modern civilization as we know it. The DCS model can help, and it may be nothing short of transformation.

Social Networking and Business Design Transformation

The synthesis of social networking and business is a concluding vision that we present here. As we will further discuss in Chapter 5, businesses have already tapped into social networks. Prime examples include the use of blogs to engage customers and manipulate word-of-mouth marketing. More recent practices also witness companies participating in cyber-games (e.g., Second Life), Wikipedia, and the so-called "walled gardens" of popular destination sites (e.g., youtube.com and facebook.com). However, it is some of the new breeds of digital service providers, in particular Google, MicroSoft, and their counterparts, that are promoting some of the most compelling innovative new syntheses. They include embedding transactions into these walled gardens and building passages among them (e.g., acting on the social activities via the embedded e-commerce sites), integrating social networking tools with traditional transactions (e.g., e-calendar triggering cell phone calls), and turning social networking resources into e-business utilities (e.g., personal homepages and files becoming Internet content for application providers) — see detailed discussions in Chapter 5.

These practices are, again, illustrations of the basic principles of service scaling and transformation. However, they are presently confined to primarily marketing applications. By fully exploring these principles, we expect *social networking* to have the promise of *being a part of any businesses' regular business*, concerning not only marketing but also production and customer services. We expect the synthesis to reflect the *integrative support for life cycle tasks and needs of persons, organizations, and society*. In fact, to be most general in scope, we firmly envision the synthesis to lead to three coexisting worldviews of the knowledge economy: *person-centered, organization-centered, and society-centered*. The person-centered view considers the whole of cyberspace as some personal playground and living environment for accomplishing a person's life cycle tasks and needs, complete with all kinds of support and services available in cyberspace tailored to his/her style and requirements. This is to put the person in control at the center of his/her world and in his/her cyberspace. This will be an ultimate model of the current trends of personalization found in e-commerce — more discussion is provided in Chapter 9.

The organization-centered view is similarly construed: putting the organization in control, orienting cyberspace to the organization's life cycle tasks and needs. It represents an ultimate goal for industrial e-business and on-demand business. So does the conception of the society-centered view, which highlights the common good and needs of all persons and organizations for the life cycle tasks of a society. Concerning society, we might mention that social networking is known to promote civil awareness and participation. When it is synthesized with businesses, civil concerns can influence business boardrooms more directly and be put to action more seamlessly because people can put their money where their mouths (or, in this case, their hands) are. *Conservation* is a point in case. The most efficient, most effective, and most immediately available alternative energy is definitely the comprehensive conservation of energy by all: promotion of green products, green life styles, and green public policies. Best yet, it is free. Collaborative grassroots efforts promoting conservation on the Web may inadvertently promote synthesis of social networking and businesses. They will have potential to reach out to the population of persons and organizations and become a society-centered view in action.

The above visions are, of course, just some of the more immediate possibilities that one can derive from the concepts of service scaling and transformation. However, they highlight a common mode of production based on collaboration and cocreation. To generalize this point, we might further observe that the person-centered, organization-centered, and society-centered practices clearly mark a stride to a *more equitable system of production, distribution, and shared governance*. The same physical world of cyberspace realizes itself for individual users and constituencies in virtually infinite number of views (virtual configurations), each catering to different persons, organizations, and society. These views are consistent with the basic proposition of cocreation of value between the customer and the provider, and hence drive the mode to permeate all economic activities. In this sense, the above visions help substantiate the notion of a service-led revolution: Service makes and provides digitization, connections, and scaling to advance and transform the knowledge economy.

The transformation is expected to have a signature property of putting persons, organizations and society in control in their own respective way, characterized by value cocreation. As such, the density of value propositions that determines the allocation of resources may more accurately reflect the needs of persons, organizations, and society — such as sustainability of the world; and the service systems that co-create these values may more fluidly evolve accordingly. The traditional definitions of industries may not accurately describe the economic activities in the new worldviews. Therefore, ultimately, new taxonomies may emerge and a new basic mode of production of cocreation may become pervasive in the knowledge economy. What we call service today may become the general nature of the future economy. We discuss this vision in the concluding chapter of the book, Chapter 9.

To recap the organization of the book: Chapter 2 continues the discussion on a new service science with a postulation of its interdisciplinary nature and some basic research problems. Chapter 3 formulates the DCS model with specific postulates and propositions as the core of the service scaling and transformation theory. The population orientation and a design method attending it are presented in Chapter 4. Chapter 5 analyzes new business designs on the Web as an illustration of the theory and establishes its relevance. Chapter 6 complements the results in Chapter 4 with a particular new design methodology for the development of service cocreation enterprise information systems. Two specific service scaling and transformation designs are shown in chapters 7 and 8 respectively for particular applications. Chapter 7 delineates a conceptual framework for instrumentation of the environment for improving global network flows such as intelligent transportation. Chapter 8, on the other hand, develops a model for accumulating and sharing independent enterprise information resources in an application population, with multiple modal data that include wireless sensor networks and enterprise databases. While the first three chapters form the conceptual foundations of the book, Chapters 4, 6, and 8 constitute a design science for innovative service systems, with Chapter 5 addressing innovative business designs and Chapter 7 a particular substantiation (application). The concluding chapter, Chapter 9, contemplates the opening question of the book: what is the big story about service? It postulates that, based on the results of the previous chapters of the book, the big picture is cocreation. It then formulates a basic microeconomic mode of production, characterized with a class of production functions, to substantiate the notion of a cocreation-based economy. The three worldviews of service scaling and transformation are also substantiated on this basis.

Chapter 2

Defining the Interdisciplinary
Nature of Service Science:
Some Research Problems

What are the grand research problems in service? Many researchers have proposed many different answers to this pivotal question, and each answer shows a particular vision for a new service science. This chapter is another effort at finding the right answer. The discussion here is formal, but still relies on logical reasoning without invoking mathematical formalism. For a start, one must first acknowledge that any comprehensive definition of a new science of service can come only from the collective effort of the field, reflecting all new results and new research paradigms obtained from all aspects of the new age of the service economy. However, we are able to use only a small subset of these results. Therefore, the particular work presented here is not a comprehensive review of the previous efforts, but a partial interpretation of the state of the art in the field. We base our interpretation on the three world views of cocreation: persons, organizations, and society. Therefore, specific objective here is to *formulate a cohesive set of basic research problems that substantiates an interdisciplinary concept of a new service science from three perspectives: value to persons, value to organizations, and value to society.* A "pyramid" thought model describes the interdisciplinary concept to the foundation for the research problems under discussion. A proposal for a national research agenda based on these problems follows the set. In this sense, the chapter provides a reference point for an intermediary step towards a research-based working definition of the new service science. With this work, the book also contributes to studies of the knowledge economy and its competitiveness.

2.1 Towards a Science of Service: An Interdisciplinary Study on the Scaling of Value to Persons, Organizations, and Society

The overarching technical problem is how to define the intellectual nature of a service science? Chapter 1 provides a conceptual framework for a particular view of service science: the theory of service scaling and transformation. This chapter broadens the view to consider a general issue: how to develop a set of basic research problems that helps to characterize a meaningful new service science?

There are, as discussed in Chapter 1, differing views about service science. For the purpose of the book, or from the perspective of service scaling and transformation, we submit that new scientific studies of service may metaphorically feature a general *pyramid-shaped body of knowledge*: The base layers cover traditional disciplines in science, management, and engineering as they apply to service; the middle layers, interdisciplinary investigations for service; and the top layers, new integrated scientific pursuit of service knowledge with new paradigms and new results. In this context, a core set of major research problems may be identified from examining the top layers of the pyramid: the possible gaps between the goals, requirements, and state of the art of service science. These problems may also dictate a *pyramid-shaped service science research paradigm*. Finally, we further submit that the pyramid may embody the three basic world views of service, or the cocreation of value: persons, organizations, and society. Figure 2.1 visualizes the above thought model:

We now review the basic concepts involved. First, the propositions of the book are interpreted according to the pyramid thought model: *Service scaling and transformation is concerned with the scaling of value to persons, organizations, and society through population-oriented cocreation systems that gain economies of scale.* This formulation recaps the essence of the discussion in Chapter 1.

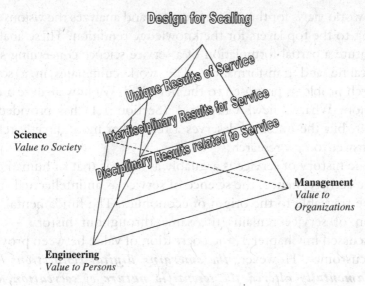

Figure 2.1: The "Pyramid" view of service science.

It recognizes the core value of cocreation for persons (customers and knowledge workers), organizations (customers and providers), and society. It also identifies the technical newness of service in the post-industrial economy for the ability and opportunities to scale service — as illustrated in e-business, globally integrated enterprises, and social networks. It follows that service scaling and transformation is a root factor of national competitiveness in the global knowledge economy, and a root source of intellectual challenges brought upon previous scientific results. From this perspective, the value rendition of the pyramid is transformed into a knowledge rendition exhibiting the scientific results required as well as obtained for the value cocreation envisioned. All layers of the pyramid are connected in a soaring pursuit of design for service scaling and transformation, and the pursuit of new results for population-oriented cocreation signifies the effort which is also a pyramid-shaped new service research.

This is a unique view in the scientific literature related to service. It may help shed new light on service research and contribute to the continuing progress of the field. The rest of the chapter is devoted to the development and justification of the concepts. It establishes three basic world views for the value rendition; and analyzes the visions pertaining to the top layers for the knowledge rendition. These analyses constitute a partial formulation of a service science concerning service scaling and transformation. The work culminates in a set of research problems proposed to the new field. We now analyze a core question: What is new? Chapter 1 (Section 1.1) has provided an answer, but the question deserves a recap that more directly relates the answer to new research.

The history of service is arguably as long as that of human economic activity; hence, the science of service as an intellectual study can be traceable to the origin of economics. The fundamental definition of service remains the same throughout history — i.e., as discussed in Chapter 1, the cocreation of value between provider and customer. However, *the emerging digital connections have fundamentally altered the scientific nature of cocreation, and this alteration demands a new service science.* An analogy is manufacturing: craft production is arguably also as old as human civilization but powered machinery had fundamentally changed it to breed the industrial revolution, and brought about its attendant new science. The new science, including materials, engineering, and manufacturing, resolved, among other things, the problems of scaling to effect better value, quality, and productivity to customers, providers, and society. The comparable service milestone is the advent of information technology (IT), especially the Internet and other digital technologies for connecting society. One might similarly argue that a new service-led revolution, substantiated with a new family of production functions using digital connections, has dawned upon our society. This service-led revolution is popularly represented by the knowledge economy which demands a new science to sustain and grow its continuing progress.

In a technical sense, all the fundamental changes can be reduced to one fact; i.e., virtually all service systems can now use digitization and digital connections. The concept of digital connections scaling then builds on this fact to convert the previous problem of service scaling to the new focus on the scaling up, down, and transformation of digital connections in any configurations of the systems for value cocreation. That is, *the studies are now substantiated by the scaling of digital connections of customers, providers, and resources to execute the cocreation for new, better, and more intensive value propositions.*

The new classes of service have the potential to work on all four dimensions of the cocreation. First, scale the customers throughout the customer demand chains to ultimately reach the entire customer population. Second, scale the providers throughout the provider supply chains to ultimately reach the entire provider population. Third, scale the resources throughout the possible collaboration of individual knowledge workers, data resources, and other production factors along both the demand and the supply chains to ultimately reach the entire population of resources. And fourth, scale value propositions throughout the life cycle tasks of persons and organizations in the economic ecosystem of human society. Needless to say, *the customer population and the provider population are ultimately integrated at the levels of persons, organizations, and society*. In a similar way, *the resources population accompanies the customer and provider populations at the same three levels*. Thus, these four dimensions of scaling are ultimately in synergism: Scaling customers, providers, and resources to achieve unprecedented *values to persons, organizations, and society*.

Therefore, comparing past and present service, *the newness is the (potential) scale of cocreation and the massive new values* that the scale (promise to) creates. Three intellectual elements are invoked in the definition of newness: cocreation, value, and scale. Therefore, the newness is consistent with the core challenge discussed above: how to scale cocreation and value. Again, this is a challenge to previous human knowledge because scaling of service is fundamentally different from scaling of manufacturing, which is not a cocreation of value but a design to expressly optimize the provider-dominated production. *Scaling cocreation is philosophically equivalent to re-orienting the center of gravity of production.* Putting *service scaling at the center of the scientific challenges* provides a perspective to any new service science. It helps, in particular, in the definition of what new studies are required beyond the previous results, and what new research paradigms must attend the new studies.

In culmination, we formulate a basic proposition here for a new service science.

Service Science Proposition 1:

A new science of service required today is an interdisciplinary study on the scaling of cocreation of value to the persons, the organizations, and society.

How significant is this cocreation scaling perspective? It challenges some traditional views. Traditionally, the science of service draws from the whole spectrum of scientific studies as service cuts across virtually all aspects of human society. Some disciplines are usually recognized as major contributors of these studies, including economic, social, and management sciences; industrial and systems engineering; and computing and biological sciences. Thus, they are usually considered as foundations for the understanding of service, and their research paradigms accepted as the pillars of the research methods applied to service. This traditional view is multidisciplinary in nature since it does not insist on the technical requirements of cocreation in these fields to discriminate their results. Although the multidisciplinary view is still valid for what it explains and can serve as a basis for the formulation of a new service science, additional knowledge that expressly addresses the challenges of cocreation scaling must be included. This new knowledge uniquely pertaining to the new science has to come from endeavors whose scope and research methods reach beyond the traditional concerns of these disciplines to address cocreation scaling — i.e., they must be from the intersection, integration, and extensions of these disciplines. In this sense, cocreation scaling helps define the middle and top levels of the pyramid thought model for a new service science.

The visions discussed in the last section of Chapter 1 may be reduced to some new unique design problems, whose solutions can be enabled by some common set of new scientific knowledge concerning population-oriented cocreation (customer, provider, resources, and value propositions). This perspective can also help formulate the previously discussed large-scale challenges in management, computer science, and engineering (see Chapter 1) with the unique characteristics of service scaling and transformation, which may in turn reveal unique new solution approaches and research methods to these problems. A common set of concepts, characteristics, and methods for these endeavors, along with the results they achieve, even just pertaining to population-oriented cocreation, will help establish the statement that a new service science uniquely improves the state of the art of service.

For example, social networks and global supply chains are two seemingly orthogonal application domains. They may pursue their own scaling in their respective ways. Each cuts cross multiple disciplines: engineering for digitization of the enterprises; science for connection of persons, organizations, and other resources and elements for service systems; and management for business designs for scaling. The scope of scaling in each case is potentially as large as the populations of the elements, and their system designs require new exogenous variables that the customer controls (e.g., browser side computing and user customization), as well as traditional decision variables controlled by the provider. These problems may be studied case by case in their own application domains. Alternatively, they may be recognized as instances of digitally connected service that subscribe to the same scientific principles and may benefit from the same scientific results. Research may be joined in pursuit of population-oriented cocreation, e.g., the methods of new cocreation information systems. The latter approach clearly promises to inspire more scientific insight and more accumulation and sharing of results.

It seems to be self-evident that interdisciplinary, rather than multidisciplinary, describes more accurately the unique studies of service scaling and transformation. Recognizing and formulating the common intellectual properties of particular service domains to guide the intersection, integration, and extension of disciplinary research will be more advantageous than custom-combining generic disciplinary results for individual service applications. Custom-combining can yield many DCS cases, each with its likely repetitive effort, but will not yield a general knowledge of the DCS model for all these applications.

The population orientation is another case in point. Research groups and enterprises can rely on sampling which will miss the promises of real-time data streams; or opt to build their own databases which, by definition, can only capture some subset of the whole space. One will expect these individual groups and enterprises to collaborate and learn from pursuing the whole population when "observing the whole space" is made technically feasible in cyberspace, since the promises of new knowledge about the population will clearly motivate them to do so. These promises are not lost on the scientific research community. New scientific research initiatives are being promoted, as evidenced in the new National Science Foundation Cyber-Enabled Discovery and Innovation Program in the USA, which is a multi-year, multi-million-dollar initiative calling for new (massive) collaborative research with new research paradigms using cyberspace technologies.

While all studies and paradigms of traditional disciplines can be applied to the new science, we focus in this book on the new inter-disciplinary pursuits that we believe the new science uniquely requires — i.e., the two new levels of results added to the base of the traditional disciplines illustrated in Figure 2.1. Again, the knowledge rendition of the pyramid is research-oriented: The first new level, in the middle of the pyramid, represents interdisciplinary studies for service; and the second, on the top of the pyramid, indicates unique, signature research and research paradigms stemming expressly from the service science. The pyramid soars to the *design* (or, applied) orientation of the new service science: the improvement by service scaling and transformation of the knowledge economy. Research pertaining to population-oriented cocreation may require the third level interdisciplinary investigation.

We now elaborate on the value rendition, or cocreation rendition, of the pyramid towards a formal, albeit partial, definition of a new service science. *Value* has three basic measures concerning service scaling and transformation: value to customer, value to provider, and value to society via service. The first two measures are derived directly from the cocreation of service; while the third recognizes the fact that both *customers and providers are ultimately connected and measured at the level of persons* (e.g., end users, stakeholders, and employees) who collectively constitute an ecosystem that we call society. Furthermore, both customers and providers comprise two basic types: person and organization; and customers and providers of the same type ultimately share common types of value. For example, an organization customer acquires services from a provider to enhance its ability (e.g., profitability) to provide services and/or products to its own customers. This value is no different from the value to an organization provider of the service. The logic is recursive on a demand chain. The same analysis applies to a supply chain, too. Both chains are ultimately reduced to persons, i.e., the end customers of a demand chain and the knowledge workers and other classes of labor as resources (production factors) of a supply chain.

Therefore, one may redefine the first two measures, value to customer and value to provider, as the value to person and the value to organization. As such, all three measures become three progressively aggregating levels of the societal value chain: *value to person, organization, and society*. Value drives service, and hence design orients service towards improving value. In addition, *cocreation* is a connection — a partnership — of the customer and the provider in the delivery of service. The concept of cocreation allows for the custom-making of a (designer) product as a service. A *service system* is also a connection — a configuration — of service *resources*, including people, technology, organization, and shared information, for the cocreation of value. A service system can be as small as a single barber shop, or as large as society. Therefore, *design* is concerned with the connection for cocreation: connecting value propositions as well as service systems and resources. Design for DCS uses digital means and the population orientation. The pyramid represents the progressive investigation of the basic problems about value, cocreation, service systems, and resources in a context of digitally connected service (as defined in Chapter 1). In this value rendition of the pyramid, design represents a new class of basic signature research for the new service science to gain new basic values to persons, organizations, and society.

The design focus ties the two renditions, value and knowledge, together. Specifically, as an illustration, the design for digitally connected service systems requires massively distributed computing, real-time optimization, and regimes and institutions for extended firms to implement, all of which are large-scale challenges to the traditional fields (as discussed in Chapter 1). The interdisciplinary study of digital connections scaling may stem from the disciplinary research addressing these challenges (the base level), from improved understanding of the gaps in these disciplines due to the interdisciplinary perspectives of the problems (the middle level), and from new knowledge gained from the understanding of the population nature of digital connections scaling (the top level). We now finalize our discussion of the pyramid and lay foundations to the formulation of research problems.

The pyramid thought model has been discussed from the particular perspective of service scaling and transformation. We submit, however, that the above discussion also shows its general relevance to any investigation for a new service science in the digitally connected world. In this general context, the top level of the service science pyramid represents the *inherent* interdisciplinary nature of any new service science. The notion of "inherent" implies some whole new perspectives, such as *how do the new problems of service transcend the previous understanding of interdisciplinary research on service?* This interpretation reflects on a longstanding philosophy of science that expands the boundary of knowledge by fusing and transforming the traditional partitions. A particular fusion and transformation sought is to unify the customer perspective with the provider perspective and thereby, hopefully, redefine many of the traditional disciplines. This philosophy, when generally employed, could lead to the incorporation of (consumer) utility functions into (producer) systems engineering; the studies of personal life cycles, into those of markets; and social institutions, into service systems. A dual version of the incorporation also exists, which could extend the results on customers (e.g., demand) in all traditional disciplines by including the results on providers (e.g., complementary products) into them.

To an extent, the unification mentioned above is already happening empirically, if not theoretically yet. Basically, much of the cocreation of value in actuality is realized through the use of common societal cyber-infrastructure, which makes comprehensive (population) data about the use and users of the cyber-infrastructure available, at least in principle. Both customer and provider perspectives are available from the same physical data as they just represent some particular logical interpretation. The fusion of user blogs into product marketing is a clear example. Therefore, this *unification* is recognized here as a fundamental principle to define the interdisciplinary nature of service; which, if proven, will naturally lead to new significant research contributing to a new discipline. The DCS model also has implications on research methods. It could join traditional disciplinary methods to enhance the formation, operation, and observation of various populations of users, providers, resources, and service systems. This prospect leads to a second principle proposed here: *population orientation* as a basic paradigm of any new service science for both its research and application.

There are other perspectives that can be applied to the new service science, of course. In general, regardless of the particular perspective employed, we expect the new service science to manifest itself in an integration of disciplinary and interdisciplinary results motivated by and pertaining to service. They are expected to exhibit unique characteristics of service due to cocreation and its scaling. We expect the new science to result in seminal principles, methods, techniques, and paradigms that amount to a distinct discipline. Ultimately, the interdisciplinary study may lead to some profound quest for knowledge on human society beyond service *per se*. For example, the "invisible hand" of market economies may become visible as digital connections record and track potentially all information about all economical activities. In a similar way, cyberspace may truly become a second living space that interacts with our traditional life sphere. How will digital connections scaling shape the institutions of the global village that they create? Can digitally connected services merge with manufacturing and thereby change the patterns of consumption? Can they facilitate the sustainability of an economy? As long as digital connections exist in the world, as shown by the Internet, these issues are relevant to any new service science.

In this general sense, the pyramid thought model is employed here to help formulate a set of research problems for a new service science. From the outset, the new service science envisioned is an applied science. Fundamentally speaking, natural sciences are concerned with *discovery*, and the basic method of research employed is generalization of data points (experiments and observations) into principles. Engineering, on the other hand, is *design* in nature, and hence the research method is reduction of general principles into particular practices (laboratories and prototypes). Encompassing both are economic sciences, (including management), which deduce principles from empirical data of the collective practices of economic activities. Similar to engineering, economics is concerned with artificial systems (macro-policies and micro-institutions); but dissimilar to engineering, its research method focuses more on discovery about the populations of these artificial systems than on verifiable particular system designs — and hence exhibiting the properties of natural sciences. Following this philosophy of science, we arrive at a general interpretation of service science.

The General Intellectual Characterization of Service Science

The intellectual properties of service are a direct encompassing of science, engineering, and economics that predicates on the deliberate design of engineering for service cocreation systems, and the scientific discovery of the knowledge of (artificial) populations for value propositions. Therefore, the basic research method features both discovery from empirical practices of the population of service and design of particular solutions for service systems.

The above characterization attempts to serve the need of a general service science, not just for defining the theory of the book. Three other general propositions (i.e., Service Science Postulates 1, 2, and 3) are also provided in this chapter and the next two, for the same purpose. Not surprisingly, however, the theory of service scaling and transformation is a particularization of this general definition.

The Intellectual Characterization of Service Scaling and Transformation

The theory of service scaling and transformation of Chapter 1 adds a clause to the above general definition: with an overarching pursuit of design for scaling of value using population-oriented cocreation.

Taking digital connections scaling for a case in point, it combines engineering (digitization), science (connection), and management (scaling). It differs from other possible encompassing mainly in its devotion to the pursuit of population-oriented cocreation, which, in turn, is characterized by a particular design science.

We use the general characterization of service science to formulate the research problems in the next section.

2.2 Some Core Research Problems: Value to Person, Organization, and Society

The pyramid thought model, with its dual renditions, leads to the recognition of some basic research problems. They promote more of a view of new interdisciplinary research than of extending traditional disciplines. The general view aims directly at the needs and challenges of new services in the new global knowledge economy.

2.2.1 *Value to Persons: Innovation of Value Propositions*

1. How to develop new genres of services to promote value to persons?

We submit that value to persons is value to a person's life. Therefore, to scale value to persons is to scale the value propositions that facilitate the needs and tasks of a person throughout his/her entire life cycle, and connect them with those of other persons to gain economies of scale. That is, develop value propositions for a person, and then create additional ones made possible by his/her connection with others. Tasks have their own life cycles. Hence, the argument applies to tasks, too. For example, a person's life cycle includes a stage of raising a family, with a major milestone in raising the first baby. This milestone is also a major task that entails a life cycle (interconnected relationships) of numerous particular sub-tasks. A **B2C** (business to customer) service on selling baby foods may serve one of these tasks, but there are many other B2C services also pertaining to raising a baby in the life cycle. They range from medical and baby care all the way to clothing, appliances, and toys. The connection of these providers creates new value for the person (e.g., the integration could reduce the cycle time and transaction cost), and the connection of such persons creates the scale to enable the connection of providers. The connection of persons also leads to social networks for like-minded persons to support one other and address their emotional needs as well as share information on the tasks and the providers. In a similar way, providers may proactively promote these connections to further their practices of value cocreation (see the next section).

This is scaling of value through scaling of customers, providers, cocreation, offerings/product lines, and resources. Raising babies is but one of the potentially unlimited tasks of a person's life cycle, and the life cycle of a task itself is also but one aspect of the potentially unlimited possibilities of connection. The same analysis applies to knowledge workers performing tasks pertaining to their job life cycles. Scaling for knowledge workers may result in new value propositions that facilitate their collaboration even to the franchising of new types of business. New genres of services could result for persons playing their particular life cycle roles. These possibilities have profound implications on many disciplines and require concerted research to understand them. The DCS model of Chapter 3 provides a formulation for investigation; however, it is but one possible perspective. It needs proof and further development, and, more importantly, other perspectives need to be investigated. *Understanding of why service can and will scale leads to understanding of how to scale value to persons.* This understanding is fundamental to any effort that help businesses compete and economies advance.

2. Can service and manufacturing (systems) be united to promote value to persons?

One can argue that manufacturing is increasingly moving towards mass customization, as customers get ever more assertive to advocate their individual needs in the marketplace. Examples include designer chips (e.g., IC fabricators) and even designer drugs, and many traditional industries have, as mentioned earlier, adopted service contracts as their new strategic products. The transformation visions of Chapter 1 all point to a direction where *manufacturing has further blurred the line with service.* Clearly, making manufacturing a service — or, adopting the cocreation mode — benefits customers. However, it cannot become reality until it also benefits the manufacturers. How can cocreation become economical to create significant new value to the end users of the demand and supply chains: the persons?

Furthermore, manufacturing may not just adopt the ideal of service. These two worlds may actually unite and intertwine to inflate new spaces of value propositions for persons. It is not inconceivable to envision a versatile infrastructure for distributed manufacturing where individual workers and machines can connect virtually to perform jobs on any scale. With this capability, *manufacturing systems and service systems may overlap on the cyber-infrastructure, and they may both connect to social networks in the cyberspace.* The connection of service and manufacturing naturally opens new possibilities for new expansion of value propositions. The DCS model, again, illustrates a possible perspective to the potential scaling and transformation that may result from combining both. However, deep understanding is needed to assess the feasibility of the combination and the scientific approaches to achieving it. In any case, with or without DCS, the stake promises to be high. Should the scientific community seriously examine the possibilities of this merger and develop new basic results to guide its culmination?

3. How to integrate social networking with service systems?

Social networking reflects on the needs of persons at various stages of their life cycles. The needs are clearly huge: Many social networks have shown astronomical growth almost overnight. In fact, we may say that social networking has taught businesses a lot about business; and the first powerful lesson is to relearn the power of value propositions based on satisfying personal socializing needs. Just consider how seemingly effortlessly many social networks scale and reach the population in their respective subcultures. ***Social networks are digitally connected services***, and their teachings should apply to other businesses, at least other digitally connected services. Businesses are indeed listening. They are participating in social networks with models ranging from advertising and marketing (e.g., visibility in the population and identification of opinion leaders) to business research and experiments (e.g., gathering comprehensive data about alternative business practices). They are also incorporating social networking techniques into their business, especially the use of blogs. Besides, businesses have always been buying social network sites to build their customer base. However, traditional businesses and social networks still largely operate on two parallel universes; even their paradigms and designs do not seem to intersect.

For example, the business models of social networks, such as Wikipedia, are fundamentally new to the business world — they do not yield direct profit from their offerings. Can these parallel universes be unified and fused, comprehensively, to promote even larger welfare to persons? One could think of the transaction aspects of social networks and their collective bargaining power as possible gateways to the merger. But, are there some fundamental similarity and logic that warrant or even guide and promote the merger? We need to understand the models of value behind the provision, innovation, and expansion of social networks to help guide the innovation of value propositions to persons for cocreation. The understanding could replicate the successes of social networks in, at least, the digitally connected services in general.

4. How to realize each person's potential as a service provider?

Every person is a consumer. But every person is also a provider in terms of performing his/her life cycle tasks for others who need them.

Providing care to younger siblings and sharing information with strangers are some humble examples. The only problem is not every person has all the means needed to provide the care and the information in question in an economic setting as, say, an employer or a seller. More generally, *every person plays numerous roles in many different contexts* related to each life cycle task, and each role involves both give and take. Hence, *potentially each role can evolve into being a customer and/or a provider* in the business sense. We might even argue that a person's ability to consume gives him/her the ability to provide, as is the case with an informed tourist who is an expert on tourism and whose knowledge can be provided to others. Even a gangster has valuable knowledge to provide to the public about, say, gangs and their lessons.

At the person level, the line between the customer role and the provider role could be blurred in the business sense, or it could be made compatible at least for cocreation. The expansion of service and value propositions envisioned above may help make the ideal a reality. The result would be a prosperous space of productivity and welfare to all individuals, whose limits are truly just up to the individual. Service scaling and transformation could be fueled by the expansion of person providers, which perhaps can create even more roles and contexts for persons to provide and consume. Is there a science of value propositions that explains and predicts the paths to person providers and the ways to unleash the innovation? How to causally relate the connections of persons and resources to service innovation, and service innovation to person providers?

5. How does value cascade in a demand chain?

The societal value chain starts and ends with persons. However, economic activities tend to focus on the immediate customer-provider relationships rather than the cascading of such relationships in a demand chain to reach the person. Therefore, to scale value to persons, the field needs to understand how value to organization customers in a cocreation relationship ultimately relates to value to persons at the end of the demand chain. This cascading is conceptually comparable to global engineering and/or scheduling of supply chain integration, where the prime company wants to "drill through" its supply chain to "see" and coordinate the engineering and production of all suppliers involved.

Deeper understanding of demand chain integration will ultimately determine the ability of cocreation scaling. It needs to include such results as how to "drill through" a demand chain to relate the value to a company's customers to the value to the customer's customers; how to reduce or aggregate value propositions in a demand chain; and how to assess the propagating effects of value propositions. The understanding will *enable a provider to better assess the total value of its service offerings to a customer*, and also to *"reverse engineer" its value propositions to a customer from the customer's value propositions to persons*. The study of complementary value propositions may lead to a new field on demand chain integration beyond the mere mirror view of supply chains.

6. How to assess a value proposition's economic promises?

Value to persons may be related to economic activities through utility theory and price theory of economics. However, value to persons, as shown in social networking, has a more general nature than utilities that can be priced. To the extent that prices ultimately guide economic activities, value needs a valuation measure compatible to price in order for value propositions to be assessable as cocreation goals. This problem shares some intellectual roots with the well-known problems of measuring intangible benefits of an investment or a new system. The fundamental difference is the scope and scale: the measurement of value to persons is at the level of individuals. For example, what is the value of knowledge to individual customers and knowledge workers? Many disciplines have to be involved, including not just economics and psychology but also life science and man-machine interaction, and much more. The scientific understanding in this area will facilitate *the transformation of value propositions to service system design, the assessment of the performance of service systems, and the connection of value to persons with value to organizations*. Without such understanding, the full value of service may never be appropriately assessed and rewarded; and service systems may face inhibitive ambiguity in its design to achieve required economic performance.

7. What are the growth models for value to persons?

How fast can service scale and transform is a function of how fast can value to persons grow and intensify. The answer promises to determine the advancement of the knowledge economy. The above research problems culminate in a problem of growth models for service (cocreation) to create, improve, and expand value to persons. The growth models should help answer *what is the maximum growth rate of value to persons, both observed and theoretically permitted,* and *how to facilitate the growth?* These models may be comparable to production functions of microeconomics, except that their level of granularity is concerned with persons as opposed to firms and industries. At this level, production functions promise to be directly relevant to the design, construction, and operation of service systems for both persons and companies. That is, economics may be directly connected to management and engineering through the design of value cocreation. On this basis, the growth models may offer an explanation to the patterns of networking discovered in the science of networks, such as the so-called small world phenomenon (discussed in the next chapter). These patterns may in turn offer clues to the growth theories for connection of persons, and help analyze whether a natural limit exists to the growth of value to persons. Unlike natural resources, which obviously have limited supply on planet earth, value propositions could not be bounded **from above**. If so, value cocreation could be freer than product creation and hence face less growth limits. In this sense, the growth models of value to persons may offer new perspective to understand the future of the global knowledge-based economy.

2.2.2 *Value to Organizations: Innovation of Service Systems and Productivity*

1. How to develop new service business designs to promote value to organizations?

The fundamental economic measure of value to organizations is profit. More refined measures also associate value to the stakeholders of an organization, including even the organization's social responsibilities. On this basis, we submit that to scale value to organizations is to scale value propositions on the tasks, functions, and offerings and product lines of an organization throughout its life cycle, and connect them with those of other organizations to gain economies of scale. That is, develop connectible value propositions for an organization, and then create additional ones to explore its connection with others. The basic concept is similar to scaling value to persons. Just like personal tasks, tasks of an organization have their own life cycles, too, which may cut across different knowledge workers, processes, and even organizations. New business designs may arise from the connection of these compatible tasks and life cycles across the boundaries of knowledge workers, processes, and organizations — i.e., the extended enterprise approach. They may also arise from connection of business models using scaling — i.e., the fluid expansion/transition approach.

Supply chain-related business designs, including industrial exchanges and on-demand business, illustrate the first type: Companies first digitized their enterprises and then connected their processes in a cross-sectional manner; they finally scaled up their connections to engage other related companies in the economy. Improvement to quality and productivity were accomplished due to global integration and collaboration; and market efficiency was acquired due to the scale. The growth of amazon.com offers an example of the second, showing not only the scaling on the customers due to digitization and connections, but it also scaled on its offerings and product lines by engaging other suppliers/providers (than publishers *per se*). This way, the company combined the B2C model with marketplace (or, online shopping malls) and some social networks, and thereby broke the limits of single company B2C.

The moral of these practices is that digital connections scaling enables innovative value propositions to companies. More analyses are provided in Chapter 5, including value propositions to a company's regular life cycle tasks such as new marketing based on comprehensive data about customer behavior and new leverages derived from its customer base. To generalize, ***comprehensive studies in this area will yield new basic understanding of why the density of value propositions vary*** *from business to business and how the distribution of the density may be altered and new business designs developed.* Furthermore, the traditional theory of how a firm minimizes the total transaction costs may be re-examined, or at least, expanded to include extended enterprises across the boundaries of firms. Previous engineering results such as **CAD** (computer-aided design), **CAM** (computer-aided manufacturing), **CIM** (computer-integrated manufacturing), concurrent engineering, e-engineering, and product life cycle management may also be expanded for the new designs that integrate tasks along their life cycles. On this note, simultaneous engineering is an example of (product) life cycle tasks integration: from product design to production.

2. How to improve non-service industries with service systems?

Service enriches an economy and enhances a society, but non-service sectors feed, build, and power the civilization. Although these two sides are clearly intertwined, their respective production systems have been kept separate; as service (cocreation) has been applied mainly to the prior, after, and support functions of non-service production, e.g., manufacturing, energy, and agriculture. This separation is not necessary, as some service industries such as consulting have always been a part of the production functions of non-service industries. To begin the research, we ask if traditional industrial service systems (e.g., those related to customer services and marketing) can be integrated directly and comprehensively into the production systems of non-service industries to improve their performance? Can home-based production (see Chapter 1, last section) be a common component of industrial production functions? *To what extent does cocreation apply to physical production systems:* Can knowledge workers of these systems benefit from a production regime where they engage in cocreation either with counterparts elsewhere along the supply chain, or with customers along the demand chain, or with both? *Can service also contribute to expanding the non-service sectors of the economy, and thereby expand itself in turn?*

More specifically, for example, can digital connections scaling help transform the physical production systems of non-service industries to promote value to organizations? Chapter 1 argues that this transformation has already started rolling in manufacturing due to the shift in focus to long-term strategic service contracts and integrating after-sale service (knowledge) into product design and production. Will the line separating service and other non-service industries be similarly blurring as well? At the least, the provision of digital connections scaling to non-service systems can be new genres of value propositions to organizations. The provision service may be provided by vendors or consultants, but may also be provided by a company in the non-service industry which has perfected its own use of the service. In either case, the synergism among service systems at different companies that employ the same models may become significant for further exploitation (e.g., population knowledge for fleet management).

Many non-service industries are subject to what economists call natural monopoly, such as utilities, telecommunications, and infrastructure. However, many others do not. Some of the possibilities mentioned above may at least be relevant to these more competitive and less monolithic industries. Perhaps (customer) service systems can be readily united to the personable non-service systems to promote value to organizations? The ultimate research challenge here is nothing short of exploring a new cocreation mode for non-service industries, and proving their compelling benefits.

3. How to gain economies of scale on knowledge and service systems resources?

How to gain economies of scale on production factors for manufacturing is clear, as it has been made a science since the industrial revolution. However, how to do the same for service is not so clear, as discussed in Chapter 1. A fundamental problem is how to accumulate one of a kind knowledge and experience from one of a kind cocreation and share them with other one of a kind cocreation? The consulting industry is a prime example: how to reduce the learning curve for solution development and/or service system design for clients? Previous results seem to apply mainly to service systems that exhibit some manufacturing properties (e.g., repetitiveness). Otherwise, they may require limiting the scope of cocreation (custom design) to fit their unspoken assumptions of recycling standard designs. The general research problem is a design science for service systems; and its particular elaboration is the scaling of knowledge and other service resources for cocreation: reducing the learning curve, improving the quality and productivity, and promoting new value propositions. We propose some partial results for the new design science in Chapters 4, 6, and 8; however, they serve to illustrate what we envision as being required by population-oriented cocreation. The real effort needed still awaits the field.

There are numerous possible approaches to developing additional results for a new design science of service cocreation systems. The field needs to sort out what works as well as what are fundamentally required. More specifically, ***new engineering and management results are needed to explain what are reusable knowledge and service resources, and how to accumulate and share them, both for the design of service systems and the value to organizations achieved through service system designs.*** Compared to previous results, the design science will address expressly the needs of cocreation scaling, such as population orientation, extended enterprises and collaboration. Ideally, even one of a kind service systems may be reliably constructed from some common building blocks in, perhaps, a CAD manner.

4. Can service scaling facilitate the large-scale challenges in engineering?

How do we resolve the large-scale computing and control problems with service scaling and tranformation? Maybe the scaling design can help simplify the problems? Or, maybe the scaling methods can help resolve the problems? As stated before, scaling service systems may require massively distributed computing that defies the single machine models of computer science (i.e., von Neuman machine and Turing machine). In addition, service cocreation may also require real-time decision-making that defies the steady-state models of control and optimization in industrial and systems engineering. Finally, service systems are extended enterprise in nature due to their cocreation characteristics. Therefore, when pushed to the ideal realm, they defy the single firm foundations of management and microeconomics.

However, can service scaling also help, rather than just causing, these problems? Can they ironically be a part of the solution to the problem they help create? Can they even help resolve the same type of problems that non-service realms also face? The answer should be affirmative if a new service science perfects the arts of comprehensive real-time data analysis and population modeling. That is, the new science may open up some new approaches to responding to these large scale challenges.

A science of large-scale service systems will develop data-driven real-time optimization to improve the efficiency, consistency, and quality of service delivery; and this paradigm may help meet the general large-scale challenges in engineering. A science of large-scale service systems will develop cyber-enabled, population-oriented collaboration to meet the operational requirements of such systems, and this paradigm may help advance large-scale computing, communication, and control. A science of large-scale service systems will develop the pursuit of value to persons and value to organizations through digital connections scaling, and this paradigm may help meet the organizational challenges of extended enterprises in management. In sum, we submit that the pursuit of service scaling and transformation can lead to a focus on *the engineering challenges of service systems scaling,* and *this perspective may help the analysis and the solution of the large-scale challenges in science and management*. The research problem here is developing these new results and meeting these challenges.

5. Can service scaling help predict the density of value propositions in business?

In other words, how does service scaling and transformation determine business and industrial renovation? The notion of a gravitational field of value discussed in Chapter 1 may actually help analyze value to organizations. The thought model compares service scaling and transformation to the gravitational pull of astronomy. Digitized cocreation elements are compared to dust particles: they connect to form ever larger service systems by the pull of (the combined) value propositions, similar to these particles forming rocks and planets by gravity. This thought model suggests that an organization (a service system) is formed not just to minimize the total transaction costs, as the traditional economics explains, but also to maximize the possibility of value propositions. Scaling extends the scope of organizing. Therefore, *service scaling and transformation may be dictated by the invisible laws of a "field of possible value propositions"*. The collection of such practices may reveal such laws and may even manifest the field. This thought model adds to the study of the density and distribution of value propositions on the business landscape. Perhaps there are some laws governing the paths of service scaling and transformation, and, through these paths, help explain the formation and evolution of industries? Perhaps, studying service scaling and transformation practices can help us understand the laws of value propositions and predict the fruitful paths of scaling?

6. How to develop knowledge-embedded cyber-infrastructure for service systems?

The Internet has proven the pivotal role that societal cyber-infrastructure plays in the knowledge economy. This is especially true of service scaling and transformation. What should be the future cyber-infrastructure? The new capabilities of Internet 2, including the enhanced bandwidth and the new accounting capabilities to facilitate sharing, are of course important. However, from the perspective of scaling and cocreation, another dimension of expansion for the future has to be the capabilities that make it easy for service systems to employ, share, and connect with one another through the societal cyber-infrastructure. We refer generally to these new capabilities as knowledge-embedded in the societal cyber-infrastructure. This view asserts that the future cyber-infrastructure will provide such embedded knowledge assistance for organizations to employ and deploy population-oriented cocreation, and to share common resources and pursue economies of scale for them. Needless to say, the future societal cyber-infrastructure will enable persons and the society to develop benefits of scale from their own perspectives, as well.

A new science of cyber-infrastructure will *develop, manage, and process societal cyber-infrastructure, with embedded knowledge assistance, to enable massively scalable digitally connected services, and to make the cyber-infrastructure massively sharable among vastly different concurrent users.* For example, the embedded knowledge will facilitate extended capabilities to allow on-demand connection and disconnection of service systems, virtual administration and security control of cyber-infrastructure. It will also facilitate sharing of accumulated knowledge in cyberspace by concurrent cocreation systems from different industries, including social networking. This research problem complements and extends the national challenge of developing future cyber-infrastructure hardware and technology.

7. What are the growth models for value to organizations?

This problem accompanies the growth models problem with value to persons. It similarly helps determine the possible paths of advancement of the knowledge economy. In this sense, it is also the culmination of the above studies. The growth models for value to organizations could analyze the *maximum growth rates, both theoretical and empirical, to population-oriented cocreation in a particular space, to particular types of value propositions, and even under specific conditions.* They may reveal the patterns of scaling of service systems and the patterns of cause-effect functions. They may be able to guide the planning and development of service systems and value propositions. They may be able to characterize companies and industries with microeconomic production functions. They may help determine new taxonomy for the economy. They may help predict a natural growth limit to digital connections and shed light on inherent security threats, which will limit DCS and the growth of cocreation.

2.2.3 *Value to Society: Innovation of Economic Functions and Institutions*

1. How to develop new service institutions to promote value to society?

Value to society is arguably at least the sum of value to persons and value to organizations. Perhaps, additional value to society can be derived from the synergism of these two types of value at the societal level, minus the conflict. Therefore, additional value to society may be identified as the contributions due, first, to the integration of life cycle tasks and needs among persons; second, to the same integration among organizations; and third, to the cross-synergism between persons and organizations. In this sense, the new genres of value to society will come from the *new genres of institutions that achieve the synergism of the new service scaling and transformation to promote new value to persons and new value to organizations in their respective life cycle tasks and needs.* What are they, and how to achieve the synergism? That is the problem calling for research.

Traditional disciplines of social sciences have accumulated rich results in this domain of research. However, a new service science may help open up new approaches and push the envelope due to its new research possibilities and paradigms. Examples include the possibility of performing "social experiment" in cyberspace (e.g., Second Life) — i.e., DCS may allow life-scale simulation without the hindrances of real life experiment in society. Furthermore, the practices of service scaling are traceable, which can lead to constructing formal cause-effect relationships, such as concerning value propositions. Therefore, business experiments and social experiments may be mutually inclusive. In this regard, business experiments in cyberspace provide a more controllable (motivational) context for scientific analysis than relying on games or other social networking means alone. For example, studying the population of some practices should help reveal whether the institutions empower every person to realize his/her potential to be a service provider; whether individual knowledge workers can form virtual extended organizations at low transaction cost, with sufficient institutional support to franchise on demand; and whether institutions exist to empower cross-industrial collaboration.

2. How to improve national competitiveness by scaling national service systems?

Societal cyber-infrastructure is a national service system. National institutions are also national service systems. The government is the most celebrated national service system. The importance of these national service systems to the national economy is well-known, ranging from positive to negative and indeed all over the map. They are among the most inertial of all service systems, too. Studying government in a context of change is next to being irrational. However, *a new service science may make this almost intractable research problem feasible, by virtue of its new capabilities of "simulating" these systems in the cyberspace of cocreation, in a ubiquitous and non-intrusive way.* That is, comprehensive empirical data of the population of government services represent unprecedented possibilities of study.

These data can come from the practices of service systems by persons and organizations, including social networking, as well as from government. Population modeling will help expose the common roles that these national service systems play, and consolidate implications to guide their development, control, and evolution. With proper modeling, monitoring DCS practices can become a surrogate of real-time monitoring of the national service systems themselves. These unprecedented possibilities of study promise to lead to unprecedented understanding of how to make national service systems better contribute to national well-being and competitiveness.

3. How does cyberspace and physical space interact in economics and society?

Cyberspace and physical space (buildings, bridges, highways, environment, etc.) are being kept largely separated in today's world. They need not be and perhaps should not be, as they are united in a person's life, an organization's life, and society's life. This logical unification can precipitate a physical unification. A first step can be as simple as adding a digital layer to the societal infrastructure and thereby integrate it with the societal cyber-infrastructure. Current examples include the deployment of wireless sensor networks on the environment and an assortment of wireless digital connectors in vehicles. With this expansion, digital connections scaling has the potential of reaching all kinds of economic activities. As such, *the invisible hand of the market will become visible in cyberspace*, on the basis of the traceable activities on the digital connections.

However, it is still unclear how cyberspace will ultimately be integrated with the traditional physical world and affect the overall design and performance of service systems, especially population-oriented cocreation. Is there a major part of the economy that can never be digitally represented and connected, and its separation natural and insurmountable from the rest? If so, then a digital economy may only be an extension of the traditional economy, not a comprehensive transformation. However, to what extent can these two economies multiply each other with the unification of cyberspace and physical space? More fundamentally, how will persons be affected by the expansion? Do humans fundamentally behave differently in cyberspace — i.e., are the cyber-world (a "second life") and the traditional world (the first life) basically parallel and do not integrate, and hence would not benefit from the expansion? The understanding will help determine the scope of service scaling and transformation.

4. How to reconcile global cyberspace with national institutions?

The new service science envisioned is inherently global in nature. The global perspective does not just refer to its scientific nature, but also recognize its premise: service scaling and transformation with a population orientation. The notion of population, as proven in e-commerce/e-business and social networking, is virtual and transcendental to national boundaries. However, the idealism of a global village runs directly into the face of militant nationalism and even the clash of civilizations. On the one hand, Internet games and other similar practices have brought people of different classes, cultures, and nationalities together like never before — a phenomenon corroborating with the ideal that cyberspace facilitates a global village. On the other hand, evidence abounds that exclusive parallel worlds clearly exist and excel in cyberspace along national and cultural identities.

A new service science may help the world understand *to what extent global service scaling can be reconciled with national institutions (interests) and even help reduce the national barriers against global collaboration for the common good.* On this basis, international institutions may be better designed to promote value to the international community through, in particular, globally integrated ente prises, global social networks, and global non-government organizations.

These international institutions may be necessary to best reconcile changes brought about by population-oriented cocreation on national regimes.

5. Is cocreation a fundamental mode of production for the knowledge economy?

If the new service science establishes that cocreation can inflate the space of value propositions and promote value to persons, value to organizations, and value to society, then the significance of service is established. If the science further establishes that scaling value cocreation can unite service with non-service activities, then a positive case is established that service may usher in a new revolution comparable to the industrial revolution. *In this case, we would expect sweeping new regimes of economic activities; what are they?* From the design perspective, we might mention population knowledge: using the information about the economy — i.e., the "visible hand" of the market, to improve the efficiency of the market and hence the performance of the economy. The design will clearly encompass economics, science, and engineering and manifest a pyramid-shaped body of knowledge, as shown in Figure 2.1. New production functions will describe and prescribe the new industries that feature extended enterprises and perhaps digital connections. New **transform** functions and taxonomy of economic activities will emerge as the results of service scaling and transformation. The research questions we ask here are, in the best case, merely a prelude.

6. How to make service sustainable and use service to help economic sustainability?

It can be argued that if service can help improve the performance of non-service activities of an economy, then service can help improve the sustainability of the economy. However, we need to understand how this can be done from the perspective of sustainability. The above research problems may culminate in creating a multiplier role for service in the knowledge economy towards sustainability: *service scales the value without proportionally consuming the destructible resources; reduces the desire for dependency on materials; and facilitates production and utilization of renewable resources.* This is a basic proposition for improving sustainability by service that the field needs to study. We need to develop the exact mechanism and dynamics to realize it.

The basic concept here is that uniting service with manufacturing and other non-service sectors is uniting the utility of a product with the product. This is a simplification of third party transactions, which may lead to reduction of the need for consuming destructible resources. In a similar way, population-oriented cocreation may change social behavior and consumer behaviors towards destructible consumption and production, as discussed in Chapter 1 (the last section). By virtue of inflating the scale of value propositions, such as making every person a service (knowledge) provider, service may enhance the society's capacity of self-conserving and adjusting.

Finally, as discussed before, service may help enable home-based sustainable production of goods and alternative energy. In addition, it may also help promote holistic healthcare and medicine (e.g., information sharing and support network for patients, and population data on medicines and treatment). They, in their own right, all represent significant research problems. To probe further: What determines sustainability of service? How do we assess sustainability of a value proposition? How do we assess sustainability of a service system? How do we incorporate sustainability into the design of service, service systems, and the service-led economic activities? We need to understand both the sustainability of service and how service contributes to sustainability of the economy.

7. What are the growth models of value to society?

Again, growth models will culminate in the research on value to society, which will consolidate growth of value to persons and value to organizations. The models will describe and prescribe the cocreation mode of economic activities for society as a whole. We expect *the models to not just aggregate the growth models for the value to persons and the value to organizations, but also guide their synergism, uniting them as a whole*, such as the facilitating institutions required for society and for the international community. The models may show the density and distributions of the innovations of institution, and predict their future patterns due to service scaling and transformation. They may show how the innovation of institutions impact on social networking, on globally integrated enterprises, and on the unity of service with non-service activities; and vice versa. But most fundamentally, we expect the growth models to relate the advancement of the knowledge economy to the promotion of value to persons, value to organizations, and value to society, through service scaling and transformation. They may help define the field for the next decades.

2.3 A Research Agenda: Population Building, Cyber-Enabled Collaboration, and an Infrastructure of Service Science Laboratories

We reiterate that the cocreation nature of service inevitably makes service ultimately person-centered (e.g., customers and knowledge workers), one of a kind, and interconnected. The interconnection stems from persons who play the roles of customers and knowledge workers, and common resources such as societal cyber-infrastructure. When digital means are employed for the interconnection, digital connections scaling becomes a core for the design of service systems and value propositions. These analyses inescapably lead to the requirement of empirical data: the continuing collection, processing, and analysis of observations from the realizations of service at the levels of persons, organizations, and society. Therefore, the field needs to build a common infrastructure for the study of the new science of service as envisioned. This notion is not fundamentally different from that of "cyber-psychology", "cyber-sociology", and "cyber-economics", where researchers study the (automatically recorded) "digital traces" of human behaviors, activities, and transactions in cyberspace. In fact, service science is supported by the same kind of data, knowledge, and infrastructure available to any cyber-enabled discovery in any cyber-assisted science.

We propose that the field embrace this cyber-assisted paradigm. Population modeling for service system design is but one example. We postulate that service science will be best advanced as astronomy has been: pondering the universe individually but using the collectively accumulated data; because no one person, group, or company can own sufficient data about the universe of service to do significant empirical research in all aspects. This paradigm is visible in the studies of social networking, but large-scale empirical data sets are not easy to come by and definitely require further collaboration.

The general concept of population-oriented design suggests immediately several particular research agendas for the field. We discuss them from a nation's perspective. Since the author is most familiar with the United States, he naturally makes liberal reference to the cases in the USA. These cases should be taken as illustrations of what a national effort can mean, rather than suggestions of imperviousness elsewhere. On the contrary, the author firmly believes that a new service science is universally beneficial to any nation, as service itself is.

Proposal 1: National Knowledge-Assisted Cyber-Infrastructure

An immediate need is to build the platform on which the population reveals and develops itself. That is, the field needs an "instrumentation" of the societal cyber-infrastructure such that service systems can conveniently employ it to promote value to persons, value to organizations, and value to society. The instrumentation should feature embedded knowledge that facilitates digitization, connection, and sharing of service systems using the cyber-infrastructure, as discussed before. The knowledge should cover the whole spectrum of cyber-infrastructure elements: users, processes, data resources, computers, and networks and telecommunications. In the case of the United States, the current national efforts such as the NSF Office for Cyber-Infrastructure should be expanded to investigate the needs of expansion and bring about the new capabilities. This effort could prove to be monumental and require a bootstrapping approach to accumulate the results. It may, however, suit city-states such as Singapore well.

Proposal 2: National Standards for Population Data about Service

To be sure, companies have individually collected astronomical amounts of data covering virtually every aspect of service. However, these data sets are mostly isolated and cannot scale to the population because they lack common standards to facilitate their joining and cross-referencing. Some industries, including IT and e-commerce, have developed significant industrial standards of inter-operation. The field of service science requires similar efforts to develop and promote open standards for adjoining research data and empirical data, and thereby scale them to the population of service. The types of data include raw data, statistics, metadata, and other necessary forms of knowledge such as models. The effort may start with particular industrial spaces which find compelling values in population modeling. Globally integrated enterprises, for instance, may be willing to help build population knowledge in order to reduce the learning curve for the design of their service systems. They may also find benefits in scaling their cocreation along the demand chain by using the population knowledge.

Proposal 3: Service Science Laboratories for Collaborative Research

Many scientific fields feature large-scale research data sets and embrace the paradigms of modeling by data — or data-driven modeling. Population orientation strengthens these paradigms. However, similar to the incentives and disincentives for companies to collaborate in industry, collaboration in academia may not be easy and sharing research data sets may not always be preferable. Deliberate efforts with common goals and benefits will be required. As a starting point, the field may confederate a network of service science laboratories to help promote the benefits and mitigate the disadvantages of collaboration. The network can provide extended creditability and resources for better research, better access to research problems, and, naturally, better funding as incentives to members, while maintaining their independence.

The endeavor may be initiated through large-scale collaborative research programs with combined funding from the industry and the government. The research programs would need to contribute clear deliverables as well as core visions and compelling research problems to the new field. The existing US National Science Foundation programs on Engineering Research Centers and Industry-University Collaborative Research Centers could be a potential vehicle. However, much more would be needed to start such new programs and launch the network.

Proposal 4: New Doctoral Programs for the New Field

A new field needs new doctoral programs to solidify and promote it. Many curricula under the general umbrella of service science, management, and engineering have been developed around the globe. At present, they tend to concentrate on (professional) master level education. It may represent some "low hanging fruits." However, to expand beyond this level, service science curricula eventually require a faculty trained in the new science. Much of the new research discussed above also requires new interdisciplinary doctoral programs to support them. Therefore, we submit that the definitive element of a new service science is new doctoral programs embodying new scientific knowledge from the new service science research. We expect these programs to be interdisciplinary and collaborative, as to reflect on the unique nature of service cocreation. In the metaphor of Figure 2.1, each curriculum would flexibly combine results from all levels of the knowledge pyramid as it sees fit. They would intersect traditional disciplines as they apply to the particular needs of the host universities, and relate them to new service science courses developed from new service science results obtained. As these new courses signify the expansion of the middle level, doctoral dissertations that reflect the new signature research would add to the top level. This body of knowledge will become the intellectual basis for service science education at all degree and certificate levels. The network of service science laboratories may serve as a locomotive for the initial development of new doctoral programs. In the USA, the development may be assisted by available government funding sources such as the GAANN program of the Department of Education and IGERT program of the NSF.

Proposal 5: National Initiative on Service Competitiveness

A nation's economic competitiveness is clearly related to her service sector, at least, because of the sheer size of this sector. However, if our analysis in the book is relevant, then service may actually determine the future competitiveness of any knowledge-based economy. The 100,000 knowledge worker-company example in Chapter 1 makes the case. Generalizing this observation to a nation, a new service science may help an economy advance through the model of the knowledge economy: scaling and gaining economies of scale. The nation that leads in this crucial area may enjoy long-lasting benefits in all aspects that a superior economy can reap. So, either the notion of a new service science is not creditable, or the time to act on it is now. An acid test may be the field's ability to convince the national leadership to significantly invest in the new science. In the case of the US NSF, new investment can take the form of new solicitations, new and expanded programs (e.g., the Service Enterprise Engineering Program of the Civil, Mechanical, and Manufacturing Innovation Division, Directorate of Engineering), and even new and extended multi-year efforts comparable to the cyber-enabled discovery initiative. In the USA, industry should also lead to move the congressional processes to start up a national initiative. Similar efforts may be launched in other countries, too, by their respective institutions.

The efforts proposed above should contribute to strengthening the field and tackling the hard problems facing service science. We present them from the perspective of a new service science. Although they clearly support our particular theory of service scaling and transformation, we submit that their significance is general and independent of whether or not the particular theory is completely correct.

2.4 Outlook of the New Service Science

Why should the government, industry, and, especially, academia care about a new service science? Is the current call for a new service science only a passing fad without scientific substance? Can it amass sufficient funding to sustain a meaningful level of new service research required of its development? We can only assume that the outlook for a new service science must be good if the field truly requires one. However, its success also requires the field to define its intellectual nature and to disseminate its value to the public, as well as to government, industry, and academia. A counter lesson is information technology. The IT field boomed around the turn of this millennium, and many IT curricula and programs were being established around the world. However, the IT field did not sufficiently answer the basic question of what is its unique intellectual nature. The field has not gone far. Now, a new service science is facing many similar questions. The field must answer and answer scientifically.

Another reference point is information systems. The IS field had a stellar beginning around the 1980s and went on to establish itself as a widely accepted discipline in academia. However, researchers are still relying primarily on other disciplines' paradigms to investigate IS problems. The question of what is the unique intellectual nature of IS seems to persistently linger. In fact, one can argue that the vision of IT reflected what IS should have been, or what it has missed. One may further argue that the path from IS to IT, and on to a new service science is a continuum: representing the same basic practical needs and posing the same fundamental intellectual challenges. They may manifest similar successes and failures unless the field learns better. We submit that the succession from IS to IT to service science reflects necessary challenges the previous scientific results: It is not an indication of popular fad, but a persistent hunger for the kind of new scientific knowledge that the knowledge economy needs. The hunger intensifies as the knowledge-based activities explode, and hence the calls elevate in scope. We may label the new knowledge as a new service science, or we may call it anything else. The problem is still the same and the buck has to stop here. Service, as formulated here, captures the spirit of the newness of the knowledge economy: person-centered, population-oriented cocreation of value. Service, as formulated here, sustains, transforms, and advances knowledge-based economies. If the field focuses on the mission and devotes to the scientific pursuit of the required research, then a new service science will succeed.

The public perception about service can be another story. The perception, or to be more precise, the value and "progressiveness" of service perceived in people's minds, has some historical baggage. As discussed in Chapter 1, traditional services tend to be labor-intensive and considered non-worthy of scientific study. In fact, the notion of service may still invoke some lingering class undertone toward service providers (e.g., masters versus servants in many cultures). The glory of the industrial revolution did not help the prejudice, either. Today's developing countries tend to target many service activities for replacement or conversion by technology (e.g., automation and mass production) to make way for non-service sectors, just like the hey day of industrialization. Even though service offers more growth opportunities than manufacturing and other sectors in the post-industrialization world, the previous perception may still stick, stubbornly.

The perception gap also reflects that the technology and knowledge-intensive nature of service has not entered the public psyche yet. The field needs to articulate a big story about why service matters. From the perspective of the book, the big story is of course the promises of service scaling and transformation in a digitally connected world which happens to be a fundamental novelty since the industrial revolution. Public awareness can also determine the outlook of a new service science. The connection between service and digital technologies, and more importantly, the connection between service and a nation's competitiveness in the global economy, needs to be made clear.

Numerous stories can be cited, such as e-commerce/e-business and the transformation of manufacturing towards service contracts. Bold, but still well-founded, interpretation can be suggested to stimulate thinking and debate. The notion of a service-led revolution is a case in point. Perhaps the most intriguing evidence of such a revolution is the totally new, Internet-based service conglomerates, such as Google, Facebook, and Second Life. These well-known stories lead the way to more fundamental realization: For example, how the innovation in social networking leads to the innovation of value propositions and hence the innovation of business designs; and how quickly, and with relative ease, new business designs using digital connections can scale. It follows that the service sector is not just a collection of service activities, but is an embodiment of innovation that promises to grow the global economy. From the perspective of the book, we hope DCS and population orientation can also contribute to substantiating the notion of a new service science for a new public perception.

In any case, a new service science promises to help the knowledge economy innovate. It is an intellectual *and* a practical pursuit. If we are wrong, i.e., if service does not hold the key to the knowledge economy, or even if it does but the knowledge economy is not the future of global competition, then the pursuit of a new service science may not go anywhere. However, if we are right, then the pursuit may be pivotal to all concerned, regardless of the appropriateness of the particular formulation that we propose here.

The next chapter develops a formal model for the concept of digital connections scaling. The model, along with the formulation in this chapter for the new service science envisioned, constitute the core of the service scaling and transformation theory that we present in the book. The rest of the book develops the details of the theory.

Chapter 3

Exploring New Frontiers: The Digital Connections Scaling Model

What does "a connected world" mean? One can take the notion for granted and brush it to the background, as many do when they discuss service science or the knowledge economy. Or, the field can substantiate it and build a science around it. This book embraces the second approach. The first step is to recognize the intellectual core of the service science knowledge pyramid of Chapter 2 and the discussion on *digital connections scaling (DCS)*, Chapter 1. As such, the three cornerstones of the pyramid are substantiated as *digitization (engineering), natural properties of connection (science), and business design of connection (management) — in pursuit of cocreation scaling*. We proceed here to formulate this basic concept in detail (the next chapter formulates the other basic concept: population orientation, which accompanies DCS). We define the DCS model, the DCS effects on value propositions, and the design propositions for growing and distributing value propositions by DCS. The model identifies these basic DCS effects: *accumulation effects, network effects, and ecosystem effects*, which reach beyond the limits of previous understanding in the field. A set of propositions deliberates on how to employ these effects, and in essence constitutes *a generic (conceptual) reference model* for population-oriented cocreation systems. The reference model supports a design science, as developed in the subsequent chapters; but analytically, it provides a basis for understanding the theoretical nature of DCS. The chapter, therefore, also assesses the complexity of DCS to establish its analytical feasibility, and suggests research approaches to studying related issues. New small world phenomenon results are obtained. The DCS model pertains to the top level of integrative interdisciplinary research for a new service science, as proposed in the knowledge pyramid.

3.1 Connection and Digital Connection

The overarching technical problem is how to discover the analytical nature of population-oriented cocreation — i.e., is it analytically meaningful? The problem has a theoretical grounding in connection. Connection is a general concept, and is immensely powerful. Its power is revealed in recent research such as the computational organization theory (e.g., Carley, 1999), cellular biology (e.g., Kauffman, 1993), and science of networks (e.g., Watts, 2003), as it provides an intellectual root explanation to some of the complex phenomena in natural and social sciences. Its popular appeal is also evident everywhere, e.g., people casually refer to a "connected" world and associate it to the newness of the world since the advent of the Internet. Digital connection, on the other hand, is not only by definition just a subclass of connection, but the qualifier "digital" may also seem superfluous. However, for deepening the understanding of the casual "newness" and doing something about it, this qualifier may turn out to make all the difference in the world, and the subclass the whole universe that we need to ponder. The previous chapters have provided arguments to justify this focus.

We recap these arguments here in an attempt to develop a comprehensive definition. Digital connection is connection by digital means. Since service science is concerned with cocreation between customer and provider, it is also a science of connection: connection of cocreation stakeholders, value propositions, systems, and resources. For the service scaling and transformation theory, this connection nature is further pronounced since the design is to scale the cocreation towards the population, to bring about new and better values to persons, organizations, and society. Connection is everything from configuration of customers, providers, and resources for cocreation to the performance of the cocreation and delivery of the value. Design of service systems is hence design of connection. Conceptually, digital connection and connection are interchangeable to the extent that digitization applies to the connection, either at present or in the foreseeable future. However, technically, digital connection is the *necessary* qualification that makes design of connection meaningful in this physical context, since connections using digital means (for representation, storage, processing, and interaction) enjoy better cycle time and transaction costs than any other means. It makes scaling technically feasible and conceptually concrete. The notion of digital connection inherits the scientific understanding of connection and does not take away any substance from a service science. However, it substantiates the intellectual nature of a "connected world."

More generally, digitization makes objects connectible, and connections scalable, as evidenced in e-business. The crucial implication is that digital connections are amenable to large-scale applications, with the unprecedented potential of reaching the entire population and domain of an application space. In this sense, a design science for large-scale service is made more immediately meaningful, in both practical and intellectual terms, by the recognition of digital connection in place of connection. Digital connections are manageable and directly amenable to design. It follows that digital connections scaling can be recognized as both an intellectual focus and a signature genre of new results to maximize value propositions and optimize service systems.

It is also worthwhile to note that digitization is not just computerization. Digitization is a transformation of objects (including persons, resources, devices, and even the environment) either by adding a layer of digital information representing them or by converting them into digital forms, or both. Digitization is also accompanied with a supporting platform of the (societal) cyber-infrastructure, which includes computers, telecommunications, and computing networks. For enterprises, digitization turns their information resources digital, their processing digital, and their communication channels digital. A unique power of digitization is its unprecedented promise of connecting and sharing: the potential that all digital elements in the world could be connected — fused, indeed — through cyber-infrastructure and be shared as a whole by any, with infinitely many possible ways of utilization. For the economy, Adam Smith's "invisible hand" can become visible in the cyber-dimension of the economy.

Digital camera and email provide two ready examples of the power. Camera for camera, the traditional optical pictures still enjoy clear advantages over their digital competitors. However, digital cameras win over the market because their pictures are digital resources that can be connected with the users' other digital resources. Users can email, edit, and publish them as they do their ordinary files on the computer; and they can integrate them with these files as well. The fax machines lost to email as a favored means of written communication for the same reason. These machines are an isolated tool that cannot fuse with others, while email is open and scalable in its connection and coupling with other digital resources. More broadly, the history of information systems is one of integration of digital resources for their users. Needless to say, the Internet offers the most conspicuous exhibit of the power of digitization.

A much larger and more profound example is concerning social networking: the "*small world phenomenon*" (due to Stanley Milgram — e.g., see Blass, 2004). This interesting postulate, first formulated a few decades ago before the days of the Internet, suggests that two random persons in the society are connected with no more than six intermediary acquaintances (called six degrees of *separation* — which could be conversely referred to as six degrees of *connection*, to highlight the connotation that we discuss here). For example, if one knows someone who knows President Bill Clinton, then she/he has one-degree connection with Mr. Clinton; and anyone who knows her/him has two-degree connection with the President. With the Internet, along with search engines and email, one could argue that the small world is poised to get even smaller. It may be collapsed on the weight of multitude social networking into one where everyone is poised to connect with anyone in zero-degree through the (global) societal cyber-infrastructure. Researchers have already observed that people from all walks of life, who ordinarily would never cross their paths, may interact in the cyberworld (e.g., via massive multi-player online role-playing games and gigantic video blogs).

This shows that people may live on (social) islands, but their many roles in life are bound to intersect, and digital connections make the intersection realizable. A president or a queen and any head of state, is also a parent/child, a sport fan, and a patient. A customer at Walmart.com may also be a member of an open technology community represented heavily by knowledge workers in Singapore and students in Cape Town. A high school dropout may be a contributor at war games, support networks for sport-related injuries, and customer comments. These people's roles in their respective life cycles may converge and meet in some common paths of (usage of) digital connections. Some common value propositions may bring some common tasks of these roles together in the small world. *Connecting roles in life cycles through their tasks using digital means is a basis for value propositions innovation.* That is, when all economic activities are connected philosophically through persons, they can be physically connected on the Web: *all businesses are complementary through proper value propositions that join life cycle tasks for persons and organizations.* This is also a design view to networks science.

Digital connections are a stride to turning the small world phenomenon into knowledge for design. The small world phenomenon means cutting out the intermediaries which, in turn, spells reduction in societal transaction cost; and both of which enable innovation. From the perspective of innovation, while digital connections represent reduction of transaction cost and cycle for life cycle tasks — for persons and organizations alike, their value propositions have to be weighted vis-à-vis the costs of connection. Again, the focus on digital connections makes the value proposition a concrete design objective. Generally speaking, the small world phenomenon is both a cause and an effect of service scaling. It always exists with or without digital connections, but digital connections makes the concept "workable". The small world concept has become a powerful research paradigm in computing sociology, information systems and some other disciplines. They tend to assume digital connections without giving it recognition.

In this context, a formal *digital connections scaling* model is formulated, which analyzes how DCS may work to innovate digitally connected service and improve their value. The scope of study is the cocreation systems that use digital means to represent, store, and process microeconomic production factors (including the service system resources), and to configure and inter-operate them to achieve common value propositions. We define quality to be a measure of value from a customer stakeholder perspective, and productivity, a measure of value from a provider stakeholder perspective. Quality and productivity are measurable at an objective level based on the physical elements of digital connections. We define the problem of improving service quality and productivity, for the purpose of our analysis, as equivalent to the problem of increasing value cocreation outcomes over the complete life-cycle of populations of customer and provider interactions. Therefore, digital connections scaling (DCS) studies how the connection of the *stakeholder populations* and *resource populations* by digital means may prove to be the new foundations of the increase in value outcomes.

As such, the challenge of improving value, especially quality and productivity, in services, including the services of transforming activities in other sectors of the economy, is accordingly focused on the scaling of digital connections and the gaining of the economies of such scaling. The above is the basic idea of the DCS model. The model is postulated to achieve three types of economies of scale: accumulation effects (the linear joining of customers, resources, and/or providers, that can be shared and reused among service systems to reduce the cycle time and transaction cost for value propositions and cocreation), networking effects (the peer-to-peer expansion among stakeholders to multiply the accumulation effects), and ecosystem effects (the total expansion of population-wide interactions to inflate the accumulation effects) due to the DCS.

The above argument for DCS constitutes the second basic postulation of a new service science proposed in the book. The DCS model itself is formulated from the following proposition. The model was first developed in Hsu and Spohrer (2008), and the next section, Section 3.2, futher expands the previous development with, specially, additional theorems. We start the formulation of the current model with the basic proposition.

Service Science Proposition 2:

The concept of digital connections characterizes the connection nature of modern service in the knowledge economy, and digital connections scaling explains how to gain economies of scale for service.

The scientific studies of DCS, then, include the digitization of resources and systems, the connection of cocreation and systems, and the scaling of value propositions and outcomes. They provide a focus for service scaling. The full model is presented in the next section.

3.2 The Digital Connections Scaling Model: A Basic Conceptual Framework for Service and Knowledge-Based Economies

The major elements of the DCS model are presented below.

The Method of Digital Connection Scaling: Digitization and Population Building

The DCS model requires digitization of service systems along each of the four dimensions: customer, provider, resources, and value propositions, and pursue their synthesis in the wholeness of the cocreation space. Specifically, the model entails scaling the customer side throughout the customer demand chains to ultimately reach the entire customer population; scaling the provider side throughout the provider supply chains to ultimately reach the entire provider population; scaling the resources throughout the possible collaboration of individual knowledge workers, data resources, and other production factors along both the demand and the supply chains to ultimately reach the entire populations of resources; and scaling value propositions throughout the life cycle tasks of persons and organizations in the economic ecosystem of human society. On this basis, the model pursues synthesis of these scaling in the populations.

The DCS Proposition: Improving Service Quality and Productivity

Improving service quality and productivity is equivalent to increasing value cocreation outcomes over the complete life cycle of populations of customer and provider interactions. Digitization reduces the cycle time and the transaction cost of connection for service systems and service cocreation, and scaling these connections decreases the marginal cost for developing new value propositions and new value cocreations, as well as the average cost for individual services. The DCS model increases value outcomes, hence improves service quality and productivity, and ultimately enhances the utility of service to the customer and the profit of service to the provider. Both quality and productivity are improved when the cycle time and/or the transaction cost of the cocreation of value are reduced, since the reduction increases both the utility of service for the customer and the profit of service for the provider. (A detailed discussion of these concepts is provided in Chapter 6.)

Postulate 1: Accumulation Effects of DCS (maximum growth: linear, $O(n)$)

The first postulate of DCS is concerned with the sheer size that it brings about by simple accumulation of resources, customers, and providers in their respective domains without also considering possible interactions. In other words, applying DCS to service systems, up to the entire population of cocreation, can expect to yield benefits (economies of scale) due to this class of effects. Innovative value propositions and business designs, as well as service systems, can be developed around the pursuit of the accumulation effects. This class of effects is based on linear accumulation and hence its growth potential is linear to the number of participants in the population built.

The accumulation effects are intuitive. Many basic economies of scaling for service are found in the accumulation of knowledge and other resources, the accumulation of providers, and the accumulation of customers. The stakeholders can share and/or re-use them for better cocreation of value (e.g., lower cost and higher revenue) and/or the development of new value propositions. For example, from the provider perspective, the accumulation of customers using the same or similar resources base decreases marginal cost and builds marketing advantages. In a similar way, the accumulation of knowledge and other resources decreases the marginal cost of cocreation for new but similar value propositions. The accumulation of providers decreases the marginal cost for collaboration, as well as for dissimilating knowledge and joint marketing for customers (i.e., the accumulation of customers and resources). From the customer perspective, however, the accumulation of providers reduces the cycle time and the transaction cost for the customer to locate the right provider, conduct cocreation, and develop new value proposition. The accumulation of knowledge (customer's experience and sophistication) and customers (peer support and collaboration) have the same reduction effect on cycle time and transaction cost for cocreation and value proposition. Many digitally connected services such as e-commerce have proven this type of economies, and their practices include incorporating social networking into their business design. The strategic service contracts sector of heavy equipment industry, such as GE's operating and/or maintaining generators for their clients, also compete on the basis of fleet information, which is a combination of knowledge and customer. The resulting customer base and knowledge base from the accumulation often become barriers to entry as well as competitive advantages for the businesses.

Postulate 2: Network Effects of DCS (maximum growth: polynomial, $O(n(n-1)/2)$)

The second postulate of DCS is concerned with *physical digital connections*, or the feasible channels of cocreation that it creates by pairing up members (customers, providers, and resources) in the population built. These channels are defined by the usual network concept as nodes (members) and edges (connections) among the nodes. The logic of networking is essentially two-dimensional. This class of effects is fundamental to cocreation system design. The more such channels are made available, the more possibilities new value propositions and business designs may be developed. The number of channels is proportional of that of the pairs among members, and hence it has a growth potential as indicated.

Peer-to-peer interactions are beyond linear accumulation and promise to scale with an order of magnitude more possibilities. For example, social networking often results in massive parallel circles formed by massively fluid value propositions. The joining of two customers for a provider means not only the possibility of accumulating these two individual value propositions, but also the possibility of developing a value proposition for both customers. The same argument applies to everything covered in the accumulation effect and promises to expand the effect by an order of magnitude. We can also consider this effect a bi-dimensional accumulation. In general, network effects are well-known in the field, but their significance is often underestimated. First, a network is not just a physical configuration; it could be role-based as well. That is, there can be numerous task-performing (virtual or semantic) networks co-existing on these physical pairs. Each channel may be a platform for any applications — i.e., it may carry any variety of semantic contents for any tasks. This potential of role-induced expansion of network effects needs better recognition. Second, these effects have yet to be formally incorporated into the design of service systems; i.e., a design science to promote and manage network effects still awaits full development.

Postulate 3: Ecosystem Effects of DCS (maximum growth: Factorial, $O(n!)$)

The third postulate of DCS is concerned with the *life cycle tasks* that persons and organizations undertake, simultaneously, on the digital connections. These tasks give rise to *multiple concurrent roles* (virtual nodes and edges) that they perform on each physical node and edge of the network; and connections of these roles represent additional possibilities of cascading and recursive interactions among all members (customers and providers) in the population that it builds. Role-based networking is high-dimensional by its nature. We can consider it "inflating" on the physical space into a logical one. In the same manner, ecosystem effects "inflate" the development of value propositions. We have discussed the basic idea in the first section, and will further elucidate it throughout the rest of the chapter (in particular, the first theorem and Section 3.3).

This line of analysis can be immensely interesting. Social networking may be the best example to illustrate these interactions and promises. Since each interaction is a particular ordered sequence, or chaining, the possible number of interactions is proportional to the permutation of all members in a temporal space of the population (i.e., the physical space augmented by the time dimension to allow for asynchronous interactions). These interactions reflect roles in the context of the life cycle tasks of a person or an organization (e.g., opinion leader/follower for a blogging topic, parent, child, boss of a job, buyer of a product, and so on). These roles are sequence-sensitive, or even sequence-dependent. Roles can only be understood in the context of an ecosystem, and cannot be "averaged" into a common number for an average member. Therefore, we disagree with some formula such as N to the power of M (number of roles per member) as the complexity of a role-based community. Just like a channel may carry unlimited types of semantic contents, an ordering may be established to reflect unlimited possibilities of roles in any semantic (application) contexts. We submit that the interactions determine the power of any social networking, and hence any business that employ social networking. We further submit that they ultimately determine the potential of all value propositions in a society.

The ecosystem effects are everywhere, but they are rarely being recognized nor discussed as it has been done here. A service system is actually an ecosystem where all stakeholders co-exist, interact, and collaborate in many different roles. In the two-customer example mentioned above, these two customers could generate many value-proposition-based pairs in the ecosystem, where the sequence of pairing matters (e.g., prime and contractor), too. Therefore, the possibilities of accumulation for increasing value propositions and decreasing marginal cost are much more than networking. The lessons of massive online games, such as Second Life, provide ample evidence for this observation. We consider the ecosystem effect an exponential accumulation.

We now expand the DCS model with an exploration of its implications. That is, we formulate some theorems of how the DCS effects may be realized into benefits for persons, organizations, and society. We present these propositions from the perspective of an existing service enterprise.

The First Theorem of Service Scaling: Build Digital Connections to Reduce the Transaction Cost and Cycle Time of Performing Life Cycle Tasks

This theorem promotes a basic premise of the DCS model: digitization reduces the transaction cost and cycle time of connection; and the connection of related tasks over the life cycles of persons and organizations reduces the transaction cost and cycle time of performing these tasks. Thus, to start the snowballing of service scaling, the enterprise should pursue maximal possible digitization of all elements involved in the value cocreation (i.e., the whole service system), and seek value propositions along the integration of life cycle tasks of both the customer and the provider.

The concept of *life cycle tasks* goes beyond the traditional notion of complementary tasks (e.g., buying a high-definition TV and buying high-definition DVD players and disks) to seek the ultimate scope of interrelatedness of tasks. "Life time" is the entire horizon of the interrelationship among tasks which can have many dimensions and spawn many different chains along each dimension. The physical life time of a person and an organization is one definitive, anchoring dimension. Many others also exist, including the life cycles of products in the market (e.g., vehicles), utility of products to particular constituencies (e.g., owning a vehicle), and tasks (e.g., raising a baby or developing a contract). Tasks are comprised of sub-tasks. Thus, the life cycle of a task is comprised of the sub-tasks pertaining to the task. As such, task life cycles are clearly recursive and can be reduced iteratively. They can also be cross-linked among dimensions to form clusters of tasks that a business design may target. Therefore, "life cycles" are definable and hence amenable to business design. The definition of life cycles amounts to a logic that inspires lateral thinking in business design. For example, connecting the life cycle tasks of an organization customer along the dimensions of its core business can lead to demand chain integration, while that of an organization provider to supply chain integration.

Chaining and clustering can be designed either horizontally across the same types of tasks (traditional service provider, such as day-care centers for children or seniors), or vertically cutting through the life cycle (e.g., person-centered or task-centered, such as "concierge" doctors or any other one-stop service providers), or in any configuration of both — a logically inspired lateral thinking. The paths of growth and diffusion of social networks best illustrate the life cycle tasks concept, and may even best reveal the opportunities for service chaining along the person dimension. Therefore, this theorem also recognizes *social networking as a natural part of any life cycle tasks*, including the integration of it into business activities. The *life cycle tasks concept is the primary guidance for identifying DCS opportunities*. It also underlies the next three theorems. (Chapter 7 provides some particular life cycle tasks for service scaling of intelligent network flows, e.g., highway administration, logistics, and travelers.)

The above theorem builds on the promises of DCS for interconnection of life cycle tasks to thereby reduce transaction cost and cycle time. Although both are some of the most basic roots to any value propositions, they can be supplemented from other aspects. The next proposition recognizes a basic logic for realizing the benefits promised by the first theorem. It is concerned with the reuse and sharing due to DCS.

The Second Theorem of Service Scaling: Gain Economies of Scale on Customers, Knowledge/Resources, and Values and Value Propositions

The first way to realize the DCS effects of the three postulates, once the digital connections have been constructed, is to scale the elements of service and service systems within the present paradigm — i.e., the customers, joint knowledge and provider resources of cocreation of service, as well as to the values and value propositions that drive the cocreation. The client-server model best describes the logic. All three classes of effects are amenable to this logic, but the constraint of not changing the paradigm practically restricts the pursuit to the existing populations of customers and provider resources. (This is a basic difference between this and the next theorems.) The knowledge of cocreation comes from both the customer and the provider (e.g., the knowledge workers); and hence the scaling will take the form of accumulating, integrating, and cross-referencing the pertinent experiences, skills, and other classes of knowledge to satisfy and facilitate the cocreation. An example of the economies of knowledge is the understanding of the entire space of particular business applications (i.e., a domain of service), or the population model. With the understanding, the cocreation (e.g., the design and development of the service systems required) can reuse some of the past results and thereby reduce the learning curve and minimize the marginal cost.

This paradigm for gaining the accumulation effect on knowledge (models) is the topic of study for what we refer to as population modeling (including a modelbase of reusable results) in the next chapter. Resources are concerned mainly with the provider, but their particular nature may extend to including the customer as well, such as a virtual organization for an extended enterprise between the customer and the provider. Examples of the economies of resources include the ASP model of e-business and the "lease" model of heavy industrial equipment (Dausch and Hsu, 2006). In these cases, the providers (e.g., Symantec for Internet security and GE for utility power stations) operate and maintain the applications and/or the products for the whole population of customers. They therefore can leverage the fleet resources — and knowledge — to optimize the operation and maintenance of individual applications and/or products for customers. This is another class of population model. The economies of values and value propositions build directly on the facilitation of life cycle tasks by the DCS, as discussed above. Therefore, they are closely related to enterprises and business designs that provide applications — see the next theorem.

The second theorem may be most straightforward since it does not call for fundamental changes. In this sense, its benefits build fundamentally on the basic concepts of accumulation and the reuse and sharing of this accumulation. These concepts are completely tangible when we bring the theorem to the level of implementation — i.e., the enterprise systems of service cocreation. At this level, accumulation, reuse, and sharing are nothing more than some concrete goals that the systems can be designed to deliver. Although the basic logic is self-evident, the design deserves further guidelines. Therefore, we now zero in on the backbone of digital service systems: *cocreation enterprise information systems*, or information systems that implement and support value cocreation in service enterprises. The following propositions further elaborate on the benefits of scaling from the perspective of information systems. The notion of *societal cyber-infrastructure* is also employed to collectively refer to all public domain digital resources and infrastructure accumulated in society, including the usual cyber infrastructure (e.g., Internet, telecommunications, and other public IT platforms) and the Web. (Chapter 6 discusses these concepts in detail.)

The first two derived propositions are concerned with openness and scalability of information systems achieved through societal cyber-infrastructure:

Lemma 1: Concerning accumulation by information systems

A basic method for accumulation is to make enterprise information systems open and scalable, to embed them into persons, organizations, and resources and to make the accumulation available as on-line assistance to customers and knowledge workers.

Lemma 2: Concerning openness and scalability by cyber-infrastructure

A basic method for making information systems open and scalable is to build them on or connect them to common societal cyber-infrastructure.

They lead to the next two propositions which help substantiate the first theorem:

Corollary 1: Concerning benefits through information systems

A basic form of benefits of scale due to accumulation is the reuse and sharing of common service enterprise information systems for concurrent cocreation of value which decreases the marginal cost of cocreation.

Corollary 2: Concerning societal cyber-infrastructure

A basic approach to implementing Corollary 1 is to make service enterprise information systems open and scalable through employment of societal cyber-infrastructure.

The above four sub-propositions of the second theorem provide a general conceptual guideline to complement particular design methods. For example, Chapter 4 discusses service systems and their design in detail in the context of a new population orientation paradigm. These propositions can guide the development of goals for the service systems while the particular methods implement these goals into specific design. Chapter 6 further develops the above propositions into a design methodology for enterprise information systems of value cocreation. In general, the results here are complementary to previous results on business strategy and information system (IS) planning. They, in particular, contribute some particular conceptual roadmaps to help broaden as well as substantiate previous methods in their ability to comprehensively create and evaluate value propositions. The methods of population orientation presented in Chapter 4 complement these propositions in a similar way: showing the scope and design approaches for the conceptual roadmaps.

The Third Theorem of Service Scaling: Develop Business Design for Concurrent Integration of Applications and Application Domains

The restriction of status quo (present paradigm) that the second theorem maintains is removed here. Therefore, this theorem seeks to achieve innovation and reap economies of scale by exploring new business designs for the service enterprise concerned. As stated above, business design is the second dimension of scaling strategies for service. For example, an important form of the scaling is the integration of different, previously separate business spaces in e-business, such as selling books together with clothes and grocery, to leverage the common e-business knowledge and resources. This integration applies to whole industries as well as the digitally connected household (the integration of entertainment, network TV, computing, utilities, appliances, etc.).

The accumulation effect of DCS is the most commonly found driver of new business designs in practice. The basic computing concept of client-server is a ready example, and its generalization into enterprise and business models is also an example. Many e-business models, including B2C, B2B, ASP, Information Portal, Transaction Portal, Consortia, and the like reduce cycle time and transaction cost both to the provider and to the customers by reaping the benefits of sharing the accumulated resources in the service systems. Many enterprise integration models also use accumulation of resources, systems, and participants as the basic means of scaling. Examples range from B2E and paperless enterprise on the administration side, to computerized manufacturing such as CAD, CAM, MES, and CIM, and all the way to product life cycle management and global supply chain integration. This type of linear scaling of business in an application domain (business space) is hereby referred to as the *application domain integration model*. It is a foundation on which additional integrations build.

The principle of networking effect is also manifested in practice, as shown in the Exchange model of e-business and, to a lesser extent, the enterprise models of concurrent engineering and e-engineering. The exchange model turns supply chains into markets to facilitate maximum exposure of both buyers and sellers for achieving the most efficient pairing of resources. Unlike the linear supply chain, the market allows a participant to network with any number of buyers and sellers in any configuration. This type of pair-wise scaling of business for applications within or across domains is hereby referred to as the *concurrent applications model*. Previous concurrent engineering and e-engineering models do not support on-demand pairing of participants, and hence is sub-optimal in reaping the possible networking effect. However, they could be refined and expanded in the new light of DCS.

Finally, the ecosystem effect is most promising for scaling business by scaling values and value propositions. A recent example is the connection of email with cell phone through calendar and other personal services by Google. The new business design, through gmail, connects social networks with transactions which are free services provided by

Google to its customer, but which are also services charged by Google to the cell phone carrier (AT&T) that the same customer may pay for. Thus, Google exploits the dual role of the user, one as a Google customer of free services and the other as an AT&T customer of for-fee services, for its advantages: to gain customers through free service provision and to gain commissions from AT&T on the business it provides (e.g., per call made through the calendar). This example shows the ecosystem effect, and also shows that the foundations of the effect are really personal values based on personal life cycle tasks. Free email, calendar, and other information services are all values to personal life cycle tasks, and since they are all related to some tasks, they can all be ultimately turned into some business processing for values to organizations and values to society. This type of concurrently integrating values across the whole society is hereby referred as the *concurrent social integration model*. These three models describe three directions in which new business designs may be identified to yield the three types of the DCS effects.

The Fourth Theorem of Service Scaling: Grow the Global Knowledge Economy by the Provision of DCS to Service Sector and Non-Service Sectors

An ultimate "super class" of service is to provide DCS for the whole economy as it applies, including all economic activities in both the service sector and non-service sectors. That is, as the new service science sheds new light on traditional disciplines and yields new results to improve traditional economic activities, the above two theorems of DCS can be applied to agriculture, energy, manufacturing, government, and all others as well. Furthermore, through DCS, the traditional service industries may even expand to improve or transform the traditional non-service industries. We might add that the pursuit of this theorem will also reflect a pursuit of person-centered, organization-centered, and society-centered integration of life cycle tasks using roles — i.e., the pursuit of full ecosystem effects on top of the networking and accumulation effects.

This vision may be futuristic, but it is not far-fetched. The emerging practices and visions of custom product and device design, personalized drugs, and home-based agriculture (e.g., aeroplantics) and alternative energy (e.g., solar panel) all illustrate the potential of DCS and DCS-based transformation of these non-service industries. As the DCS principles may apply to any enterprise to facilitate the (open and scalable) connection of their stakeholders and systems, the DCS service that effects these applications promises to become a transforming activity that propels the growth of the knowledge economy. In pursuing this ultimate playground for transformation, the life cycle tasks concept of the first theorem can serve as a tool to seek out particular opportunities for concrete business design. *After all, there is only one world and only one life for each one of us in society.* Agriculture, manufacturing, energy, medicine, education, and entertainment are all just some aspects of this synergistic ecosystem of tasks. Analyzing and pursuing life cycle tasks promises to reduce the abstract concept of the ecosystem effects of DCS to the level of business for the identification of concrete opportunities of this theorem.

The above four theorems provide a basis for proving whether digital connections scaling is a basic approach of improving service systems in the knowledge economy. It also promises to be a general way of improving any knowledge-based economic activities. The first two theorems are directly implemented in the new IS design methods of Chapter 6, the intelligent network flows models of Chapter 7, and the new information resources collaboration and sharing designs of Chapter 8. The last two are indirectly assisting these new results by guiding the future directions. Along with Chapter 5 which corroborates all four theorems with empirical evidence of new business designs on the Web, *the rest of the book establishes a de facto proof of the above theorems.* On this basis, we submit that the DCS model complements the previous results in the field for design of business strategy and systems. Finally, these propositions may be embodied in some microeconomic production functions to formally relate the ideas to service scaling designs for economic productivity analysis — or, relating the DCS model to the knowledge economy. Chapter 9 is devoted to this analysis.

Finally, one will still want to establish these propositions at an analytic or even mathematical level. For example, the above argument penetrates the presumption of doubt of the model's empirical relevance and thereby establishes its empirical feasibility to an extent. However, what is its inherent complexity — *is it scientifically feasible to promote these theorems*, and to what extent? We start to ponder this basic question in the next section.

3.3 The Analytic Nature of the DCS Model

We need to understand the mathematic nature of the DCS model such as the analytic properties of the postulated effects, in order to be certain of its full application to assist in service scaling analysis and design. The study may be based on empirical data, simulation, pure mathematics, or any combination of these four. Regardless of the methodology, the study is subject to the model's basic nature. First, we review the dimensionality of the model. The physical elements of digital connections are three-dimensional in nature: the surface of earth and space (e.g., the Internet plus satellite-based telecommunications, and earth-bound nodes plus air-borne users). However, the semantic contents of digital connections includes inherently a fourth temporal dimension since the connections are asynchronous, or have built-in time lapses. This is not surprising. The surprising complexity stems from the multiple simultaneous uses of the physical connections: virtual connections. The *basic four-dimensional space inflates into a virtually infinite logical space when the roles of the persons are included*. That is, when digital connections are represented in terms of their nodes, each node may play an unlimited number of roles — the virtual nodes — in the ordered sequences of interactions over time, or just simultaneously.

This observation suggests that mathematical modeling of digital connections is hard. Even more moderate attempts such as simulation modeling can be difficult as well. Therefore, one may need to consider the nature of particular applications and add qualifications to the model. Using empirical data to build the model is the ideal way. In any case, complexity is compensated by potential benefits: the enormity reflects the promises of the DCS effects postulated as well.

Any results that promise to shed light on the analytic nature of DCS can help its application.

A theoretic reference point is found in the science of networks, due to Watts and Strogatz (1998) who provided a mathematical model to explain the analytical nature of connections in biology, society, and some other intriguing networks. Many applications of the network science, including public health and social networking have relied on this model to construct their theoretic basis, especially those that investigate the small world phenomena in open communities. However, new results are needed for the higher dimensional space facing DCS.

In general, massively high-dimensional spaces possess unique properties that cannot be extrapolated from the physical space; and they may even be counter-intuitive. For instance, the volume of a unit sphere approaches zero when the dimensionality approaches infinity. Simulation provides a viable approach, in lieu of mathematical analysis. It may also supplement the latter, or be employed to generate results that may be generalized into mathematical expressions. In any case, the analytic nature of the DCS effects determines the limits, natural patterns, and strategies of how service systems should proactively design these effects into their value propositions and cocreation configurations. We submit that, to the extent the DCS model helps explain digitally connected service, the analytic nature of DCS addresses some of the fundamental questions in the research problems of Chapter 2, such as a Moore's Law for service innovation, theoretic growth rates of social networking, and the natural "gravitational field" for (the distribution of) value propositions.

The analytic investigation may start with a focus on the networking effects. It may also start with certain assumptions and constraints on the ecosystem effects to simplify the complexity. For our purpose, we attempt the first approach here. We refer to the usual two-dimensional network as the basic network, with node representing persons and resources, and edges representing connections. By extension, we refer to the *role-based higher dimensional virtual networks* as *hyper networks*. Each *hyper node* of a hyper network may correspond to roles of a single node of a basic network, but may also represent a collection of the basic nodes based on their roles. For example, a hyper node may be a forum, an open community, or a massive online multi-player role-playing game — or just a particular collaboration scheme on an extended enterprise. The *hyper edges* represent accesses to hyper notes. The hyper network degenerates (reduces) to the basic network when the number of roles considered at each node is one — i.e., the case of not considering roles at all.

Using the concept of small world phenomenon from Milgram (see Section 3.1), any pair of nodes connected by a single edge has zero degree of separation; and in general any pair of nodes connected by a minimum of n edges (i.e., the minimum path between them consists of n edges) on the network has n-1 degrees of separation. We apply the same definition to hyper networks. However, due to the congregating nature of hyper nodes, multiple basic nodes may congregate in a hyper node. Therefore, we define all such basic nodes belonging to the same hyper node as having zero degree separation on their basic network. Any pair of basic nodes connected through an exogenous hyper node has one degree of separation — or, in general, the degree of separation on a basic network is n-hyper +1 where n-hyper indicates their degree of separation on their hyper network. For example, two connected forums (hyper nodes) are separated by zero degree, but their respective members are connected to members in the other forum by one degree separation. We now turn to learn from the basic networks — i.e., the networks science.

Many simulation models exist in the field which studies the general phenomena of networking from many different disciplinary perspectives. We cite below a particular work by Dr. W.K. Victor Chan of Rensselaer Polytechnic Institute that studies the growth of connections in a particular open community — as a representative result on the small world phenomenon (see http://sigma.dses.rpi.edu/ROSL/content.asp?id=120&sid=180). In the model, members talk to each other with a uniform probability of p ~[0, 1], and each new talk establishes a connection between these two participants. The above cited source provides a real-time simulation to show the growth of connections from scratch. The figures provided there capture the dynamic growth as connections are generated in the simulation. The main figure shows the whole network as it grows, and some other (smaller) graphs record the patterns of the growth. The simulation parades a series of tantalizing formation of *hubs of connection* — a common phenomenon reported in the field. In this sense, the network and its growth patterns demonstrate the small world phenomenon mentioned above.

For our purpose, we recognize the *formation of such hubs as a signature property of the small world phenomenon*. This property helps explain why the six-degree separation postulate may be true, and how it may work: these hubs make fast connection of "remote" nodes feasible, just like international travel is made shorter by hubs of airplane flights. We note that these hubs of connection are a result of *population evolution* at the grass root: they tend to emerge naturally from the logic of networking itself. In actuality, the logic is, of course, application space-specific. For social networking, the hubs may be opinion leaders who emerge by natural selection (direct democracy at work). For enterprise information systems, they may reflect key resources in terms of software objects and sharable data/knowledge (entities, relationships and processes). In the real world, such selection may be influenced by wealth, status, geographical locations and the like. In the simulation, however, it measures the power of pure chance — i.e., the uniform probability distribution employed for the random creation of talks. Still, hubs formed. It shows that *by natural selection alone, some centers of gravity will dominate any networks*. The point that matters is, of course, the selection is subject to *design*: it is influenced by some underlying conditions and rules that the designer can manipulate, perhaps by employing the DCS model. The knowledge of the small world phenomenon ought to be treated as knowledge for all levels of design in the knowledge economy. Analyzing the selection and designing it, therefore, is a natural objective of the analytic investigation of the DCS model which has to be done to account for various conditions for various populations. The analysis itself is a proof of the need for population orientation since it has to be population-based: grass roots, bottom up as opposed to top down as in some traditional design paradigms.

We submit that the small world phenomenon applies to the hyper networks as well. Obviously, it promises to help make the pursuit of networking effects feasible: *any customer, provider, resource may find any other customer, provider, and resource for collaboration* in a reasonable manner with reasonable transaction cost and cycle time. Based on this observation, we present the following generalized postulate, which helps justify why it is feasible to promote the DCS theorems:

The Small World Phenomenon in Service Scaling and Transformation Postulate

1. *The phenomenon exists in networking effects, and hence helps promote DCS.*
2. *The phenomenon exists in ecosystem effects, with an upper bound of degree of separation equaling its degenerated case, the basic network; and hence helps DCS.*
3. *On average, any pair of hyper nodes is separated by no more than one degree in the hyper network, and* **any pair of basic nodes is separated by no more than two degrees via the hyper network.**

We refer to the third part of the postulate the *two-degree separation* postulate of DCS. It deserves some explanation, although the statements are presented as just postulates. The basic logic is simple: hyper nodes are in fact proactive facilitators for networking. For example, a forum of some common theme is not recognized in the basic network, but it is a hyper node that recognizes the commonality of some basic nodes according to the common theme. In this sense, it is the result of proactive recognition to connect nodes that would otherwise not be connected — we discussed this point in Section 3.1. Such recognition — e.g., a prince shares a common interest in a movie star with a janitor — may not be amenable for direct connection in the basic network without the hyper node; and yet it has the flexibility of being virtual to allow it to be implemented on demand. In other words, hyper nodes transcend the usual barriers or blind spots of the basic network, and they are subject to *design*. Clearly, the hyper network does not diminish the connected nature of the basic network; it only enhances the latter. We expect hubs to exist in the hyper networks, too. Therefore, these hubs of hyper nodes help to further reduce the average degree of separation on the basic network. The end result of the logical argument is the postulate of two-degree separation under DCS.

New lines of research may be inspired from the above observation. We expect the results to be helpful to promoting the propositions of the DCS model, and thereby shed light on the design of service scaling and transformation at all levels. At present, it is still possible to suggest some general postulations about the implementation of the DCS model without specific analytic results. We present one, in particular, to launch an investigation into the growth pattern of service scaling and transformation in the knowledge economy. Figure 3.1 visualizes the general pattern postulated.

The growth reflects the realization of DCS in the population, regardless of its reference to any particular application space or society, as measured by the number of DCS effects experienced over time. The measure, in theory, can be the physical digital connections

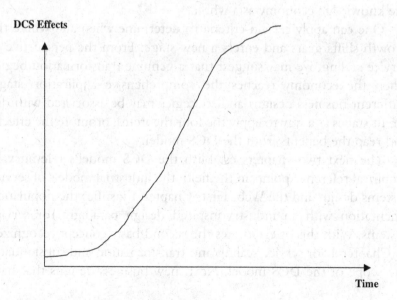

Figure 3.1:   Growth of the DCS effects in the knowledge economy.

established — i.e., the networking effects; but can also be some indicators of ecosystem effects by virtue of a production function of DCS. The figure does not specify on this measure since it is intended as a general thought model. Its basic logic, the growth rate, is related to the general concept of acceptance rate or diffusion rate, which applies to such common fields as new ideas, new technology, or simply, changes. A cross section of many fields of science has accumulated numerous results, both empirical and theoretic, about change and innovation. We propose below a postulate based on a common notion emerging from these results:

The Growth Pattern of Service Scaling and Transformation Postulate

An S-shaped growth path — slow initiation, followed by rapid general application, before the change reaches maturity and slowly runs its course — will characterize service scaling and transformation in the knowledge economy envisioned.

Based on this postulate, we expect the growth of DCS to follow a similar pattern. This is true for particular population as well as for the knowledge economy as a whole.

One can apply certain criteria to determine when and where the growth shifts gears and enters a new stage. From the perspective of service scaling, we may suggest that a genuine transformation begins when the economy reaches the comprehensive application stage. Different business designs and strategies may be associated with different stages as a way to apply the four theorems, promote the effects, and reap the benefits from the DCS model.

The next two chapters establish the DCS model's relevancy to empirical reference points in the field: the industrial models of service systems design and the Web. First, Chapter 4 justifies the population orientation with an industry-inspired design paradigm for service systems. With this, it elaborates the second basic concept recognized in Chapter 1 for service scaling and transformation and substantiates the scope of the DCS model. Next, new business designs that have emerged on the Web — or have been developed to employ the Web for business, are analyzed in Chapter 5 with predictions offered. The analysis proves that the service scaling theory of the book assumes a parallelism between the Web and the DCS model. Their growth patterns are expected to be similar.

Chapter 4

The Population Orientation Paradigm and Cyber-Enabled Knowledge System Design

Does service require a different kind of design science? The answer depends on whether the field intends to tackle large-scale value cocreation. Traditional design science was inspired by physical products, systems, and infrastructure. It encompasses results from, for example, industrial and systems engineering, operations research and statistics, and information systems. It has been successfully applied to many types of service operations found in hospitals, call centers, and large offices. These operations tend to be amenable to automation and, in this sense, tend to share many characteristics with manufacturing and construction operations. However, knowledge-intensive value cocreation is different: They tend to be one of a kind as shown in consulting. Chapter 1 analyzes this problem in detail. This chapter deepens the analysis and proposes a solution using DCS. It starts with recognizing the core concept that only the collection of all cocreation practices — the *population* — can show reliable patterns for designers to adopt and yield *reusable design results*. The duality of the concept is that DCS can help build the population knowledge — i.e., *cyber-enabled design*. Reusable results do not have to match perfectly with new cocreation needs to be useful; they only need to help reduce the learning curves i.e. they only need to be relevant. The population is by definition the maximum source of "relevant" (as opposed to "exact") results. Therefore, *service scaling not only reaches the population,*

*but also uses the population to reduce the learning curve for design —
this is the full meaning of population orientation*. Digital connections make the population visible for studying, modeling, and reusing
for new cocreation design. A population modeling methodology and
a particular *modelbase* method are developed to help accumulate and
reuse knowledge resources for service systems, and add to the previous design science.

4.1 Population Orientation: Reaches to the Population, Study of the Population, and Design with Knowledge of the Population

The overarching technical problem is how to reduce the learning
curve of population-oriented cocreation? As stated before, the service
scaling and transformation theory of the book has two basic
concepts: digital connections scaling and population orientation. We
now elaborate the second concept and move to develop a particular
design method to help implement it. The core logic that we present
here as a core conceptual contribution is to turn the population of the
population-oriented cocreation into an ally to facilitate cocreation
design. The rest are technical details (which of course matter and
which we address here, too).

The DCS model, presented in Chapter 3, is by definition concerned with the population of the application domain. However, one
may argue that all scientific endeavors are also similarly concerned
with the population of their subject matter and always seek population knowledge. Therefore, by this view, it is superfluous to recognize population orientation in our formulation of a new service
science. We disagree with this argument on the basis of the adverb:
"similarly". For the DCS model, the population is "attainable"
directly in the scientific endeavor proposed, and will be literally
incorporated into the studies. However, many other sciences rely on
samples — often timed in very limited sizes — to infer about the
population. In a general sense, we submit that any scientific study that
employs statistics to substitute for observed population knowledge

(e.g., probability) is not similarly concerned with population as the new theory here does.

Furthermore, we submit that much of the traditional design science is concerned about closed systems, controlled (or even proprietary) application domains, and finite planning horizons, such that the design can be comprehensively proven in laboratory settings, by simulations, or using (relatively small) samples. This paradigm of design is proven insufficient in a digitally connected world. An evidence of this ineptness is the so-called "data-rich, information-poor" phenomenon that many in the field have argued (e.g., see James Tien, 2007). It basically refers to the fact that the world has been inundated in (real-time and online) data that it generated (from its digital connections), while the scientific field (including all decision sciences) has not been able to derive much information (useful knowledge) from them. Although a number of interpretations and implications are possible following from this, an obvious fact is inescapable: serious gaps exist between the new types of data generated and the previous results that analyze data — i.e., the previous results are not sufficient for studying and using the new data. Otherwise, why is the field unable to catch up with the data? Can it be just the lack of will to do so? These data, quite simply put, are due to and reflect digital connections scaling.

We wish to bring the argument one step further and submit that, from the perspective of designing for service scaling and transformation, the real problem facing the world is *theory-rich, data-poor* — i.e., similar to the situation that the field of astronomy used to face (as discussed before). The field has endless supply of theory about service and value cocreation (and this book is but another addition), but very few comprehensive empirical data to prove or disprove them. Astronomy started to change in the 1960s with massive new observations, and today it enjoys a renaissance, thanks to new digitally connected massive observations on ground and in space. Now, a wealth of population data is helping rewrite the entire story on the universe. From this perspective, we may interpret the call for a new service science as one to change the theory-rich, data-poor phenomenon. That is, the endeavor of developing the new service science will feature more population data and better theories supported by these data. The following statement summarizes our argument: digital connections in our society are accompanied by new data which require as well as promote new paradigms of research; and one such paradigm is the population orientation: reaches to the population, study of the population, and use of the population knowledge for service system design.

The above argument is general and not dependent on the particular theory of service scaling and transformation of the book, although it inspires the particular results that we present. Therefore, we recognize this idea as the third basic, general proposition for a new service science.

Service Science Proposition 3:

Digitally connected service deals directly with the whole population of value cocreation where comprehensive knowledge is attainable from digital connections; and service system design should rely on common, reusable results developed from the population to reduce the learning curve.

It has three underlying concepts: reaching out to the population, studying the population, and designing with knowledge of the population. The first one is fully embedded in the DCS model, and the second is also being increasingly understood and practised in the field, such as the social networking research conducted in related information systems and computing sociology. Therefore, we elaborate on the third concept — designing with knowledge available in the population, in the rest of the chapter. Our work is geared *at a technical level of knowledge systems design*, including a particular design approach and a particular knowledge repository method, proposed here for implementation of this concept.

In a broader sense, a population orientation for design has implications and philosophical grounding beyond service *per se*, let alone being limited to digitally connected service. Fundamentally, human society is a distributed world. All knowledge, resources, and stakeholders of all economic activities are distributed physically, logically, and geographically. No single person and no single organization possess the total picture of the wholeness in real time; nor can anyone hope to possess it with the remotest possibility of succeeding. However, digital connections make this distributed world whole in cyberspace. It becomes conceivable that one can have access to some meaningful versions of the total picture in real time under some reasonable conditions. Population orientation is the recognition and pursuit of the total picture, in real time as well as in persistent, archival data. This orientation accompanies the DCS model and is a signature paradigm of studying service scaling because DCS functions in the population. This orientation may lead to some new basic approaches to understanding how to gain the DCS effects discussed in Chapter 3, and hence it may become a new basic research paradigm that characterizes the new service science envisioned. Therefore, it becomes possible that a new design science for service systems will be one that develops the benefits of population modeling. We should add that the population orientation applies to the study of all three dimensions of service cocreation: value to persons, value to organizations, and value to society.

4.2 Design with Knowledge of the Population: The Cyber-Enabled Design Approach

We first analyze in detail why the traditional design science originating in the industrial revolution does not work sufficiently for service; viz., why does the model of computer-aided design (CAD) work for product engineering, but not for service cocreation? The basic argument is that products are finite, self-contained, and closed. Thus, the challenges of CAD are containable in a stand-alone box (albeit connectible with other boxes over the cyber-infrastructure) affording a comprehensive set of standard product engineering tools and functions to design engineers. In contrast, service systems are less neat and their design accordingly requires all help that one can get in the extensible field. Therefore, the counterpart of CAD for service systems will be more comparable to *a window into cyberspace* than a self-contained box, *seeking available experiences and knowledge from any source, in the form of application domain (business components) models, simulation models, and optimization models.*

To substantiate further, we note that in both cases the designers equally need to draw reusable results from the population to design systems for any applications. The contrast rests in the fundamental differences about "reusable results for the population of applications" between services and products. CAD can and does tap into the science of physical production. The CAD capabilities, along with their international standards such as STEP, represent reusable results defined in the science for the population of products. Their definitiveness is enabled by standardization of parts, rationalization of engineering, and optimization of manufacturing which, in turn, are possible because physical products have fixed forms and lasting structures that are subject to physical constraints verifiable by physical sciences. These constraints also regulate the resources, facilities, and systems that make the products. Therefore, it is possible to embody into a stand-alone CAD system a definitive set of generic data representation methods (objects), engineering analytics (algorithms), and graphics (solid modeling) to support an efficient design process that generalizes and scales to the population of applications. Additional capabilities of inter-operation (e.g., Blackboard, processes library, and application ontology) can also be developed to allow for concurrent engineering and even comprehensive collaboration throughout a supply chain.

However, service is utility-oriented, not physical product-oriented. The utility, the cocreation of value, tends to be perishable (no shelf life and cannot be stocked) and subjective to the particular consumer of cocreation. Thus, the science of physical products does not apply to service, and does not derive physical constraints for service design. Furthermore, service can be co-created in many different ways for the same utility, and hence service systems can be one of a kind for the particular cocreation implemented. As such, it is unclear whether past experiences and designs were optimal or even can stay relevant to future systems. Therefore, reusable results of service systems are difficult to define, generalize, and scale for the whole population of applications. These fundamental differences between services and products have been detrimental to the adoption of CAD ideas for service. In addition, knowledge workers are not amenable to standardization, unlike parts and machines. Their predictable, standardized scheduling and assignment (compared to the availability of "bill of materials" in manufacturing) are elusive. The above analysis indicates that a new design science is needed, and will manifest itself in a population orientation for service systems.

From an empirical perspective, the modeling of the abstract service, elusive service operations, and fluid service systems is a modeling of the service population, or the abstraction of the whole space of service system applications, from their basic value to their architecture and implementation in information technology (i.e., their IT solutions). This existential approach may not be applicable to all kinds of services, but it is attainable by services that rely on cyber-infrastructure to produce — i.e., DCS, as discussed earlier in the book. For this case, the on-demand employment of cyber-infrastructure itself provides a concrete, observable, and definitive reference point for the service systems that operate on it. Modeling the population in this domain enjoys additional benefits, such as the fact that these service systems have a definitive closure in the form of their IT solutions. This closure enables a rational process to lead any conceptual abstraction to this IT-based design, and thereby reduces the arbitrariness of design and increases reusability of (IT-based) design resources. We refer to the above concepts and goals as *population modeling: abstracting the available knowledge in the population and thereby making it feasible for design of service systems*. It represents the rationalization process based on which new designs can be more easily developed, evaluated, and parameterized for implementation. Population modeling requires *an open and scalable representation method, a cyber-infrastructure-based repository of population models, and a methodology* to implement it. All three components become a part of the design science for service systems.

We now analyze why population modeling has to be open and scalable. The simple argument is that the population is by definition open and scalable. Population modeling has to be evolutionary, in order not only to capture the comprehensive experiences and knowledge accumulated in the entire field today, but also to accommodate future experiences and knowledge on an on-going basis to respond to future needs. It follows that, technically, the population models (i.e., repositories of all modeling resources) have to be represented and organized in a way that they are searchable for designers to identify what they need from the huge collection, and, equally important, for them to be able to connect to other similar results that other enterprises may have developed. The population is certainly much larger than any one company can capture. In addition, these modeling resources need to be interrelated to support joining, zooming in and out of them; such as relating business logic models to the appropriate analytic models that evaluate them and guide their employment in many alternative configurations for many alternative designs. Again, this inter-relationship means that different classes of knowledge (in the form of various models) have to be represented and organized in an integrated way. Ideally, these analytic models should be generic enough for each to correspond to a type of business logic model, or a number of particular models that they are able to evaluate.

The ideas of population modeling presented above are inspired by the DCS model discussed in Chapter 3 for service scaling. However, their intellectual roots can be traced back to certain results in the field, including some industrial practices of population modeling in their own proprietary contexts. For manufactured products, industrial standards and universal coding of parts have been commonly employed for decades and which are a form of population model. Industrial data dictionaries and standardized concepts, including scholarly studies of ontology (e.g., see Kalfoglou and Schorlemmer, 2003) have been developed to facilitate inter-operation of data and knowledge systems in both manufacturing and service. For service expressly, the field has also recently witnessed the development of industrial reference models for particular application domains (e.g., Dausch and Hsu, 2006) and open software objects formulated as Web services. Related industrial topics also include business services, service-oriented architecture, and service-oriented business application (e.g., Erl, 2005). All of which are applicable to industrial service system design.

However, for companies developing massively customized service system solutions in large quantity and compressed time horizon, such as those in the consulting industry, these results are far from sufficient. They need firm understanding of all the possible business processes that their clients may require at present and in the future. They also need proven knowledge to construct and configure software solutions for these processes in perhaps a pre-fabricated way with predictable performance. From our perspective, the industry needs sufficient population models. To satisfy this need, many companies have embraced the idea of developing comprehensive business component models from which they can draw to develop future systems. That is, population models in some form of business components are typical in a company's proprietary design portfolio when they attempt to build their consulting knowledge base to reduce the learning curve of new projects. A prime example is IBM's paradigm consisting of the component business modeling (CBM) approach and a comprehensive set of key performance indicators (KPI) for capturing particular application spaces, one by one (e.g., see Chebakov *et al.*, 2005; Nayak *et al.*, 2007; Nigam and Caswell, 2003 and Sanz *et al.*, 2007). The effort is clearly predicated on the principle of accumulation.

These industrial results provide a promising starting basis for researchers to develop population modeling methods as well as particular population models. However, they are insufficient to satisfy the goal of population modeling as envisioned here for service scaling. For the purpose of designing massively customized and evolving service systems, these results in and of themselves do not satisfy the requirements of openness, scalability, and verifiability. The basic problem is, while satisfying their proprietary needs, the previous industrial results may aim at being self-contained and become isolated from each other. As discussed above, no one company or organization can be expected to really own the knowledge of the whole population. The fact that the previous proprietary results are in fact less than satisfactory to capture the required knowledge of the application spaces intended is ironically advocated by the fact of the industrial push to a new service science. One would expect the push to be frivolous had they already mastered the art and science of service systems design. The above analysis leads, again, to the need of an open and scalable representation method for knowledge of the population, so that the field can possibly collaborate and expand to cover the whole population. That is, the field must develop the technical feasibility of collaborative population modeling even though the collaboration requires managerial will to happen. It is our postulate that such managerial will is a function of value. If it pays to collaborate, then collaboration will happen. If the population orientation is required, as proven in the value propositions that it generates, then companies will adopt it and make it a reality. We submit that the history of adoption of the open technology is precedence.

Finally, concerning the cyber-infrastructure-based repository, its scope must encompass both the particular industrial results as mentioned above and the generic design results in the academic literature. That is, the population models and their modeling resources to be assembled cannot be confined to the needs of proprietary application only (e.g., business component models), but should also reflect the goals of generalization (e.g., analytic models). To be specific, we consider the scope of the knowledge to be represented which is a central issue of population modeling. Business components are necessary knowledge since they capture the work done in an enterprise, and therefore guide the analysis of the allocation of resources across the enterprise. The knowledge of business components must be accompanied by the knowledge to evaluate them since a component can be implemented in many alternative ways. This observation leads to the inclusion of analytic models in the design knowledge of population models.

Therefore, the core design knowledge is expected to take the form of, at least, data and knowledge models for business logic (e.g., business component models) and simulation and optimization models for evaluation. The open and scalable representation method required will actually be a meta-representation of these models and modeling resources. For example, a population model may be a repository of business component models, simulation models, and optimization models which integrate in a meta-representation method of all modeling concepts and structures representing these models. The repository may be distributed across the community over the cyber-infrastructure, so that designers anywhere can query the repository and draw necessary results from it, either for use as a component of the service systems being designed, or for use as a tool to facilitate the design tasks at hand. That is, both a particular design and the evaluation of the alternative designs can draw from the design knowledge contained in the repository. Even simulation and optimization models can be applied to the evaluation, as well as being incorporated into the designs.

The above discussion substantiates the population modeling paradigm proposed in the book to accompany the DCS model for service scaling. Clearly, of the three components pertaining to the concept, the open and scalable meta-representation method is a core element required of population modeling.

We present in this chapter a particular meta-representation method for population modeling of service systems. The method is referred to as the *modelbase* whose initial design was first discussed in Hsu and Wallace (1993). The complete scope of a modelbase includes the representation method itself, the collection of all three types of modeling resources: business component, simulation, and optimization, and a cyber-infrastructure-based implementation of the representation method to manage these resources for both population modeling and the use of population models in the design of service systems. Although a particular representation method is proposed here to substantiate the concept, we contend that the notion of a modelbase is general and independent of the particular method employed.

Now, we can formally define an approach to designing service systems with knowledge of the population. It is referred to as the *cyber-enabled design* (CED) approach. The CED approach employs population modeling to develop a searchable modelbase, and implement and maintain it as an evolving window into cyber space for the design of service systems. The CED approach also calls for, as well as assumes, some open community style of collaboration among persons and organizations.

4.3 A Methodology of Population Modeling: Identification of Reusable Models

A design methodology of CED may be formulated around this central idea: Population modeling can start with a rather limited scope which still captures some core classes of knowledge to be meaningful in the application of the CED approach. In other words, we propose that the population models do not have to be perfect or even conceptually comprehensive to be useful in service systems design. A design does not have to be 100 percent supported by the population models to be considered as gaining benefits from such a paradigm. The goal is really *reducing* the learning curve and *improving* the reusability of the accumulated results in the population models. Compared to 100 percent custom development of a service system, a 70 percent, 50 percent, or even 10 percent reusability can be a significant improvement. The real importance is the ability to continue gaining — i.e., accumulating — new results to enhance the comprehensiveness of the population models as the practices continue and additional experiences are obtained. This is a crucial form of reaping the DCS accumulation effects for service system design. It can be a strategic advantage that established significant companies enjoy over their younger and perhaps smaller competitors. Conversely, if a population model cannot evolve and grow, then it is actually doomed upon creation for the design of future fluid service systems. Therefore, a core, unyielding technical requirement of population modeling is really an open and scalable meta-representation method for the population models. The methodology presented here adopts this approach: *a practical starting core built on an uncompromising design to continuously grow.*

An overview of the methodology is as follows. The starting core is proposed to comprise of select industrial results from business components modeling and proven analytic models in simulation and optimization from the public domain literature. The IBM results of CBM are identified here to be a reasonable starting point of acquiring industrial knowledge. Next, the scientific publications accumulated over the past decades in relevant fields offer an exceedingly rich mine of analytic models complete with computing algorithms and experimental or empirical data. They have seldom been reused or combined for new or different applications even when their underlying analytic logic permits these applications. The methodology calls for mining this mine of models, and make them reusable and connectible through the modelbase. The business component models chosen can provide the immediate scope of search for these models from the literature. In fact, they may determine the requirements of the analytic models, since the latter will either represent or take part in individual component models and their configuration, at all levels of aggregation. Concerning the modelbase, the previous metadatabase results will serve as the starting point for the development of this particular design. All classes of models selected will be represented and then stored in a repository structured according to the metadatabase model (see the design details in the next section). We discuss these core building blocks below.

The CBM Approach

Analyzed from a scholarly perspective, CBM reflects the principles of component engineering and information engineering to verifiably abstract the application domain. Its basic logic is reasonably generic, and hence one can expect its results to be logically compatible with those from many other industrial sources that follow the same scientific principles. To illuminate this point, we describe how the CBM approach works. Based on the open publications — see especially Nayak *et al.*, 2007 — the approach begins with determining the essential elements of the business architecture of any service-oriented enterprise. The core business architecture elements are described through various metamodels that provide abstraction of business architectural domains in terms of such fundamental concepts as business value, business structure, business behavior, business performance, and business policies and rules. The interrelationships among elements can then be captured through the occurrences of these concepts. The results are represented in standard data and knowledge concepts such as the unified modeling language (UML). An overarching conceptual modeling framework guides and drives the modeling to move down the ladder of specificity from the top concept of business services and globally integrated enterprise to business value (strategy), and progress from there to business structure (components), business behavior (operations), business performance (KPI), and business policies and rules, level by level. Business information modeling bridges these concepts and their implementation into IT solutions.

For the CED approach, we envision the CBM metamodels as results that describe the *types* of elements for all digitally connected services, guide the development of particular models (instances of the types) for the particular application space. These particular models are the object of accumulation by continuing development, collaboration and evolution. They are to be evaluated (simulated, optimized, and parameterized) and represented in the modelbase for design use. When implemented, the designers can configure CBM metamodels through the CED window to provide a roadmap of developing particular component models for particular application domains. These metamodels prescribe the types of business components that should be modeled, not the components themselves. The particular components are the building blocks of the particular design of service systems and relate to particular analytic models. These components are developed for particular application domains at varying level of aggregation, and can be made proprietary with some collaboration design. In other words, although the CED adopts an open community spirit, some of the detailed solutions and implementation design may be left to proprietary development. The present open technology practices again offer plenty of precedence and lessons that can guide CED.

Moreover, how companies use any modeling resources in the modelbase, including business components, is strictly the companies' own business. For example, IBM advocates (e.g., see Nayak *et al.*, 2007) a methodology of building a CBM Map to capture the core business architecture of service-oriented enterprises in an application domain. The methodology determines the types of competency that enterprises in the domain need to possess in order to complete successfully (the columns); and then organizes these components into the levels of accountability (the rows). It also interprets a business component to be related strongly to a business service — i.e., a particular business component is designed to provide some particular business service, and it also consumes service that other components provide. The notion of business service then leads to the modeling of business behavior that describes business operations, which determine the particulars of the service systems required and ultimately lead to their IT solution and implementation. The concept of a service agreement is employed to culminate in the identification of business service for a service provider. Accordingly, a service ecosystem model, expressed in UML, is developed to represent the context of service agreements for the application domain concerned. Clearly, other methodologies of using even the same components are possible. As long as the components built have generic logic beyond their immediate development by the designers, they can be used in some generic way in multiple contexts.

Simulation Models

They are identified from three perspectives to capture the widest spectrum of component models possible: intelligent agents for modeling persons and personal behaviors (e.g., Bonabeau, 2001), mathematical programs for modeling queueing classes of components (e.g., Chan and Schruben, 2009), and the toolset-based traditional simulation modeling for component models that are not amenable to either of these two perspectives (e.g., generic tools and solutions — e.g., see Baker, 1998). Simulation models serve two roles: representing component models and their configuration, and supplementing component models. Individual simulation models can be combined to represent the design of a service system and predict the performance of the design. This view of simulation modeling goes beyond the traditional brute-force simulation. It envisions simulation to also capture human factors (i.e., behaviors through interactions) in a service system at a high level, with a goal of understanding and identifying unknown outcomes, or verifying expected consequences, if certain rules or policies are enforced.

Therefore, simulation in the CED context not only evaluates design alternatives in the sense of comparing results to identify better component configurations, but also evaluates in the sense of alerting designers about a configuration's potential pitfalls that would otherwise be hard to identify. The mathematic program approach of simulation also provides sensitivity analysis and other information that traditional simulation lacks. Collecting all these models in one shared modelbase promises to help advance the knowledge of simulation and facilitate the integration of all three perspectives.

Optimization Models

These are decision models employed for evaluating business components as well as for evaluating the results of simulation. Since the literature contains many proven models for various service applications and generic processes that apply to certain service operations, they effectively represent a "models' mine" that we can tap into for building a comprehensive modelbase. It turns out that optimization models tend to be well abstracted in terms of algorithms and boundary conditions, and hence are particularly promising as targets of "mining the models mine". Conversely the vast collection of models developed over the past decades deserves to be better utilized and reused. The mining recognizes, including possibly modifying, the past models that describe closely the business component models created.

Optimization models help determine the parameters and boundary conditions of the component models. A collection of generic mathematical algorithms will be similarly identified for the purpose of evaluation and analysis of simulation results, as well as for employment in the simulation itself. These algorithms are expected to be a subset of the commonly available results in software libraries of mathematical programming tools. The focus of this effort will be stochastic optimization, including the generic service agent models that capture key variability and uncertainty characteristics in services delivered across the cyber-infrastructure — i.e., the DCS. The "models mine" in the supply chain literature provides a ready starting point for the collection of stochastic optimization. These service agent models can be complemented by stochastic control models that determine how systems of service agents that are jointly responsible for service delivery should be designed, controlled and managed. These service system models can be integrated using stochastic network algorithms to determine how service systems should be networked and orchestrated in a global setting ensuring that local optimality and global efficiencies are simultaneously realized. Again, collecting these models in one shared modelbase promises to help advance the knowledge of stochastic optimization and make it a tool for service systems design.

The Modelbase Method

To represent models, the method must represent at least three types of basic information resources: data, knowledge, and analytical models. The classes of data and knowledge are recognized directly for the CBM results since business components are represented by UML and other usual data and knowledge modeling concepts of the information engineering field. The other common data and knowledge modeling methods in the field include object models and entity-relationship models which are consistent with UML. All these data and knowledge models of service systems are in essence classes of *metadata* that can be represented and stored in searchable repositories, too — i.e., some databases of metadata, or metadatabases. Therefore, a metadata representation method needs to not merely represent the particular design of individual systems, but focus on representing the collection of such individual models in an integrated manner for the metadatabase. This is the same concept as the integrative collection of models in a searchable modelbase. Therefore, the modelbase method is an extension of the metadatabase concept to integrating models.

However, the list of metadata models that satisfy this requirement is short. Many results in the scholarly literature are methods for constructing a common schema for multiple databases, including global schema integration, federated registry, conceptual dictionary, and repository of enterprise metadata — see Chapter 8 for a technical review of this topic. They do not necessarily lend themselves to representation of business rules, processes, and objects that comprise component business models. Furthermore, many of the industrial metamodels, or common schemas and reference information repositories, tend to be based on some application ontology whose practicality, openness and scalability are not necessarily proven or even promised (e.g., the e-engineering effort at GE and the ebXML registry information model by Oasis-UN/CEFACT).

The metadatabase model that we adopt here for the modelbase differs from all the above results. It uniquely develops an ontology based not on applications but on the general theory of modeling, i.e., the above-mentioned concepts of objects, entities, and relationships that application (data and knowledge) systems use. Such an approach promises practicality, openness and scalability, insofar as the modeling concepts remain relevant to new applications. The next section shows how this metadata representation method may be expanded to also represent analytic models and thereby substantiate the modelbase method. The modelbase advances the knowledge of information engineering to help reuse analytical models together with data and knowledge models.

In sum, the above methodology promises to yield an implementation for the CED approach and achieve population modeling. The capability of design evaluation (via simulation and optimization) addresses the problem that service tends to allow for many alternative designs, and the new open and scalable modelbase of all models enhances the ability of *evolutionarily* modeling the population. The simulation and optimization models required are generic in nature since they correspond to the (types of) component models. Therefore, they can be abstracted, modified, or combined from representative results in the field for particular application domains — i.e., from mining the models' mine, with necessary generalization and modification. Significant new development of models is expected to be the exception rather than the norm.

4.4 A Representation Method for the Modelbase Using a Metadatabase

The modelbase method represents all the component models, simulation models, and optimization models in an integrated and searchable way. Since it employs the metadatabase model as a basis for the design, the previous metadatabase results are reviewed first. We then show how they can be extended into a modelbase.

The metadatabase is a common schema for an open community characterized by heterogeneous, distributed, and autonomous systems. Its theoretical and practical foundations have been established in several dozens of scientific publications since the late 1980s — e.g., see http://viu.eng.rpi.edu. The references at the end of the book contain some of the representative sources by the author. The metadatabase model recognizes a basic set of generic information modeling concepts, including entity-relationship-attribute, object-classification, rule-condition-action-fact; and implementation concepts of software, hardware, application, and user. They constitute the ontology of the metadatabase. This set of concepts encompasses standard modeling tools used in the field, such as the UML constructs. To the extent that these concepts are applicable to capture the constructs of all enterprise data, knowledge, and analytic models, they readily give rise to a set of common *types* of metadata of information modeling. Therefore, the metadatabase representation is *logically* open and scalable in accommodating any data, knowledge, and analytic models consistent with these concepts. In this sense, it is a logical ontology for modeling metadata, whose utility has been demonstrated through an application to narural language database query — i.e., it is shown to be capable of supporting natural language query interpretation and processing (Boonjing and Hsu, 2006). The metadatabase functions at three levels of enterprise information integration (Hsu, 1996): information repository (metadata) management (Hsu *et al.*, 1991), global query (Cheung and Hsu, 1996), and databases inter-operation (Babin and Hsu, 1996). Extended results are provided in Levermore and Hsu (2006).

The original semantic representation (conceptual schema) of the metadatabase (Hsu *et al.*, 1991) is shown in Figure 4.1, with a focus on representing multiple data models and rule-based models. The metadata types are incorporated into the ontology of an extended entity-relationship-attribute model called TSER (two-stage entity-relationship), which encompasses object orientation and uses an

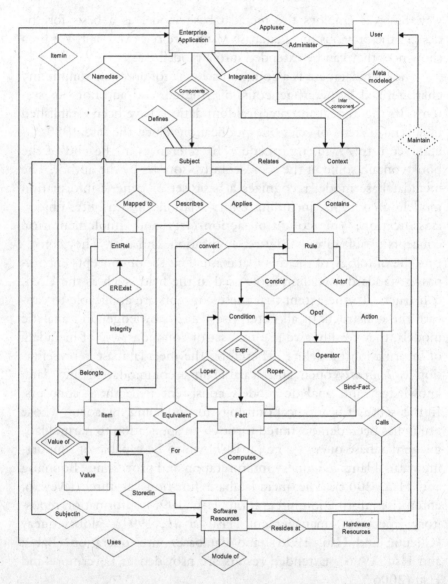

Figure 4.1:   The common schema — the conceptual structure of the metadatabase.

attendant translation methodology (Hsu *et al.*, 1993) to correspond objects to the TSER ontology. Each icon in the figure represents either a table of metadata or a particular type of integrity control rule. The meta-tables are categorized into four interrelated groups:

users-applications, database models, contextual knowledge, and software and hardware resources.

The database models group is comprised of metadata types that define application data models for enterprises. They include subject (comparable to object and view), entity-relationship, and data item. The meta-relationship "define" supports recursive subjects, showing the super sub-hierarchy between subjects in a bill-of-materials manner. The contextual knowledge is structured in terms of the metadata types rule, condition, action, operator, and fact. These types constitute a rulebase model as a particular representation method for rules (Bouziane and Hsu, 1997).

The condition and action metadata types represent the declaration of conditions and actions for the predicates of rules, both of which are further substantiated with operator and fact. Fact corresponds to data items of the database models, and thereby integrates database models with contextual knowledge. These two groups are further linked, in one direction, with the aggregated definition of users-applications, and in the other, with software and hardware resources. The user-aplication group is defined as representing multiple enterprises, application families, and user interface types (including natural language input) of the database models and their contextual knowledge. The software and hardware resources group represents the particular computing platforms, networking middleware, and other IT solutions involved in the implementation design of the databases and knowledge systems.

The equivalent meta-relationship cross-references data items from one application data model to their equivalents in others. Together with the conversion routines represented in software and hardware resources, they achieve data semantics reconciliation for the community. This part of the metadatabase model is also recognized to be a core set of metadata that a distributed metadatabase design can use to install in local sites and facilitate peer-to-peer data reconciliation and collaboration (Hsu *et al.*, 2006). This conceptual schema defines the metatables of the metadatabase, which in turn is implemented and processed as a standard relational database.

Application information models are "saved" into the metadatabase by first reverse-representing their constructs (e.g., the object types) into the neutral TSER constructs, and then entering this neutral representation (e.g., the metadata) into the corresponding metatables in the metadatabase. Thus, an information model will have a number of entries in a number of metatables in the metadatabase representing it. New information models are added to the community in the same way, using the neutral method TSER. This process extends to the modification of existing models represented in the metadatabase, too. This conversion process is amenable to using a CASE tool, while the insertion and updating processes are just ordinary relational operations. Thus, the metadatabase does not need to shut down during the insertion and update. In this sense, the common schema, i.e., the metadatabase, implemented as a relational database, is *operationally* open and scalable, as well.

The metadatabase model includes a distributed design to support data fusion. Chapter 8 elaborates on this concept. The distribution design is centered on a minimum metadatabase to be resided at participating sites to facilitate collaboration (information sharing and exchange) among them. Any site that supports a thin database (e.g., a system on a chip) can participate; this includes some of the advanced wireless sensor system and RFID (radio frequency identification) tags.

The global equivalent metatable is the only necessary element of any minimum metadatabase design. It is also possible to reduce the software and hardware resources metatables of Figure 4.1 and include them in the local metadatabase to support the implemented IT solutions.

Although the previous metadatabase model is concerned primarily with data and knowledge representation, it has also been proposed to be applied to managing analytical models (Hsu and Wallace, 1993). We further develop the possibility here. For this application, models are represented at three levels: the metadata that describe a model, the core logic, or algorithm (e.g., the pseudo code), and the software implementation. The metadata are directly construed in terms of the TSER concepts, with modifications to suit the model definitions. The logic is stored as text, or a character stream, in the modelbase. The software implementation is referenced (by pointers) in the modelbase but actually stored separately as BLOB (binary large objects).

The modification of the metadatabase model for the modelbase is concentrated on the design of particular attributes that represent models. These attributed are listed in Figure 4.2, which relate the elements of the metadatabase model (i.e., the conceptual schema in Figure 4.1) to the basic concepts and constructs of analytical models. Both the logic and the software implementation of a model may be further reduced into rules and programs, respectively, as well as being considered as a single, aggregate "rule" and a single program. In other words, multiple levels of reduction are allowed by the recursive nature of the schema to either "zoom out" to the level of whole models or zoom in to individual rules and routines. We envision a new design science for the sharing of modelbase that "normalizes" (or, consolidates) model resources up to the level of individual rules and routines, in a way similar to the data normalization method that characterizes the science of database design. Such a normalized modelbase promises to facilitate maximum flexibility in model sharing, reuse, and aggregation. The modelbase attributes in Figure 4.2 support this concept.

The anchoring constructs in the modelbase representation method are Subject, representing models for an application; EntRel, representing normalized, sharable models; Rule, representing logic; and Program, representing software implementation. They are also the anchoring constructs for the metadatabase. Therefore, the basic structure of Figure 4.1 remains unchanged, but the meta-attributes of the constructs of the structure are changed, as defined in Figure 4.2.

To populate the modelbase (creating and saving models into the modelbase), the effort will focus on two primary activities: the representation and organization of the CBM results, simulation models, and optimization models according to Figure 4.2; and the reduction of some composite analytic models into some common reusable modules shared by these models. The results of both activities will be the model resources that the modelbase represents and saves. The results from the first will show the models as they were in the literature, or as how the applications will use them (the user views); while the second will be the normalized resources that can be flexibly assembled and reused to form new models as well as to recover the original ones

Modeling Construct Representation for the Modelbase:

System (eco-system/CBM map/overall management-decision-operation systems)

Application (application domain/meta-models)/*i.e., meta-models for applications/*

Subject (application/model/component/IT solution)/*i.e., models for an application/*

Context (associations between models)

Item (parameter and decision variable)

Rule (model structural rules, solution logic/procedure and operation/assertion)/*i.e., logic/*

Condition (constraint, function, and mathematical/logical statement)

Action (feasibility, optimality, and mathematical/logical statement)

File (input, output, and other interfaces)

Program (executable algorithm/code)/*i.e., software implementation/*

Model Resources Representation:

- **Meta-Entities**

System (Systname, descript, addedby, dateadded, uname)

Application (Aname, SubAname, descript, addedby, dateadded, Uname)

Subject (Sname, SubSname, descript, addedby, dateadded, Uname)

Context (Cname, descript, addedby, dateadded, uname)

Item (ItemCode, iname, represent, length, domain, descript, defvalue, addedby, dateadded)

Rule (Rname, rtype, descript, addedby, dateadded)

Condition (Condid, iname, operator, value)

Action (Actid, acctype, exemode, actcont)

EntRel (OEname, PKey, AKey, descript, addedby, dateadded)/*i.e., normalized models/*

PR (PRname, PKey, AKey, descript, addedby, dateadded)

MR (MRname, PKey, AKey, descript, addedby, dateadded)

FR (FRname, Dant, Ded, descript, addedby, dateadded)

File (Fname, ftype, accessmode, descript, addedby, dateadded)

Document (Dname, doctype, numpages, author, addedby, dateadded, descript)

Hardware (Hname, htype, location, comnet, addedby, dateadded, descript)

User (Uname, Aname-usagename, position, phone, office, address)

Program (Progname, descript, language, addedby, dateadded)

Figure 4.2:   Model resources representation using the metadatabase elements.

- **Meta-relationships:** mostly binary relations associating meta-entities

Relates (Cname, Sname)

CondOf (Condid, Rname)

Describes (Iname, Sname)

Actof (Actid, Rname)

Contains (Cname, Rname)

Applies (Sname, Rname) etc.

Figure 4.2: (*Continued*)

(the first). This recursive structure is captured by the similarly recursive concept of subject in the TSER ontology. In sum, the modelbase has two meanings: the open and scalable meta-representation method and the cyber-infrastructure-based repository of modeling resources (models) structured according to the representation method. *The repository itself can be distributed, and its management separated between the proprietary knowledge (e.g., IBM CBM) and open knowledge* — see below.

Now that the elements of the CED approach have been established, a possible CED prototype design using the cyber-infrastructure can be contemplated. Fundamentally, implementing the modelbase over cyber-infrastructure will result in a software realization that we call the CED system. The implementation can use a central global modelbase server, or distribute the copies of the modelbase at major sites of the community. Both approaches promise to work because the modelbase handles only metadata whose frequency and quantity of retrieval and update are expected to be limited, unlike real-time transaction data in ordinary distributed databases.

The central server approach will be efficient on a modelbase management but requires some central authority that can be controversial for all participants to accept in a collaborative environment. The multiple copies approach will maximize the autonomy of participants at the cost of complicated metadata management issues to synchronize all copies, which, however, can be achieved with a variety of methods. The performance of the modelbase in either approach should not make discernible difference to most users most of the

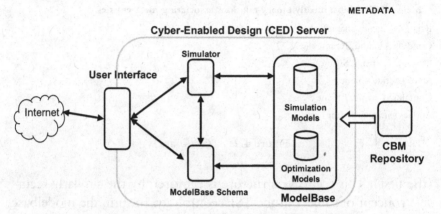

Figure 4.3:   The CED prototype architecture.

time. Some mirror sites will accompany the central server, of course. The modelbase itself will be implemented in a relational database system, with additional management functions created as an added shell to the underlying database management system, either at the global server site or the local participant sites. In either approach, the CED system consists of a number of components as depicted in Figure 4.3.

It should be noted that the CBM repository is separated from the rest of the modelbase in the design, in order to allow for proprietary control of the industrial knowledge of business components. This way, the CBM repository can be physically located at the company site, under the company control, while logically connected to the modelbase server. The modelbase schema is the software implementation of the meta-representation of all three types of models in the modelbase — i.e., the structure of the database of the modeling resources. The rest of the components are self-evident. The software implementation of the CED design and the system's inter-operation with other similar results is beyond the scope of the book. The openness and scalability of the modelbase for CED can be established at a conceptual analysis level, based on the openness and scalability of its foundation, the metadatabase model. The extended metadata auery language (exMQL) (Babin and Hsu, 1996; Cheung and Hsu, 1996 and Levermore, 2006) of the metadatabase model can be adopted to query the modelbase, too.

We now use a simple example to illustrate how the CED system may reduce the learning curve in developing a service system. Specifically, we discuss how a modelbase can facilitate new simulation to reuse past models either in full or in part. A CED scenario goes like this. A service provider is chosen to develop an organ transplantation supply chain solution for the Canadian provincial departments of health. The company has developed particular CBM results for healthcare space and certain classes of supply chain applications, all of which have been saved in a modelbase; but it has not worked for the particular organ transplantation problems. The clients of the solution also require their own versions of certain business processes involved to satisfy their own quality policies and regulations. The company recognizes that the basic logic here is similar to the logic that they have worked on before, and decides to tap into the CED, to leverage the available results from the community as well as reuse their own previous results. Therefore, it embarks on the development by following the metamodels and conducting the necessary analysis, with the modelbase at their disposal.

In this case, the modelbase would have stored CBM application domains as entries in the Application metatable; CBM metamodels as entries in Subject with possible decompositions; the generic KPI and other generic UML objects as entries in the EntRel; and the application-specific UML objects as entries in Subject. Attributes and rules/methods would have been represented and stored as Data Items and Rules, respectively. A set of basic views defined on the modelbase would also have reconstructed the original UML models by, when activated, retrieving and joining the pertinent results in the modelbase, all through ordinary relational operations. Querying the modelbase, as the scenario continues, a set of specific UML models are identified to indicate the objects of analysis, such as the goals of the business service.

In addition, simulation models from all application contexts are also identified for possible retrieval since the UML entries are associated with analytical models whose logic apply to them. Among them, simulation models of some liver transplant supply chain systems in the United Kingdom and a few other organ transplant supply chains developed for a few other countries are discovered. Their core logic has been reviewed to be sufficiently applicable to the problem at hand. Finally, a variety of simulation models is developed from reusing these results for the particular business service objects identified. They evaluate the alternative designs for the components. This scenario illustrates possible reduction of the learning curve throughout the development life cycle of service systems.

The population orientation of a new science for service scaling is elaborated in this chapter. The discussion begins with the general concept and concludes in a specific design method inspired by the DCS model. The new results include the CED concept and the modelbase method to guide the accumulation of particular reusable knowledge for particular application domains. Together, *they support the second theorem of DCS* for modeling knowledge, and expressly contribute a population modeling paradigm to the design of service systems, to support reuse and sharing of, for example, the component business models, simulation models, and optimization models accumulated in the field. The reuse promises to achieve economies of scale for accumulated industrial experience and scientific knowledge, as well as to bring verifiability to the design of service systems.

The CED approach requires industrial effort to make it a reality. In fact, in the context of a service science, it is ultimately related to some of the proposals we make in Chapter 2, such as national standards and collaborative service science research laboratories. The design method presented here may in this sense be received as a substantiation of why and how those proposals may help industry develop their service systems. Of course, in the end, whether or not the effort will come depends ultimately on whether or not the approach helps. Although any new ideas need proactive championing, no champion can replace the value itself. We do not know if the particular formulation and design of the approach will ever be tested for its value, but if the concept of population orientation for service system design is right, then some form of population knowledge constructed in the spirit of DCS will eventually emerge.

Beyond service *per se*, in a broader sense the modelbase method may have bearing on accumulating and sharing scientific knowledge for collaborative research in other fields as well. For example, the science community can benefit from an open source technology that supports the general sharing and reuse of the scientific knowledge accumulated in all scientific literature. We submit that the basic ideas of the modelbase deserve further investigation, including possible normalization of all three forms of knowledge concerned, as a starting point for a new technology to facilitate cyber-enabled scientific discovery.

The chapter has provided two major results for service scaling: establishment and substantiation of the population orientation, and development of a new design paradigm, CED, and its attendant method, the modelbase. They contribute directly to service systems design, and therefore help illuminate the integrative research required of a new service science. In a general sense, these results link Chapters 3 to 6, 7, and 8.

Chapter 5

Quintessential Digitally Connected Service: New Business Designs on the Web

What will be the next waves of the Web? No one can answer this question with certainty. However, one may try to analyze how new designs have emerged in the past, what was the general logic that propelled them, and then try to infer for the future. This is what the chapter tries to do. It provides an explanation for the stories of e-commerce/e-business, social networking, and other Internet-based enterprises with the help of the service scaling and transformation theory. By extension, it also sheds light on these stories' continuing evolution. In a nutshell, we submit that the first decade of the Web since 1993 is largely explainable by the first theorem of the DCS model, while the second decade also exhibits the second theorem and even some evidence of the third. Therefore, the full-fledged logic of the third and fourth theorems is expected to increasingly describe new emergent designs in the coming decades. The analysis has a few implications: First, the Web is the quintessential digitally connected service, including its operation, its applications, and all the economic activities that support these applications. Second, the Web can be a quintessential proving ground, too, for studying service scaling and transformation, as well as a source of inspiration for the theory. More broadly, the Web will continue to serve as a momentous thrust for the S-curve transformation of the knowledge economy postulated in Chapter 3. Besides the theory, the chapter has a more general appeal in its own

133

right: It can be used as a stand-alone *tutorial* of new business designs using the Web. That is, although the theory is responsible for a unique and hopefully deeper analysis, the review itself is neither limited to nor distorted by the theory. Representative revenue/business models of e-commerce are also included to strengthen the chapter's tutorial value.

5.1 The DCS Difference

The overarching technical problem is how to innovate business designs for population oriented cocreation? The Web plays an important role in the search for an answer. In retrospect, the Web has evolved from a humble platform for posting documents to one that carries much of the social and economic activities on its shoulders. Everyone knows why social networking, Internet-based commerce (e-commerce), Internet-based enterprise (e-business), and all other public and private activities using the Internet are good: in one word, "convenient". The first theorem of the DCS model as presented in Chapter 3 is a fancy way to explain this word. However, convenience alone does not spell transformation; at least, not directly. It can start snowballing towards transformation, but will need additional momentum and perhaps even additional helpers to make an avalanche. We recognize some of these helpers from the collected experience of the Web, and use them to try to foretell the future Web. That is, we apply the other theorems as well, and indeed we apply the whole theory to lay a conceptual framework of analysis. With the framework, we logically infer the future for the Web as a transformation leader for the knowledge economy. The focus of our review is e-commerce, e-business, and social networking.

Retailing is cocreation of value between the customer and the retailer. As every luxury car dealership and every upscale clothing store would say, making shopping a fulfilling personal experience for their customers is a critical success factor to them. This factor extends to the active cultivation of personal relationships with the customers and potential customers, using all information they can gather on them. Unfortunately, this practice is costly and requires resources.

Most retailers whom ordinary people have the chance to deal with do not belong to that league. They may not be in a position to pursue the well-known best practice in any service of fulfilling cocreation. In any case, they settle into getting by with treating their customers as faceless John or Jane, without any pretense of attempting to lure them back service. If this is not entirely true with traditional mom-and-pop stores, which rely on none other than the proprietors' sheer brain power to relate to repeat customers within the confines of their locality, then it is certainly the case when these stores grow in size or are substituted by megastores of giant discount chains. Everyone knows this kind of story by heart. We may quietly point out that this abundantly shows *the failure of service to scale up* — service operations on the provider side may scale up but not their *value cocreation* for customers. In fact, customers have been made to sacrifice value (happiness of life?) for material cost in this unbalanced scaling, with or without their consent. Such is the case of service scaling by non-digital means.

Digital means are altogether another story. The Web, or e-commerce, proves that scaling by digital means can be cost-efficient while also preserving value cocreation, at least relatively speaking. The transaction systems itself, after digitization, is reusable and sharable, and hence its development can be more affordable (diminishing marginal cost) on the basis of accumulated customers. More fundamentally, the system is amenable to personalization for individual customers to help preserve cocreation. Using the Web, i.e., digital connections scaling, every customer is by definition a distinct node complete with personal data that may grow by additional connection. Moreover, every transaction is also automatically recognized and recorded, and accumulated over time in relation to the commodities being sold as well as in relation to the customer. This *population data* is available almost merely by the asking, since they are technically by-products of the digital connections. Therefore, the intelligent and diligent moms and pops not only can scale up their operations, but also scale up their "brains" in digital form to scale up their value cocreation in catering to the individual customer — and no longer confined to a locality.

On this note, one may in fact argue that the new population data is bound to be more comprehensive than the trusty, rusty traditional ways of relying on store records alone, since traditional records never capture customers' unrealized intents and are difficult to cross-reference on demand. Comprehensive data promises to yield powerful new knowledge for value cocreation and innovation. For one thing, understanding personal intents, preferences, and style can lead to innovation of transaction systems to enhance fulfilling cocreation. For another, one can recall the lateral thinking predicted in the first theorem of the DCS model, that new business designs can follow the chaining and clustering of the tasks that persons or organizations must perform during their respective life cycles, in any combination of any dimensions of the tasks and cycles. Population data holds the key for such analysis of complementary value propositions and revelation of business opportunities.

For the moms and pops that employ DCS, this means that they can think more strategically and will have better chances to change, to branch out, to convert, or to merge their traditional business designs and models to leverage what the Web has to offer. For example, small tailor shops can link to form upscale clothing suppliers for customers located in small cities or remote regions. They can even form specialty clothing co-ops for moviegoers who idolize movie stars and mimic their dressing. The latter practices can be further generalized with links to dealers anywhere in other trades to offer related paintings, pictures, or gifts around any possible theme: movies, businesses, politics etc.

This *fluidity* is only possible with the Web due to the latter's unique "equalizing" power. Cyberspace sees no inherent divisions in trades, commodities, and industries when it comes to connecting them with digital means, as it sees little difference in who can or cannot use the digital connections because of sex, race, and nationality. The four theorems of the DCS models indicate that even a mom-and-pop store has a relatively level playing field on the Web to function like a multinational conglomerate: selling and buying globally, innovating globally, and moving in and out of different trades globally. This cannot be said for any mom-and-pop outside of the Web.

Thus, the real difference DCS makes that promises to transform the knowledge economy is its capacity to help *inflate the change throughout society*. This observation leads to the basic conviction that *the Web sparks and continues to fuel the S-curve transformation of the knowledge-economy* as predicted in Chapter 3.

The stories of amazom.com and Google, which have become common knowledge in the field, offer proof of the conviction. However, we wish to point out that their ongoing revolution reflects a growth from the first theorem of DCS to the second, when analyzed from the perspective of the service scaling and transformation theory. As everyone knows, Internet bookstores have simplified the value chain of publication, but at the same time have complicated the value chains in many other traditional industries. Therefore, the story of amazon.com has two sides: First, it digitizes the retailing of books (direct digital connections to customers and publishers) to combine retailers and wholesalers in the value chain of publication. This is the reduction of transaction cost (including the cost of the traditional storefronts in retailing channels) and reduction of cycle time for everyone involved, as advocated by the first theorem of DCS. Second, after having reached a significant scale (the accumulation effects of DCS), it applied lateral thinking and branched out to non-book commodities to tap into its customer base for additional business. This lateral movement implicates the value chains of other industries and forces the issue of concurrent configuration. Again, the core logic for this concurrent business to happen so smoothly is the simple fact that book buyers have other life cycle tasks to perform which involve purchasing of other goods. The same technical platform that amazon.com built to sell books can equally support DCS for retailing of other commodities on the same basis of accumulating customers and value propositions. This is another part that the first theorem of DCS advocates and the second grows.

In theory, amazon.com or any other online book store can opt to stay in their current space, buying from publishers and carrying only books and their complementary goods; but they can also in principle easily move into almost any other retailing space and/or further simplify the publication value chain. The only constraint seems to be the industrial barriers that already exist, such as the business logic behind the division of book selling, publication, and writing. For example, if amazon.com should cease to buy books directly from publishers but to provide connections between customers and publishers in order to save the huge cost of carrying inventory, then publishers could also move into retailing to replace amazon.com and save the huge markups for themselves. It is only the fact that amazon.com buys in huge quantity from them that keeps the publishers at bay — i.e., the current division still makes more sense to them than their expansion by DCS to selling directly to readers.

To generalize, the business situation today is inherently delicate and major changes can happen at any time, due to the connecting power of the Web. There is no birth right for any middle business to exist if they do not offer sufficient value to both sides. Therefore, the whole value chain of the publication industry today (i.e., customer (person) — retailer/wholesale — publisher — writer [person]) is in an intriguing or even tenuous state of balance. Any link of the chain can break out of the status quo and reach out to the whole population of the chain, such as what some writers/artisans have chosen to do — to directly sell to readers on the Web. In this case, the entire publication value chain is collapsed into a direct person-to-person relationship. The only determinant to whether this practice propagates throughout seems to be the value propositions involved: which business design ultimately amasses the most purchasing power to succeed?

For amazon.com to offset the cost of maintaining a huge inventory, they need to scale up value cocreation for both their customers and suppliers. From this perspective, the most fundamental competitive advantage that amazon.com has built is the *population knowledge* which is even more important than the customer base they now own since customers come and go but the knowledge accumulated stays. The second theorem of the DCS model is pertinent to some recent strategies at amazon.com, such as the practice of recommendations and cross-referencing. The logic may be expected to continue to describe the further exploitation of the competitive advantages due to population knowledge at amazon.com. This line of strategies may one day permit Internet bookstores to do away with their huge inventories and become a pure service provider — i.e., when they have accumulated decisively more knowledge to enable them to provide more formidable value cocreation to customers than any other in the industry can, so that publishers would have to rely on them and outside contenders who do not have such knowledge could not touch them.

Google is another interesting case. It has taught businesses a lot about business, such as how to use the Web's open community and free service spirit to build customer base for immediate business benefits (new business models). Google also shows why it is prudent to shoot for the stars and aim at the whole population of the business space (new search engine-based technical models), and what is lateral thinking on the Web (new business designs). It started as one of the best search engines on the Internet to reduce the transaction cost and cycle time of connecting to Web sources. Again, the first theorem of DCS offers a general logic to explain its initial success. However, unlike the other search engines and information service providers before it, Google swiftly moved to build unprecedented knowledge bases by digital connections as well as acquisitions (e.g., satellite images, youtube.com resources, and a digital "universal" library) and put them to new value propositions. This growth may attest to the second theorem of DCS.

Again, these practices (e.g., Google Earth and its embedment into many information and transaction sites on the Web) demonstrate the virtually unlimited possibilities of digitization, digital connection, and scaling along personal and organizational life cycle tasks. They corroborate with the DCS model. Some of the emerging practices of Google, as discussed in Chapter 3 under the third theorem of DCS, have progressed to new heights towards innovative business design. We wish to recognize that the third theorem of DCS expects more new developments to come following these emerging practices. Ultimately for the knowledge economy, we further expect the Web to continue expanding its business designs to cover traditional industries. In this sense, we expect to witness new waves of practices from Google and other innovative companies to reflect the fourth theorem of the DCS model. Google is indeed poised to be among the first to explore as well as exploit ecosystem effects since it literally owns the population of Web search.

From the perspective of the service scaling and transformation theory, social networking is not only a major class of values and value propositions, but also a major way to identify values and expose life cycle tasks for persons. That is, social networking has inherent implications on business by virtue of value propositions. Social networking sites represent stand-alone digitization of traditional social activities among persons (peer-to-peer connections for certain roles of life), and their successes reflect the promises of DCS as the first theorem advocates. For example, youtube.com, facebook.com, and spike.com have each registered huge success with an astounding growth rate. However, they have not been commonly connected to business beyond the usual marketing activity such as advertising. This is unfortunate for both sides since important values (to persons and to organizations) can be co-created by their connection. As Chapter 3 explains, social networking is more directly related to business than merely being some object of propaganda; because, philosophically speaking, socialization is an integral part of a person's business life, too. If a person's social activities and interests are intertwined with his/her other activities and interests in life, including buying, selling, and working, then how can social networking be unrelated to business? It is only a matter of understanding this fundamental fact and putting the implications to work, as the concept of life cycle tasks indicates and the propositions of DCS explain.

Consider a recent business deal between facebook.com and Google, which did not materialize due to privacy and other issues involved. The former would have put the vast amount of information resources that it has accumulated at the disposal of the latter for provision to businesses as Internet contents. This would-be example illustrates the logic of the second theorem of DCS. The story does not end here. Since social networking sites usually do not generate revenues directly from the services they provide, their success can only be attributed to the values they create to persons which indicate the directions of value propositions, e.g., finding like-minded persons for discussion, extracurricular activities, and business ventures. These directions can be logically configured around tasks that intersect with businesses, such as the subject matter of discussion, transactions involved in the activities, and the ventures themselves. Therefore, social networking may reveal life cycle tasks and new value propositions for cocreation, as discussed above. It may pervasively accompany new business models and designs that pursue the logic of the third and the fourth theorems.

This view is actually another delineation of the *person-centered perspective* discussed in Chapter 1. It promises to help link all business tasks at the level of persons, since all economical activities are ultimately concerned with persons in various roles. Person is a common denominator for all. The recognition leads naturally to the conclusion that *social networking can be integrated with value cocreation, as a part of customer practices and knowledge worker practices to enhance their abilities to go about their life cycle tasks on the job or in life*. Through this integration, social networking can impact all other economic activities that involve persons — i.e., the entire economy.

The integration can take many forms. For example, an organization can provide social networking as a business service to customers and/or its employees. It can also incorporate social networking into its business practices on the Web. Since businesses have already incorporated social networking tools into their marketing practices (e.g., blogs), further integration is mainly a matter of will and finding the right value propositions. The DCS model may help guide the search for value propositions, especially identifying the logic of exploring life cycle tasks (of the customers and knowledge workers) to expand the business design. In this sense, the practices of customer comments at amazon.com and many other e-commerce sites should not be the end of their employment of social networking, but only the beginning. More innovative social networking can clearly lead to a better customer base on which they can expand their business in more ways than just carrying non-book goods. In this sense, the big story about social networking is its promise to be a part of service scaling and transformation for the knowledge economy.

We now review the representative or prototypical business designs on the Web. For the S-curve transformation, the review shows an evolution pointing to the possible synthesis of these designs to breed new designs. For general reading, the review also serves as a tutorial on e-commerce/e-business and social networking.

5.2 Review of Business Designs on the Web

The Web has offered many particular business designs which provide in various degrees some specific ideas for developing digitally connected services. We review them one by one and discuss how they may be expanded and/or combined in the light of the four theorems of the DCS model. We recognize five categories for them in order to provide some organization: Internet commerce, Internet enterprise, social networking, Internet utilities, and technology and system providers.

5.2.1 *Internet Commerce*

In this category, the Web is employed as the platform on which to conduct retailing and business procurement. This is the original and narrow definition of *e-commerce*. The category includes some of the best known business designs using the Web. Virtually any business can adopt some of these models at a cost reasonable to the business and with value propositions beneficial to all its stakeholders. There are many providers and many technologies available on the Web to suit almost any budget and any need, including free solutions from open source communities. From the perspective of service scaling and transformation, this category explores primarily the Web's potential of connecting a provider to its customers, but ignores many other possibilities with the Web — such as connections among customers. Some designs, especially auctioning, feature limited and controlled interaction among customers for self-policing (e.g., peer reviews). These noteworthy practices, unfortunately, have stopped short of promoting participation as a tool of scaling, such as employing social networking and other possibilities to grow the participant pool.

Scaling in these designs is largely one-way: individual businesses linking to more customers, and hence the first theorem describes most of the basic value propositions found in this category. Some business designs reflect truly forward-looking innovation, at least at the time of their conception. Among them we single out the marketplace concept, which represents a powerful stride towards implementing the third theorem of DCS.

B2C (business-to-customer: individual business sites for retailing, marketing, gaming, etc.): One of the most venerable business designs on the Web, its original meaning refers to just about any kind of Web site that conducts business (selling to) with customers. However, since vastly different business designs have emerged from this prototypical idea, the meaning of B2C has been narrowed down to refer expressly to individual businesses that sell to persons on the Web. A significant percentage of organizations and persons in digitally connected economies have engaged in this design, one way or another. Our discussion in Section 5.1 about amazon.com and mom-and-pop stores pertains largely to this design and explains its common benefits. In addition, the practices of B2C have permeated from the "usual suspects" such as Internet retailing, Internet banking, and Internet ticketing to all corners of society, ranging from Internet-based cartoonists and other artisans all the way to universities (e.g., admissions/recruitment) and politics (e.g., fund raising and meetings).

As illustrated by amazon.com, the B2C design does not have to be aligned rigidly to the confines of traditional business spaces. That is, the idea itself is general enough to include such practices as the businesses' moving in and out of different clusters of business opportunities as they pursue complementary value propositions revealed by customers' life cycle tasks. In other words, a B2C site can sell anything and buy anything on demand, due to the *fluidity* afforded by the Web. Equally significantly, the digital nature of the Web allows *B2C connections to be embedded* (i.e., *embedded B2C*) into any other site using any business design, including social networking. For example, a news article about a book that amazon.com sells can include a hyperlink on the book to bring the reader of the article to the precise homepage selling the book at the online bookstore. This idea extends the original concept of hyperlinks from linking homepages to also linking online businesses on the Web in a completely on-demand manner. The practice may be technically simple, but its business implication is enormous — meaning that there is no such thing as pure business or pure information services, and no such thing as isolated business designs or business models.

The big picture is that this design is fundamentally consistent with the notion of person-centered and organization-centered views of a digitally connected world (see Chapters 1 and 3). Therefore, *we expect B2C to eventually evolve into a cyber-dimension of every person and every organization.* That is, the design will continue to exist, expand, and more significantly, evolve into a platform supporting the transformation into a person-centered or organization-centered knowledge economy. In this transformation, *we expect the design to incorporate many other designs on the Web to promote the values to persons, organization, and society.* For example, a person offering skills for hire on demand, or acquiring services on demand, or soliciting any activities related to his/her life cycle tasks, is a person amenable to engaging in *personal B2C* to sell as well as to buy on the Web. It should also be abundantly clear that *social networking and personal B2C cannot be separated,* and the separation may not even be desirable. By extension, the same can be inferred for the *interrelationship between social networking and organizations* to the extent, at least, that *customers, knowledge workers, and other stakeholders are all persons.*

Online Storefront (a B2C site that does marketing only): This design can be defined as a subset of the B2C model since it focuses primarily on the informational value of a Web presence for persons and organizations. However, it deserves to be given a separate identity to recognize its wide applicability as a practical initial step to using the Web for business that any person and organization can afford to do. In a broad sense, all college students have their online storefronts if they maintain personal homepages and link them to their resumes.

The common benefits of this design lie basically in its ease of updating the information contents that the business wishes to post. To take this marketing goal seriously, however, the storefront model needs to align with some (non-transaction based) informational designs (see below) to make it work: Attract visitors and promote the host business. That is, online storefronts need word-of-mouth effects.

B2B (business-to-business: business procurement, supply chain activities, and collaboration): When the "C" in B2C is replaced by "B" — business, then we have another venerable design focusing on business-to-business commerce, with similar basic functions and characteristics as the B2C design. In other words, a simple view of B2B is that it is a B2C where the customers are organizations. All properties of B2C apply to B2B as well. However, because organization customers have significant characteristics beyond those of individual customers, such as the magnitude and complexity of transactions, the B2B system requirements tend to be oriented more towards collaboration or even cocreation. More sophisticated B2B activities have led the model to additional business designs to support, especially, supply chains, as discussed below. In general, we contend that the basic model of B2B is similar to B2C, and they differ mainly in the business space with which each deals. They may be combined in analysis.

B2C Shopping Mall (collection of B2C sites for one-stop shopping): The same business logic that spawned department stores and shopping malls before the age of the Internet bred online shopping malls (or "business spheres") on the Web, too. The original examples include yahoo.com and geocity.com which tend to be portals to many independent B2Cs whose operation is beyond the portal's direct control. Later models offer more integrated presence and operations throughout the shopping mall, as exemplified by travelocity.com and orbiz.com. In any case, the destination site (the shopping mall) and its participating B2Cs are by design independent of each other in ownership as well as in operation in this business design. Each shopping mall, especially the more integrated ones, is in and of itself a B2C destination site selling commodities to (persons) customers, except that it does not own inventories: the commodities that it sells not only come from their participant companies but also are being sold under these companies' individual control. The business relationship between the shopping mall site and the B2C sites that are "parked" on it is actually B2B. The shopping mall site tends to offer technical solutions and lease their Web platforms to their clients to conduct B2C on it, as a business model for this B2B practice.

Clearly, this design is a form of DCS, to accumulate as well as tap into the customer base, the provider base, and the system base. The benefits of this design actually reflect the benefits of the scaling of the digital connections realized at the shopping mall. Clearly, the success of this design depends on the added value propositions that the collection of B2C sites can yield: how compelling is the value of this one-stop shopping to the customers' performing their life cycle tasks? Again, in addition to reuse of the accumulated resources, the particular business design of an online shopping mall must make sense to propel cocreation of values among all stakeholders in order for it to last and prosper.

The *life cycle tasks* concept helps to identify compelling value propositions, as shown in the success of the model for the travel business where car rental, lodging, and other tasks pertaining to travel are hosted under the same roof of the destination site. Many earlier practices of this model failed despite their hosts' name recognition — a counter-example that proves the same point. In general, the shopping mall ideas are advantageous for developing fluid clustering of B2C sites at relatively low cost, for common or complementary life cycle tasks. In fact, a grouping of such tasks becomes a particular application domain or business space. A critical success factor is an integrated theme and streamlined operation for tasks grouping. The B2C shopping mall design is especially noteworthy for small businesses. For example, antique stores may form collaborative Web presence to collectively promote their business and gain benefits of the scale so built. Neighborhood stores may also join to promote the community and in turn gain from the accumulation of customer base. Both represent application of the DCS model by the first theorem: value proposition according to life cycle tasks.

B2B Shopping Mall (collection of B2B sites for one-stop supply chain needs): Unlike the shopping mall concept for B2C, which has become relatively stable at a plateau, shopping malls for B2B practices are booming. One example is alibaba.com. The difference seems to lie in a simple fact: the B2B shopping malls are designed for supply chain needs which are a clear dimension of any company's life cycle tasks. We expect such B2B shopping malls to also accumulate common system resources in other aspects of supply chain operations, such as finance and logistics support, and tap into them to gain benefits of scale for their clients (the participating B2B sites). Similarly, these destination sites can scale by proactively facilitating formation of on-demand supply chains for their clients. Clients may match their life cycle tasks and collaborate and transact via the site. In other words, the B2B shopping mall model is amenable to converging with the industrial exchange model to be reviewed below.

Consortium/Communal Cooperative for B2C or B2B (jointly developed online shopping malls for closely knit groups): This is a model of collaboration. It can reflect either an extended enterprise (e.g., a consortium of companies based on a medicine supply chain) or a theme-based community (entertainment). Compared to the shopping mall model, the collaboration model goes deeper and involves proprietary control. That is, the participants tend to own a piece of the co-op, and may not enjoy any independent presence and/or operation at the destination site. This business design is natural to participants belonging to a group closely related by their (common) life cycle tasks. Therefore, they can develop sufficient value propositions to justify going another step beyond the usual online shopping malls and jointly develop their group consortia or co-ops; share a common Web presence as a group; and pursue common or complementary life cycle tasks (the theme). It is a digital version of the industrial guild model.

Examples include the consortium by Johnson and Johnson and the communal collaborative enterprise by Italian knitting mills in the Alps region (many of which are allied with the Benetton Group). Surplus commodities sale sites (e.g., hotwire.com for travel) are also a prototypical example. This business design may be exceedingly fitting for business collaboration to develop extended enterprises on the Web, especially for forming on-demand alliance or a "task force" among participants. Social networking is the best way to explore communities while life cycle tasks are a coherent logic to identify value propositions for the collaboration. However, as the level of fluidity increases, new forms of organization may have to be explored and employed to assure accountability and business control.

Auction/Marketplace for B2C (integration of B2C systems to conduct massively distributed assortment of transactions): This design shares some fundamental properties with B2C/B2B shopping malls, such as the destination site itself being a B2C/B2B with the participants of the site being its customers. Differences are also fundamental. One signature property of a marketplace site is its pricing mechanism: instead of fixed pricing by the B2C participants, marketplace sites set prices (mainly) by direct auction between the buyers and the sellers (the many businesses and the many customers). Furthermore, while participating B2C/B2B sites in an online shopping mall maintain their own identities and may use their own systems and Web presence designs, participants in an auction or marketplace site do not have their own integral, persistent existence on the site. Their existence is commodity-based and commodity-centered, all defined by the destination site at the run time. Therefore, the whole site is a single B2C and B2B in one.

However, a far more intriguing observation has it that an auction/marketplace site mimics theoretically how the whole economy works. As ebay.com and other major successes illustrate, a marketplace site with sufficient participants is an ultimate online shopping mall for customers. It is on demand, customer-centered, and hence it is helping to fulfill the customers' performance of their life cycle tasks. However, in practice, current marketplace sites share a fundamental limitation: they deal only with material commodities — i.e., manufactured products. We expect to see new marketplace sites catering to services, and combining all these functions. Ultimately, we expect to see market sites join and grow together, in a way that the DCS model describes.

Also from this DCS perspective, we expect the separation of B2C and marketplace sites to blur. Just like many small businesses are selling heavily on eBay while maintaining their own B2C on the side, what inherent value propositions justify perpetuating this separation and against the merging of these two designs? Why does a marketplace provider not facilitate both? At the minimum, why do B2C and marketplace sites not work together? Evidently, the key determinant for either side of the argument (the separation versus the integration) to excel is value proposition: which makes more value sense? We submit that the four theorems of the DCS model have identified the inherent logic for generating value propositions pertaining to this analysis. For the last two theorems to fully work, network effects and ecosystems effects must be fully developed for the business through, likely, social networking. Ironically, although a populous marketplace is consistent with social networking, the latter has not been explored by any such sites.

Auction/Marketplace for B2B — Industrial Exchange (integration of B2B systems for on-demand business): This is almost a mirror image of the above auction/marketplace model. However, some major differences do exist, which may account for the different levels of success that each has experienced: industrial exchanges are not booming. As the analysis of the B2B shopping malls asserts, the supply chain is a natural focus of life cycle tasks for companies. Both shopping mall and exchange models target this business space which is by definition generic and huge. The difference is the level of transaction support that each seeks to provide. From the very beginning, industrial exchange providers sought to integrate supply chain activities for all industries and developed new generic systems and technologies to suit the vision (e.g., see Glushko *et al.*, 1999). Examples include perfectcommerce.com (formerly commerceone.com), ariba.com, and freemarket.com.

Compared to eBay, these systems involved more complex processes with higher threshold (requirements) for their participants, and their customer base is by definition smaller and more difficult (costly) to cultivate. While eBay is a mass sale in the B2C style, the pioneering industrial exchanges would have to develop one user at a time like a consulting company. As a result, they did not succeed as envisioned, and many surviving sites focus now on low end supply chain integration similar to B2B practices, and have effectively become hard to distinguish from B2B shopping malls. Some sites succeeded in particular application domains — e.g., covisint.com for the automobile industry. In general, an industrial exchange is referred to as public if both the buyer and the seller sides are open to participants; and it is private if certain buyers own it for their own procurement. From the perspective of service scaling and transformation, the industrial exchange model makes sense and its logic is fundamentally right. It is a good way to implement the DCS model. The issue is only that the model needs a practical way to accumulate value propositions to give it momentum in the gravitational field of value. Perhaps, it requires other easier practices of DCS to set the stage by enhancing popular designs such as B2B shopping malls, so that it has the basis to overcome the high threshold problems.

Our comments on the future marketplaces for B2C also apply here. The business design can benefit from common themes across life cycle tasks, such as *a habitat for persons as well as for organizations*. A *community/habitat exchange* can integrate B2C, B2B, and service providers on the basis of members' common needs. A critical success factor is, of course, that the exchange must generate sufficient value propositions based on the whole versus the components of the habitat/community. The more mature digital connected service has become, the more likely that such value propositions will be developed and realized in abundance. The time of industrial exchanges, or some reincarnation of this model, will eventually come.

Information Portal (information services for life cycle tasks): The original implementation of this design is none other than straightforward collection of URLs of select Web sites — or a clickable table of contents for the Web organized according to some taxonomy conceived for Internet users. Incidentally, such taxonomy is nothing more than a particular view on the categorization of life cycle tasks. Along with the initial search engines, this model helped propel the Web to world prominence because without them the Web is useless to layman users. yahoo.com is a major pioneer. The initial model soon became insufficient and even inappropriate, as the Web quickly grew beyond the point where any table of contents can be maintained meaningfully for the whole community, or even just for some small select subset. New search engines have become the only sensible way of locating Web sites in any category anywhere, new or old, known or unknown; and everyone uses them. However, the notion of a convenient portal for all required information is still appealing, except that now its scope must be highly particular to allow its contents to be precise, accurate, and up-to-date. In fact, as long as search engines remain less than accurate and their results clumsy to integrate, information portals will continue to save users transaction cost and cycle time.

It follows that new information portals need be oriented for particular life cycle tasks of the intended users — e.g., map requests, medical information, stock trading and finance services. This also means that the new portals cannot rely on URLs only, since switching back and forth among many URLs is unwieldy and the information piecemeal. To serve the purpose of tasks support, the portals need to work at the level of contents, that is, to provide original, edited (compiled), or at least annotated information. As proven by the earlier information portals, the basic value of this model is its information services provided free to users. Therefore, information portals are consistent with marketing as a basic tool to attract viewers and promote the site. Although an information portal can charge user fees or use any other business model to generate revenues, and some sites do (e.g., in finance), the most promising use still seems to be treating it as a free service. From the perspective of service scaling and transformation, we recognize the model as a basic tool for promoting cocreation of value to persons and organizations.

For example, a B2C site can incorporate an information portal for the tasks that it targets (e.g., for the products it sells, the use of the products it sells, the needs of the customers of the products it sells, or any other life cycle tasks on any dimension). In this case, a Bed and Breakfast (B&B) B2C site can provide an information portal for tourism in the region, for the transportation to the region, for the

B&B industry in general, or for any other topics pertinent to the targeted travelers, as a way to attract attention to its site. The DCS model, again, predicts that information portals can benefit from seeking accumulation of information resources, and the providers of information resources can benefit through, surely, social networking. When sufficient information resources have been accumulated, then the information portal can easily become an information utility site (see below) for the Web, to reap its promises for reuse in other information portals. This observation converges to the assertion that on the Web, *business designs are fluid and amenable for connection and scaling*, digitally.

Transaction Portal (transaction services for life cycle tasks): The notion of one-stop transactions actually provides a working definition for person-centered or organization-centered e-commerce. This vision is perhaps best illustrated in online banking, which wants the customers to entrust and delegate to the bank the handling of all payments for them, in addition to handling their accounts at the bank destination site. This vision, which reflects the DCS concept, makes perfect sense for banks since checks are an ultimate paper trail in our economy which can be digitized and connected rather easily from a technical perspective. In fact all finance accounts and transactions are ripe for integration if money is completely digitized. The precedence in credit cards has offered plenty of results for banks to expand their success to checks and beyond. Banks can enjoy all the savings (fundamentally in terms of transaction cost and cycle time) from this automation and integration, plus more control of the whole process and better assurance of its quality to their customers. The problem is with customer acceptance and collaboration.

The customers, persons and organizations alike, are supposed to gain, too, in the form of convenience of paying bills in going about their life cycle tasks. Are these value propositions sufficient to offset the issues concerning trust and control? Is an online banking transaction portal a step towards customer-centered transactions, or one for bank-centered total purview of the customers? However, not all transaction portals are so one-sided in favoring the provider in the power balance, which determines the gravity of these trust and control issues. One such precedence is a transaction portal for relocation, which will handle different businesses related to relocating ranging from moving to reconnecting cables and identifying doctors' services at the new location. This is a business design developing value propositions based on the life cycle tasks of helping the customer relocate. Compared to marketplaces, which are one-stop shopping portals for an assortment of life cycle tasks, the transaction portal model is more focused on a cohesive task-based theme. More interesting is the logic that the model is extensible to becoming an agent for the customers by providing proactive services as a surrogate.

This notion of an agent on the Web — or *cyber-agent*, is precisely the big picture of this business design. It has the potential to grow into *some digital protégé, or CEO, for the customer.* The cyber-agent can be an implementation approach to realizing the vision of a *person-centered and organization-centered Web*. Evidently, the more mature the digitally connected service has become, the more easily a transaction portal can be developed profitably to serve as a cyber-agent for customers. In this vision, the collaboration among these transaction portals, as well as the interaction between them and the rest of the Web, can help showcase the DCS model. The prospect of such collaboration also substantiates the concept of ecosystem effects being a basis for developing new value propositions. The concept of a personal wizard presented in Chapter 9 is a vision based on the cyber-agent.

5.2.2 *Internet Enterprise*

If Internet commerce is interpreted as applying the Web to a company's external business, then Internet enterprise is applying the Web to a company's internal business. The range extends from a company's administration to its core business, and even to its transformation. This is also a narrow definition of *e-business*. More broadly, people in the field tend to use e-business and e-commerce interchangeably; however, many also interpret the former with a connotation that includes the latter but not vice versa. We adopt the second view. In any case, Internet enterprise may not require more costly technology than Internet commerce does, but it can be more involved in the sense of precipitating sweeping internal changes. Previous practices tend to show digital connections scaling on enterprise processes, knowledge workers and other resources, and immediate suppliers but they have basically refrained from similar connections to customers. The scaling sought tends to be one-way, too: enterprise to employees. However, more progressive practices have also attempted to leverage their DCS platform and cultivate pervasive interpersonal relationships among employees, as a foundation to facilitate their collaboration on the job and accumulation and sharing of work experience. Overall, Internet enterprise complements Internet commerce, and there is no inherent logic to separate these two categories forever. We consider both the first and the second theorems of DCS to be descriptive of the driving force behind Internet enterprise.

Intranet and B2E/B2M (business-to-employee/business-to-management: company portal for administration activities): One of the earliest models applying the Web to a company itself, this business design obviously makes perfect sense to any enterprise. The question is what should be the scope of the company portal? What should follow the practices of company intranets, which include (clickable) company directories, human resources documents, and other mundane administrative processes? Should the portal be connected, for example, with the company's production databases as a common user interface to facilitate cooperation across the enterprise and thereby enhance its core business? Should some key external constituencies who are on the mission critical path also be included, with necessary controls and firewalls being put in place? In other words, is Intranet merely an administration tool or also a production tool? Different answers to these questions give rise to different models and implementations of this general business design with different value propositions. Some practices seek value propositions in turning digital company directories and other mundane resources into a potent knowledge base to support on-demand collaboration among knowledge workers. Some others seek to incorporate social networking of employees into the Intranet. Still others conduct some workflow management processes (e.g., recruitment, proposals, and shipping/ receiving) and asset management processes on the Intranet. The examples are unlimited. Evidently, the Intranet logic is also the DCS logic that we discussed above for supporting the life cycle tasks of an organization.

Paperless Enterprise (digitization of pro forma enterprise processes): This umbrella name includes all such recent concepts as e-sales, e-supply chain, e-workflow, e-meeting, e-administration, e-learning/training, and much more. The basic idea is simply to digitize all stand-alone enterprise processes, with a definitive measure of removing paper trails from the enterprise. A deeper connotation of the term is integration of these processes by digital connections. Some companies, e.g., Cisco, have claimed impressive savings to the tune of billions of dollars a year. One would think that this number may have included intangible benefits all of which have resulted from the transformation, since "paperless" is only the appearance and beneath it lies the reduction of organizational transaction cost and cycle time. However, if it has not, then the figure must adjust upwards to truthfully indicate the total benefits. From the perspective of service scaling and transformation, going paperless is actually a working definition of digital connections of enterprise processes.

E-Enterprise (complete digitization of an enterprise, especially the core business): As paperless enterprise is specific about its goal, e-enterprise is broad in its scope. The concept applies to all enterprises in all sectors, including of course manufacturing, agriculture, energy, healthcare, and government, as well as service *per se*. In fact, many results pertaining to this concept have their roots in manufacturing (e.g., agile manufacturing and concurrent/simultaneous engineering). This general class of enterprise models clearly distinguishes itself from the other e-business designs in its conspicuous focus on the totality of the enterprise. That is, the digitization goes to production and any other mission critical areas of the enterprise, not just administration, sales, or procurement. For example, an early push by GE is focused on concurrent design over a supply chain — the e-engineering model. Other industrial thinkers also commonly put the concept in the context of enterprise integration.

From the perspective of the service scaling and transformation theory, *e-enterprise is the digitization and connection of all these enterprise elements: users, processes, (information) resources, computing, and (networking) infrastructure;* and thereby gain benefits through scaling these elements up (e.g., knowledge base) or down (e.g., simplification and consolidation of processes) or transformation (e.g., knowledge worker-centered support). Or, more simply, it is the application of DCS on the enterprise itself. All four DCS theorems are applicable to e-enterprise (and its extension: the e-extended enterprise). This definition leads to an analysis that previous practices in the field tend to miss: the central role of knowledge workers in an e-enterprise. They ignored how knowledge workers can be better networked to enhance the accumulation of knowledge from them, and how the accumulated knowledge may be shared among them to support their life cycle tasks on the job — i.e., knowledge worker-centered virtual enterprise. This is how we believe that the DCS model may shed light on e-enterprise to further advance the concept. Needless to say, the provision of e-enterprise is a major class of DCS which triggers transformation of the client. Since e-enterprise applies to all sectors, this service applies to all sectors as well. Our earlier assertion that DCS may help transform the entire knowledge economy is based partially on the success of this harbinger.

On-Demand Business (consulting; or real-time custom production and co-production by customer order): The notion of on-demand business was promoted by IBM. However, it has its own logic since it makes sense. The notion, in theory, is as broad as e-enterprise but, in practice, its primary concern seems to be consulting and IT industries. From the outset, the phrase may sound like a platitude since consulting, or any service for that matter, is by definition on demand.

Its challenges, or indeed the profound implications, are revealed only when one considers the scaling issues in previous practices. That is, when a company conducts its business on a customer-centered-and by-order-only manner for *many* customers, repetitively, then how can it achieve efficiency at a level comparable to mass production? In addition, an on-demand business solution provider has to consider the immediate customer's customers (the demand chain) — i.e., it conducts on-demand business to provide solutions for its clients to conduct on-demand business. This is a cascading of on-demand business on the provider's demand chain — and by extension on its clients' demand chains as well. The value propositions here are clear: (cascading) on-demand business makes the business agile and most effective in providing maximum value to its customers, while at the same time it is able to do this efficiently to sustain its price competitiveness. This seems to be a universal ideal for any business that has been evading the field.

The above analysis shows that *on-demand business is cocreation in nature* and hence faces exactly the same challenges as the general field of service in requiring a new service science. To be even more theoretical, the notion of "business" here can include non-service activities as well. Therefore, on-demand business implies two things: First, the business design is a model of *adding a mode of customer-centered cocreation of value to all industries*. Second, cocreation may become the basis of a science for all businesses, to the extent that the model works. On the note of *a science of cocreation for all businesses*, we refer to the visions stated in Chapter 1. They point to the possibility that any company can do cocreation.

This is not surprising to consulting companies; however, it can be tremendously refreshing for manufacturers and other traditional non-service industries. The field has witnessed ideals such as mass customization and agile manufacturing which are by nature on-demand manufacturing; but these ideals have been difficult to achieve (e.g., an automobile maker sells custom-ordered, designed, and manufactured cars at current mass-produced prices). A humbler goal is to focus the on-demand business only in the service industry. This limited interpretation still requires new basic results, otherwise it risks sounding awfully familiar against the backdrop of previous practices — isn't it always the case that everyone knows?

Therefore, on-demand business requires pushing the envelope and seeking out new frontiers and new scientific results that support it. The field might as well consider the possibility of a science of cocreation for all businesses. The newness in the business design of on-demand business must be the recognition itself: The reaffirmation of this long-held ideal implies that the previous cocreation practices are less than satisfactory — i.e., they have not really achieved the goal of on-demand business. We respectfully take this business design to mean a value proposition of doing more and achieving more for the traditional ideal, and submit that a new service science as proposed in Chapter 2 may help accomplish it: help transform businesses into the mode of cocreation.

Globally Integrated Enterprise: This phrase was coined, again, by IBM (Palmisano, 2006). Nevertheless, it embodies a new, theoretically profound recognition: *Any enterprise has a global context, and the Web makes this context tangible* (i.e., the Web makes any enterprise amenable to globalization). An all-encompassing example is the generic notion of the global supply chain — extending from the retailers (e.g., coffee shops) all the way to the end producers (e.g., coffee growers) which may be located all over the world. Virtually all multinationals today involve hosting their business in Asia, Africa, Australia, Europe, and the Americas; and giants household names are stellar examples of this model. Although this concept is customarily associated with large industrial companies for good practical reasons, it does not have to be so. A mom-and-pop coffee shop is a globally integrated enterprise, too, if it cares to work on its global supply chain by employing the Web (e.g., contacting the coffee growers by email). The recognition has a fundamental implication: since every enterprise has a global context, the models of e-enterprise and on-demand business ought to be interpreted within the context and practiced for this context — may be *an e-globally-integrated-enterprise, or e-GIE*?

5.2.3 *Internet Utilities*

The sheer size of the Web means the sheer size of its users, information resources, and systems. It also means the sheer opportunities of *sharing and reusing* them. However, this will not happen by itself: Someone needs to accumulate the users, resources, and systems, and make their sharing and reuse practical for others. Therefore, doing just this has become a major class of business design, as reviewed below. This class builds on the logic of the first theorem of DCS, but it also proactively develops value propositions whose logic is described by the second theorem. Business designs of the category is B2B in nature, but they may actively employ B2C (usually in the form of free information services to persons) to help their accumulation. In fact, some of the most celebrated accumulations on the Web happen to come from social networking. Thus, they prove the *versatility of business designs on the Web*. An enterprise may use multiple designs simultaneously, as well as switch among them with relative ease. In any case, this category offers some of the most direct illustration of the service scaling and transformation theory: *gaining benefits by accumulation and sharing* for massive, concurrent cocreation of value to persons, organizations, and society.

ISP and User Tools (Internet Service Provider: basic utilities for persons and organizations to join the Web): Two types of this business design have emerged since the inception of the Web: one for persons and another for businesses. The first personal type is the origin of this class of practices and continues to drive its innovation. The second type may offer Internet access at many levels of different sophistication, from end-to-end to point-to-point and network-to-network. Small businesses can easily find many low end services to "park" their Web sites at negligible cost; but cost of high end services to host international Web businesses using generic ".com" domain names, can go very high. Both types use subscription or leasing as the basic business model (revenues). We focus our review here on the original ISP/tools model for persons. A sure way to gather Internet users (for use as prospective customer base) is to give them Internet access, a search engine, and an email account. The early ISPs and user portal sites, including AOL.com, Yahoo.com, and hotmail.com have proven this over and again. Even eBay.com finds its origin in the free email tools that it offered which amassed the initial customer base for it to launch the auctioning business.

This basic point remains true today, notwithstanding the fact that users' requirements have multiplied manyfold and the threshold for new comers has become seemingly unattainable. Another powerful concept established from the beginning is free services: Internet users cherish and celebrate the culture of an/ open and free community. It remains as powerful as ever, and the relatively recent ascent of Google into global dominance has eloquently proven it, once again. Therefore, Internet utility sites tend to charge their business clients who use their utility services, but support free services to the end users who help build the utility. The ISP model is traditionally a fee-charging B2C but it has now really become a utility for cyber-surfers. In a sense, the split between business ISPs and person ISPs is due to this split in the business models. Person ISPs are increasingly becoming a free service; for example, cable carriers throw an ISP as a "gift" to subscribers. As a free service, person ISPs are also becoming a marketing tool and/or a source for acquiring Internet utilities.

Obviously, for practices aiming at persons, the value of building an enormous *customer base* outweights the heavy investment required for a successful ISP or other tools. The twist here is that the immediate customers (e.g., email users) may not yield any direct revenue for the site, but they can indirectly contribute revenue to it either through other applications on the site that generate revenue (e.g., fee-bearing sales and services) or through other sites that sell to these customers (embedded B2C, advertisement, and the like). Again, *free services and for-fee business are just two sides of the same coin because customers and free users are just two different roles of the same persons* who can switch between these roles easily. The life cycle tasks concept helps identify these roles and design the embedded B2C (or any other business models) to generate revenue. On this note, we wish to stress that *customers and knowledge workers are also just two roles of the same persons* who have little reason to keep these roles isolated when they see the value to switch between them.

ICP (Internet Content Provider: leasing information resources to other sites): Traditional publishers of travel books and newspapers are among the first to offer their accumulated information contents to other sites that need these contents (e.g., travel information portals). In fact, the ICP model can be compared to news agencies (e.g., Associated Press) supplying contents to news media (e.g., network television and newspapers). Since digital information resources are easily editable and revisable, while not physically consumable or destructible by use, they can be shared and reused many times over by many different users in many different ways. Therefore, the most natural business model for ICP is subscription rather than sale to account for the inevitable and even profitable ensuing update. The transaction nature of ICP is B2B, except that the ICP operates on the hinterland of its subscribers to support the latter's business, e.g., B2C.

The big picture here is that on the Web, *any owner of original digital content* — writings, documents, images, photos, videos, drawings, music, songs, movies, etc. — *can become an ICP* and the threshold of entry is as low as any Web site — a sharp contrast to the situation facing ISP. For example, a freelance writer can be an ICP for some information portals and so does anyone who has accumulated any information resources interesting to others. Closer to today's business practices, an information portal containing original content can also operate in the ICP business design for any other sites, destination or not, which may find use for this content and vice versa. The ICP model is a good supplement to B2C for a person or an organization to reap business value from the Web. In this sense, it is also a tool to promote person-centered and organization-centered views of the employment of the Web. Social networking, again, can be a very fertile field for developing ICP values, as proven by (the business interests in) youtube.com, facebook.com, flickr.com and other similar sites that are powerful at accumulating information resources. If one wonders how Wikipedia.com can make money, then ICP is a ready candidate for the answer.

Internet Resources (technology, hardware, and transaction systems) Provider (leasers of Web resources): As shown in Oasis.com and other forerunners in the field, this business design can be considered an ISP for significant businesses where the focus is not so much on basic access and other tools for basic Web presence, but on heavy-duty IT systems of data storage, processing, and communications for significant Web-based enterprise. These heavy-duty systems tend to be offered on a leasing basis and shared among such businesses. They also tend to be offered separately as particular Web (component) technology (e.g., Internet data storage to support globally distributed application systems), rather than as an enterprise process or any integrated all-encompassing enterprise solution. Sometimes, the notion of a (resource) portal is also used to describe the concentration of such resources. The design allows specialization to gain on scale and help user businesses leverage on the scale. This is a definitive example of the second theorem of the DCS model at work.

5.2.4　*Enterprise Services*

Similar to Internet utility providers, enterprise service providers work in the background of Internet enterprises and enable their systems. However, unlike the former, who lease particular technology, information resources, and stand-alone systems to company customers, the latter lease primarily solutions in the form of enterprise processes and applications to customers. This category can grow into supporting all applications of DCS. All four theorems of the DCS model are expected to contribute to describing the basic logic of value propositions for this genre. Since both the providers and the customers in the category belong to DCS, providers are expected to practice what they preach. For example, if IBM excels in providing on-demand business to globally integrated enterprises, then the company itself is expected to be an exemplary e-GIE. One may consider this class of business designs as the core beneficiary of a new service science: they promote, they develop, and they use it.

Online Vendor (providers and consultants of technologies, soft-ware systems and solutions): We include traditional IT vendors at all levels of the Web in this category, ranging from Microsoft and Oracle to Computer Associates and SoftBank, and all the way to Cisco and AT&T. So, the definition is based on the provision of enterprise solutions to implement any of the business designs on the Web. Online vendors are themselves Internet enterprises, and often provide their solutions online through the Web. Dell's practices of direct sale and technical support online are a well-known case. Security vendors (e.g., Symantec) have gone further: they install security control soft-ware on PCs and connect them to their global server so that the server can *monitor the population* (the global network of PCs) and execute the control (e.g., suspect lists and blacklisted keywords) based on this *real-time population information* gained from individual PCs. This de facto design allows the global security server to take con-trol of the local PCs, just like hackers would do. The difference is of course the accountability that legal businesses abide by: these vendors are restricted by what they agree to do and how they do it, while the hackers are constrained only by what they are able and willing to do. Similar practices are found in MicroSoft and many other solution vendors where they update their software remotely and virtually automatically at their will. This automatic connection also allows MicroSoft, for example, to gather information (e.g., about bugs in their software) online from the whole population.

   Therefore, *population knowledge*, or more broadly, a *population orientation*, is the fundamental newness about online vendors when compared to traditional vendors. The new breed ought to exploit this difference as a critical success factor. The population knowledge advantages showcase the second theorem of DCS, and point to a strategic direction to further advance this business design (i.e., all vendors go online). Many online vendors may expand their online practices into the main stay of how they deliver their products, and thereby effectively make their products a service (e.g., becoming an ASP — see below). To push the analysis further, one may argue that MicroSoft faces just one choice for the future: It may have to convert to a global PC operating system server directly running PCs networked to it, rather than continuing to sell stand-alone operating system software designed for independent installation and operation on presumably isolated PCs. The server route may be the most efficient and viable way to fend off viruses and hacker attacks on ordinary PCs, none of which is isolated on the Web.

ASP (Application Service Provider: leasing solutions online to clients as their enterprise processes and applications): The OEM (original equipment manufacturer) model may best describe the ASP concept. The host enterprise out-sources some of its enterprise processes (e.g., payrolls) or applications (e.g., airline ticketing) to a vendor (the ASP; e.g., ADP and sabre.com) who operates the processes or applications from its servers which are connected to the client's enterprise systems or Web presence. The ASP always works in the background of the client's systems, and the processes/applications they provide usually appear as an integral part of the client's Web presence. An example is the airline's ticketing engine provided by sabre.com, which is included in many travel sites as well as airline sites. The ASP model differs from ICP and Internet utilities mainly because it focuses on enterprise processes and applications. In contrast, the ICP model provides information contents while Internet utilities tend to provide particular technology and generic component systems that enterprise processes and applications use. In the case of ISP, which arguably provides solutions, the solutions tend to be for personal use as opposed to supporting businesses. An online vendor can readily become an ASP if sufficient value propositions exist, as discussed above.

Although an ASP may require certain particular technology that a vendor does not (e.g., see Tao, 2001), the main difference between these two business designs may actually be in the business models that each employs: vendors sell while ASPs lease. Similar to the case of online vendors, the ASP model also enjoys the advantages of scaling and a population orientation, which pose the model for pursuit of the second theorem of DCS. The big picture is that *online leasing makes software products a service*. Therefore, the ASP model is a leap of mentality that should continue to push for new possibilities of DCS. In particular, previous practices of ASP tend to be fixed on configurations for routine processing. They may be opened up for new designs as *agile and on-demand ASP*.

SaaS (software as a service) and On-Demand Service: These emerging concepts can be related to the ASP model. In fact, they may accurately be described as some models of on-demand ASP: on-demand development, operation, and reconfiguration with other software solutions for (fluid) enterprise processes and applications. The notion of *on-demand reconfiguration* is the newness here. It requires enterprise software solutions to be generic as well as versatile in their functions. In a way, this concept is also comparable to Web services, except that the latter is concerned mainly with object level software components (with an open technology flavor), while the former deals exclusively with enterprise processes and applications. However, as the notion of object is scalable, the conceptual differences here may not be as large as they appear.

The big picture here is, again, that these concepts pertain to the general effort of tackling the issues of quality and productivity in IT *software cocreation*. From the perspective of the service scaling and transformation theory, this category of services are concerned with the software dimension of the scaling and transformation. That is, they are also a part of the effort towards a new science of service. We may draw a stepwise linkage of Web services–SaaS/on-demand service–on-demand business–globally integrated enterprise (eGIE) along the progressive scale and scope of solutions for enterprise that each addresses. In this sense, we submit that the results presented in Chapter 4 contribute to the design of software systems for these enterprise models.

5.2.5 *Social Networking*

Most Internet users do not consider social networking as a for-profit activity, and much less as any intentional business design. This view is correct, of course. However, we still put it here as a category of new business design because social networking inherently supports the person-centered view of the Web. Our business activities and social activities are but different renditions of our life cycle activities. Social networking enhances our conduct of life cycle tasks on the Web, including business. More significantly, social networking and business have been proven to be related (even by hackers) and have started to intertwine. We might as well face the fact and analyze it for the benefits of all: person-centered, organization-centered, and society-centered views. As stated before, we consider *social networking to be the most important method of studying life cycle tasks and of promoting the network effects and ecosystem effects of DCS*. In this sense, it is a part of the basic logic of the DCS model.

P2P (peer-to-peer: individual "walled gardens" of socializing activities): This is the original form of social networking, pure, direct, and innocent like our childhood. It has grown in sophistication as the underlying technology matures: Initially, cyber-surfers talk to each other using peer-to-peer tools such as instant messaging and (text and music) file transferring provided by some destination sites (MSN.com and Napster.com). Then blogs evolved (e.g., buzz.com and nytimes.com) to support grassroots freelance writers to create, comment, and exchange ideas on all topics. Writing very soon expanded to realms of videos and images, as well as music, as blogging expands (e.g., flickr.com and youtube.com). In parallel, deliberate networking activities seeking peers also emerged from the initial peer-to-peer contacts among college students (the original FaceBook.com), social (meetup.com), and professional (linkedin.com) interest groups. Some of the more intensive focus areas such as gaming, mating, and job hunting have distinguished themselves and become B2Cs; and some others evolved into hybrids of peer-to-peer social businesses, with a prime case found in the so-called massive multiple player online role-playing games (MMPORPG) — e.g., World of Warcraft and secondlife.com.

Both free sites and for-fee sites exist in this space. However, even the more technology-intensive providers who tend to charge registration and/or user fees offer free social networking services beside the core gaming business. All the above have become part of our mainsteam culture today and a significant part of many people's daily lives. They all *accumulate information resources,* including their socializing activities themselves, *while accumulating customers.* However, the scope of social networks goes way beyond these immediate walled gardens. A much more significant garden exists on the Web that is walled only by the limits of the peer-to-peer tools that people use. That is, to the extent that everyone on the Web can email and by email can exchange, share, and accumulate virtually any digitized content that each owns, the whole of cyberspace is the playground for any social activity in any form and shape that people care to initiate — whether they are directly related to business or not. Or, simply put, people use the cyber-playground to conduct their life cycle tasks. Hence, it ought to be designed as such.

The open source/technology community is a telling example. It is *both personal and business-related*; and it is also a social network (consisting of unlimited number of sub-networks) formed on demand for the people, by the people, and of the people, where only the common goal (set of tasks) that people share defines and drives the community. Such *networks and sub-networks are life cycle tasks-based*: their formation virtual (and associated with roles); their practices unlimited; and their existence simultaneous. These communities are the big picture of social networking, not the destination sites *per se*, because they can help us to go about our life and our business. The DCS model taps into this observation and formulates how social networking may facilitate service scaling and help transform the knowledge economy.

Business on P2P (business use of P2P practices): Advertising is perhaps the most natural means of tapping the accumulated customer base at the walled gardens for business benefits. However, the homepage advertisement has many severe limitations that hinder its effectiveness. Aside from the well known issues such as space (e.g., small "real estate" on a screen) and intrusion (e.g., abrasive pop-ups and cookies), the appearance of the advertisement itself often causes uneasiness among cyber-citizens who are accustomed to the free spirit of the Web. This can lead to more serious issues such as compromising users' trust in the host. The trust factor explains why sponsoring links, for example, is always a delicate practice for search engine destination sites and information portals. In fact, Google originally committed to advertisement-free integrity in its search results, in order to distinguish itself from its already established competitors, and the strategy worked in winning over users. Therefore, the best business practices seem to be synthesizing business interests with the social activities themselves — the more naturally integrated these two views are, the better chance for the business interests to be realized. Two major types of synthesis have emerged thus far: embedded B2C (including embedded advertisement, sales, and related activities) and participatory promotion (including marketing, extracting business intelligence, and other studies). Some of the practices can be carried out unilaterally, either by the P2P sites or by the business that wishes to tap into the sites; but many require business agreement and even cocreation between these two sides. The embedded B2C model is explained above under B2C.

For participatory promotion, blogging offers some of the earlier practices. Companies scan blogs to gather marketing information and even try to influence customer opinions. Some of the practices can be controversial and have crossed the border lines of legality or morality outright (e.g., paid and company-engineered blogging). More sophisticated uses are found in, e.g., Second Life, where businesses create their own avatars to play their roles in the virtual reality world. This way, a real world company can function in the virtual world and experiment on anything they like, from products and marketing to personnel, without (perhaps) the real world's restrictions and consequences. Needless to say, the image and success of the company in its second life can impact on the same in its first life to the extent of what the participants of the MMPORPG can reach. Clearly, the possibilities are limited only by imagination, and lateral thinking or even swirling and three-dimensional thinking are needed to help the design. However, the principles embodied in the first and the third theorems of DCS, especially pursuing life cycle tasks and concurrent applications, can shed light on the thinking, too.

In general, the more the *users' life cycle tasks* performed at the walled gardens (e.g., talking about movies and jobs) intersect with *their life cycles tasks* at the businesses (e.g., buying movies and job hunting), the better the businesses can synthesize and embed their business into the social networks. Finally, the P2P sites have their own business needs (e.g., technology, systems, and applications) which represent opportunities for their solution providers. The twist here is that social networking is fluid by nature, and hence the business needs should be adapted frequently as well. This means that solutions for social networking enterprises may require higher degrees of cocreation than many other enterprises do. The cocreation may, for example, demand that the providers do fully and persistently participate in the walled gardens.

Business Resources from P2P (Internet utilities: covert or overt customer base and information resource base): The basic idea has been explained above under ISP and ICP; that is, the customer bases and information resources gathered at any sites (hosts) can also be generic utilities for other sites (clients) to employ. Traditional businesses have long established the practice of gaining on customer base and resources through business acquisition; however DCS makes the outright acquisition optional since it makes such customer bases and information resources sharable and reusable by many. In one word, it makes customer bases and resources potential "utilities" on the Web. The applicability is often determined by the degree to which the host sites' customers overlap with the clients' in terms of their characteristics (not just their direct propensity to purchase the clients' products). In general, the more comprehensive the customer base and more generic the customer information are at the hosts, the more generically applicable — and hence more valuable — they are to the clients.

By this measure, social networking sites promise to provide some of the best candidates for producing such utilities for the entire Web, because they are centered on persons, generic and whole, to whom customers (and knowledge workers) are just some *roles* they play in relation to certain *life cycle tasks*, as discussed above. The facebook.com example is a ready illustration. The persons at this walled garden are the same customers at the businesses that they patronise, and the same knowledge workers at their jobs. Thus, the information resources about them at facebook.com are immediately applicable to all these businesses and employers, and their social networks formed within the garden are similarly relevant to their activities outside for marketing and recruitment. This example is but a beginning. The review here is about two things: First is the fact that social networking sites build user bases and accumulate information resources, both of which can be (and are being) turned into customer bases and business resources either for direct business at these sites (covert utilities) or for use by their clients (overt utilities). Second is how to do this. Once again, the analysis leads to the basic concept of life cycle tasks as the core of an answer to the "how" question.

Social Networking at Businesses (P2P as an integral part of regular B2C, etc.):   Many Web businesses have adopted blogs as a supplement to their B2C sites to gather customer input and promote customer relationship. These earlier practices, which tend to be coupled directly with their products (e.g., comments on news articles and books) and limited to the companies' own customers, are being increasingly expanded to make blogs a marketing tool to recruit new customers and develop new products (e.g., at news sites). The premises here, however, are that these ideas are amenable to being expanded even further along two basic dimensions: one is employing the full practices of P2P, not just blogging; and the other is to integrate P2P into any business design to enhance them. An immediate application in the second dimension is the B2E/B2M model but all other models can use the same ideas, too. The basic logic here is very simple: P2P helps implement DCS for customers, for providers, and for the cocreation of value by customers and providers on the Web. For example, a company portal (intranet) with a full P2P embedded in it can facilitate its enterprise towards an on-demand business. When the P2P practices are expanded to its customer base, current and potential, then the on-demand business' marketing and cocreation processes will benefit evidently. When they are applied to its supply base, on-demand e-extended enterprise, or eGIE may result.

For e-commerce, large B2C may offer P2P as free information services to customers and gain on building the customer base. Small B2C may join force and/or leverage on what the walled gardens have to offer. The resultant population and population knowledge promise to contribute beyond marketing *per se* and facilitate the cocreation of value itself. Therefore, a full circle of Internet commerce and enterprise is connected through P2P, with the conceptual effects of this connection reduced to concrete benefits for life cycle tasks that link the customers and the providers. We discussed this concept from many perspectives of the above business designs since it is a culminating idea to forecast new business designs on the Web. For the service scaling and transformation theory, social networking is the basis for realizing network effects and ecosystem effects of DCS to explore roles and life cycle tasks for value cocreation. It helps DCS, helps implement its model and the population orientation, and helps advance the knowledge economy. Again, social networking may be the catalyst to bring about a person-centered Web.

We make one more observation before we conclude the review of Web businesses: A rule about finding the "killing applications" for the Web is there is no rule (i.e., outside, perhaps, pornography and gambling). No one predicted the magnitude of success of P2P auctioning on the Web before ebay.com. Google came out when everyone thought Yahoo and its companies were the name of the game which would not change overnight (but it did). youtube.com inflated into the giant that Google bought, under Google's wary watch who obviously thought it had foreseen all. In this sense, maybe everyone is entitled to making some bold predictions, and our share is the statement that the best kept secret on the Web is ***the potential of P2P becoming a mainstream strategy with every Web business design***.

5.3 Representative Revenue/Business Models for e-Commerce

The above review includes a number of generic revenue/business models that different business designs on the Web have employed for generating revenue or business benefits. We consolidate them in this section. They may be applied to all Web businesses, but customarily, we consider their scope to focus primarily on e-commerce.

Sales (including donations): This is the most traditional and direct way of making a profit on the Web. The requirement is obviously that the business must have some "products" to sell. If these products are in traditional physical forms, such as vehicles and clothes, then traditional material flows such as inventory, logistics, and shipping are required. This aspect often represents the downside of B2C since traditional stores may not require as much, especially shipping (e.g., comparing online supermarkets to traditional supermarkets). Therefore, material flows need to be integrated into the sales model and become a critical success factor for e-commerce, especially for perishable goods (e.g., freshdirect.com). On the other hand, e-commerce has the potential of digitizing some classes of traditional products and delivering these digital products online. Books, movies, and music are apparent examples. The list is actually not short, although its scope tends to be limited to those consumed through the eyes and ears.

By the same logic, many services can be made into digital products and delivered online, too. Counseling of all types is a case in point. In a broad sense, education may also belong to this class. Once digitized, more choices of revenue types become available. For example, movies may be sold, leased, or bundled with other digital products on a one-time charge, per view fee, or flat rate, or even offered for free. In fact, any of the business models listed below can be applied to any digital product of any nature in any scheme. The choice is mainly a matter of business strategy. More fundamentally, digital products can become a service if they are not sold but leased. The logic is similar to ASP, as discussed above.

Another twist of sales on the Web is the widespread use of donations: donations to Internet artisans as well as to wikipedia.com, for example. This form seems to fit best 'the cause-related P2P. Fundraising for non-profit organizations and politics is another major domain of donation. Donation goes hand-in-hand with word of mouth (see below).

Advertisement (on the host site): For a B2C that does not have any obvious products to sell, digital or otherwise, advertisements may be the most common source of revenue. The requirement is obvious, too: the site must have sufficient "eyeballs", or a user base, to warrant any interest from other sites. Therefore, the advertisement is a viable model for an e-commerce site to "cash in" on its already established, significant customer base. But if it does not have one, then it must grow its customer base first. In this sense, the revenue model of attracting advertising to it is predicated on the model of growing a customer base, although the converse is not necessarily true — there may be even better ways to tap into the customer base than advertising. Advertisements, on the Web take many forms, as it does in the traditional world. Typical forms include (clickable) icons and slogans, pop-ups and flashers, sponsored links, and, most promisingly, *embedded B2C*. We have discussed these forms in the above section.

Advertising on the Web has a unique property that its traditional counterpart can never achieve: it may be digitally connected to viewer actions, such as clicking on the advertisement. This means that an advertisement's effectiveness may be directly and immediately accountable to allow its fees to be linked precisely to the consequences, e.g., the number of clicks. Moreover, since the actions (e.g., clicking) may spell sales on the spot, the advertisement fees may also take the form of commissions on the sales. Finally, for the advertisers, e-commerce advertising affords them the "population data" (e.g., clicks and follow-up actions) to study the effectiveness for improvement. This investigation promises to be more accurate and comprehensive than any traditional sample-based follow-up studies on traditional advertising.

Free (Information) Services as Advertisement (the word-of-mouth model): This model is aimed at building customer base, and can be employed by any Web businesses. By itself the model does not generate any revenue, but it will eventually, as the customer base grows (see below). Therefore, this is also a growth strategy for starting, say, e-commerce and social networking. The free services they provide fall into a few classes. A common type is simply the digital products that they sell (or lease), in such schemes as preliminary services (e.g., basic membership), trial versions (e.g., software), and introductory offers (e.g., books and book chapters). Retailing of traditional products can also develop digital (information) companions of these products, such as e-books/videos and virtual reality presentations for their cars, gears, and intimate attire. These digital companions can then be given away as introductory gifts.

But more interesting is additional innovative possibilities. Using information portals is one, where a Web business can create information services for its customers to help them in their life cycle tasks, which are presumably but not necessarily related to the ones that bring them to the business in the first place. A golfing gear B2C, for example, can use an information portal on PAC tournament schedules and a P2P site specializing on soccer may start with an information portal following the niche of quarter-finals of the upcoming football world cup. A challenge is obviously how to maintain the portal and stay always a step ahead of the followers. On this note, we submit that the most powerful way to keep a customer relationship site such as an information portal always in sync with the users is to make it P2P: let the customers define, maintain, and further develop it, with the host's willing sponsorship. The big picture is the *word-of-mouth model*: it has the quintessential network effects and ecosystem effects on the Web, and hence the ultimate advertisement weapon for Web businesses. If word of mouth does not work in the large-scale non-digital traditional world, then it works in the DCS world.

Contract with Fixed Pricing (flat service or leasing fees, levels of memberships, and fixed formula of compensations): This traditional type of revenue is actually the sales model for services.

It is dominant in the traditional consulting industry, and is especially suitable for large-scale and/or open-ended value cocreation. The model fits equally well for Web businesses in the Internet enterprise category since they tend either to be an extension of traditional consulting or to share similar business logic with their traditional counterparts. The pricing usually takes the form of flat fees for delivering a solution and/or running the solution. Using performance-based compensation either as a supplement to the fees or as a self-contained pricing is also commonplace. The model applies to other categories as well: Internet commerce, Internet utilities, enterprise services, and social networking. The difference is that, for these categories, contracts may not be the best model or may be used in combination with other models. The flexibility comes from the fact that services on the Web (e.g., running B2C software or a host of social activities) have physical ramifications (e.g., the use of tools and platform for digital connections in selling and socializing) that may render them directly accountable to both sides of the cocreation (customer and provider). This is true at least for relatively stand-alone services with well-defined finite boundaries and conditions, as long as they are deliverable and conductible by digital means. The situation is similar to what we have discussed above under sales for digital products and advertisement.

Flat fees often take the form of memberships in the case of B2C that supports social networking (e.g., tools, platforms, and information). Flat rates work best in these typical situations: when the services can be framed as a product and sold as one; when the uses of the services are convoluted and/or numerous; or when other ways of costing involve too high a transaction cost and/or opportunity cost (e.g., goodwill and customer perception) for them to be advantageous. The big picture is the *versatile nature* of digitally connected services and digital products, including the possibility of integrating them. Just like cell phones may be offered for free as a part of a calling plan (service contract), would PCs and even industrial equipment be offered at deeply discounted prices as a part of a service contract by service providers who operate these products? Conversely, would the makers of these PCs and industrial equipment become global servers and charge their clients by the use and performance of these products (user fees), with or without a service contract?

User Fees (transaction-based charges: commissions, clicks, fees to participate, etc.): User fees may be the purest libertarian economics. It is the retailing version of fixed-priced service contracts (as compared to wholesale). The specific forms of the charge must depend on the forms of the business: commissions may be appropriate for embedded B2C; per click charge may work best for the online advertisement; and fees to play may be the name of the game for MMPORPG. This model is also natural for inclusion into an otherwise fixed pricing contract, as additional fees beyond some flat rates for additional usage above certain thresholds. This practice is common, and well-understood, in traditional businesses as well as in cyberspace. The big picture here is that its transaction cost may be minimized on the Web as opposed to traditional practice. That is, it may be more viable and advantageous for this model to be universally employed on the Web than anything that traditional economics has predicted for it. Or, *the Web may be amenable to libertarian economics*.

Customer Base as an Internet Utility: The basic ideas behind this model have been discussed above under social networking and ISP, for example. The profound point is actually simple: any accumulation of users/customers on the Web can be a user/customer base for any other websites as well — just like the fact that any accumulation of information resources can be a utility for the whole Internet. We further point out here that this model has potential to become a norm on the Web if appropriate revenue/business models are developed. Previous practices are largely limited in two forms: advertising, which is the easy way of "providing" one's user/customer base for other sites to tap into; and acquisition, the obvious but costly way. Both are well-known. However, some middle ways are necessary for the model to be universally applied.

The fundamental concept is to explore and exploit the complementary value propositions based on life cycle tasks between the customer base provider site and its customer base using client sites. Embedded B2C is the best example: the more the customers and their tasks at a client site are integrated with the provider site, the more effective the embedded B2C (of the client on the provider) will be. In other words, the model requires careful design to achieve business synthesis between both sides. Strategic alliance, virtual (extended) enterprises, and other forms of traditional enterprise collaboration can be applied on the Web, too, except that the Web promises to make these models even more viable, flexible, and practical as far as connecting their customer bases is concerned. For example, using embedded B2C is a proven way to connect businesses. Developing fungible credits between them (e.g., linking the credit earned in an MMOPRPG site to real world benefits, similar to frequent flyer programs and credit card points programs) is also promising. Both designs spell enterprise collaboration.

But the most widely applicable way is perhaps the most basic form of promotion: word of mouth through exposure. That is, the business connection does not have to be always immediately yielding tangible gains in revenue; rather, it could be just for the connection in the customers' minds or on the playgrounds. For example, a mere co-location or sponsorship can matter materially in building name recognition and customer perception. Obviously, the notion of embedded B2C can take many forms and be made universally applicable if business gains are broadly defined and measured in this way. Obviously, appropriate business models are necessary to consolidate the business relationship between the provider and the client. To accomplish this, the revenue models of fixed-pricing contract, including leasing, may be the most viable way to account for indirect benefits for the clients, while user fees may be the best fit for direct benefits.

To conclude, we recognize a set of *critical success factors* for new business designs on the Web from the discussion presented above. They apply directly to new business planning for e-commerce, but are also relevant to planning in all other categories on the Web.

Vision: innovation of value propositions. Generic innovation of value propositions comes from reducing transaction time and cycle time for persons and organizations to go about their life cycle tasks on the Web. Translating this concept to particular business practices gives specific value propositions. Therefore, business-specific innovation will identify the customers, formulate their life cycle tasks, and relate these tasks to the particular business. The DCS propositions may provide a reference model for analysis.

User/Customer Base: promotion through word of mouth. Advertising in the traditional way fits businesses in the traditional way. Innovation on the Web requires innovation of advertising and promotion, too. Traditional advertising is always costly to scale up; however, community building in a P2P manner may not be. Free and value-added information/transaction services and portals deserve to be considered. A Web business always needs to strive towards self-promotion on the Web.

Agile Business Designs: reconfiguration of business models. Success on the Web needs successful exploitation of unique Web promises. Digital connections of a Web business' resources, systems, and customers provide flexibility and versatility to the business, because they lower the variable cost for changeover from one model to another, or a combination of many. A Web business should explore these possibilities to update its designs and models. This update can be vital both for staying competitive and for growth.

Sustained Revenues: combination of revenue models. A sustainable business always requires sustainable revenues. This cardinal rule can become obscured on the Web since building user/customer base itself is a viable business model (e.g., in play for acquisition), too. However, revenue-bearing value propositions must be defined, and-better yet-proven even for sites that aim at building customer base. In this case, the revenue models promise to help the host site valuate its customer base.

Retention of Users: accumulation of opportunity cost to leave. Users/customers need good reasons to stay with a destination site, since choices on the Web are numerous and easy. The value of the products the site provides is of course key. Notwithstanding, the business also needs to create personalized "assets" for the user/customer to accumulate at the site (e.g., contacts and information resources). The accumulated assets are the opportunity cost for the customers to leave, and the fear of losing them becomes the deterrent against their leaving.

Reputation/Word of Mouth: occupation of business high ground. As stated above, visions and business designs/models must be agile. Therefore, the immediate users/customers do not necessarily represent the whole potential business space. A business needs to poise itself for possible reconfiguration, and always seek out the network effects on the Web either directly from their customers or indirectly through their customers. The bottom line is simple: 360-degree reputation by word of mouth.

The review in this chapter helps guide the planning of Web-based enterprises and value cocreation systems. We now move to system development itself. We present a design methodology for developing the backbone systems of service — cocreation enterprise information systems, in the next chapter.

Chapter 6

A Design Methodology for Service Cocreation Enterprise Information Systems: The DCS Contributions

How to make enterprise information system (IS) adequate for service scaling? Traditional enterprise IS methods do not distinguish cocreation from production. However, population-oriented cocreation requires further discrimination. The appropriate design methods have to assure agility, openness, and scalability for the systems to support customers and knowledge workers in one of a kind value cocreation. From the perspective of service scaling and transformation, previous results can use additional linchpins to make them work better — in particular, they need a new design methodology to focus on cocreation IS that scales up, down, and transforms the knowledge economy. This chapter develops such a methodology. The methodology defines and builds DCS through immersing or even *embedding IS elements* into *societal cyber-infrastructure*, which includes the Web and other public domain digital resources, as well as the usual cyber-infrastructure. Therefore, the cocreation uses IS to use the Web, and uses the Web to use the IS. The methodology of embedding becomes a central theme for implementing DCS on service cocreation enterprise IS. In this methodology, a cocreation IS becomes a mechanism of employing and deploying IS elements, available on the Web as well as within the enterprise, to customers and knowledge workers of population-oriented cocreation, including *embedded assistance*. This approach realizes the person-centered nature of cocreation and support service scaling and transformation. A concept model of a *societal cyber-infrastructure sharing schema* is also presented to accompany the methodology.

6.1 General Principles of DCS Enterprise Information Systems Planning

The overarching technical problem is how to support virtual configuration of service systems required by population-oriented cocreation? Since enterprise information systems are the technical backbone of service systems, the problem is also one of how to design *service cocreation enterprise information systems* that support both customers and knowledge workers of value cocreation and scale to the population? We explain these research problems below.

In the total schema of the service scaling and transformation theory, Chapter 4 presents a new design method for population modeling to reduce the learning curve of population-oriented cocreation. These results contribute to system development tasks ranging from representing the business goals demanded to the software construction of enterprise information systems designed. However, their scope does not include the design of such systems. The general results in the field support system planning and analysis (e.g., see Alter, 2008), except that they tend to cater to systems envisioned for providers' internal use as opposed to customer-provider value cocreation. The latter features task-based virtual configuration of system elements. The population orientation also represents additional requirements, especially openness and scalability, to previous results. Therefore, many proven methods need extensions and supplements to satisfy the goals of population-oriented cocreation.

On the business strategy front, Chapter 5 analyzes the new business designs that have emerged so far on the Web from the perspective of the service scaling and transformation theory, in particular the DCS model. The analysis also extends to their further innovation. In addition, Chapter 3 also adds a set of propositions (i.e., the four theorems of the DCS model) representing some basic logic for planning value propositions for DCS. These results amount to a conceptual reference framework for recognizing the directions of innovation and developing visions. They can help formulate the goals of population-oriented cocreation enterprise information systems. In a general sense, the results in Chapters 3 and 5 supplement the previous methods of business strategy and contribute to the planning stage of service enterprise information systems design: setting the goals of cocreation for the information systems; specifying the basic functional components of the system; and assessing the technical correctness and feasibility of the system logic. To be sure, the field may need concrete results (e.g., Yourdon, 1989) more than any generic models, especially not on business strategy and system planning. However, the DCS concept may help the previous general planning methods to focus. That is, the DCS logic is concrete and specific in terms of propositions. For example, the four theorems of DCS suggest specific directions to look for innovation: where to identify business opportunities and/or business limitations.

The planning stage is followed by a (high-level) logical design stage in the usual system design life cycle. The sub-propositions of the second theorem may help the transition from broad business goals to functional goals for information systems design. Once the functional goals are formulated, particular design methods can take over and develop the systems (with the CED being a candidate method). This is a standard practice in the field. The rest of the paper provides a design methodology to assist the standard practice. That is, in a way similar to how the DCS propositions may help general planning methods to focus, the proposed methodology aims at helping the usual design methods to identify solution approaches. Again, service scaling and transformation through DCS is the overarching guidance of the methodology. We define the theme below, where *the newness is cocreation* — the technical goal of the information systems:

Design Principles for Cocreation Information Systems (IS)

Follow the second theorem of DCS, especially the lemmas and corollaries, to gain openness and scalability; use an element orientation to embed the IS into societal cyber-infrastructure; and configure concurrent cocreation along demand and supply chains.

The rest of the chapter develops the concepts and methods of these principles. The specific requirements in each system development case will determine how these DCS results may be employed. However, regardless of the applications, the employment always predicates on insights gained from the DCS concept. For this reason, this section will elaborate on some of the basic principles, or axioms, underlying all DCS results in order to shed light on their general application. Foremost, we review the principle of reduction of transaction cost and cycle time which has been asserted earlier to be fundamental to all value propositions for all information systems but not been sufficiently explained. We will do so here.

Reduction of Transaction Cost and Cycle Time

We submit that all sensible value propositions for information systems can be traced ultimately to this root cause. Consider this fact: the field has never settled on how to comprehensively assess the benefits of IT investment. Firms tend to rely on such measures as return on investment (ROI) to evaluate their IT projects, although it is well known that ROI does not account well for intangible benefits, which happen to be crucial contributions of IT and information systems. This gap helps explain why firms have failed to account for the value of their IT investment based on formal methods while empirical evidence (e.g., anecdotes) have attributed their business success to IT — such as the case in the so-called "productivity paradox" of the late 1990s and early 2000s. The economy did not register much productivity gains compared to astronomical IT investment, at a time when the whole society was witnessing an IT-driven new economy and benefiting unequivocally from the IT boom. More specifically, the field has difficulty in properly accounting for the contributions of information systems to the microeconomical production functions of firms for society.

A broader and more appropriate measure is found in the concept of *organizational transaction cost* — see Williamson (1985), which examines the whole enterprise and accounts for both tangible (e.g., savings on labor) and intangible (e.g., effectiveness) returns. Incidentally, this school of thought theorizes that firms embody the optimization of organizational transaction cost. An organization is brought into being to process information (transactions) for making the right decisions and taking the right actions to accomplish the organization's goals. The interesting point is that the abstract notion of organizational information processing becomes concrete for digitally connected enterprises, and measurable through their information systems. That is, the processing on enterprise information systems not only corroborates organizational information processing; it, to a large extent, is the organizational information processing. Therefore, contributions to the processing represent contributions to organizational transaction cost for the enterprise: processing with DCS information systems versus processing without, and processing with improved DCS information systems versus processing without, and the like. That is, the contributions are measurable in terms of the reduction in organizational transaction cost and total (enterprise) cycle time which are a function of the individual processes' transaction costs and cycle times. It turns out that both are concrete and measurable concepts on their information systems' performance.

Cycle time is evidently measurable, such as the time to market new product development at the high enterprise level, and the throughput (service or physical) of a process at the system level. It is related to transaction cost, but it is not necessarily reducible to it. For example, if a cycle consists only of sequential processes, then the cycle time is determined (proportional to) by the sum of the process transaction costs. However, if it is not, then the total cycle time could be more a function of the sequences of processes than a function of the sum of the individual transaction costs. Naturally, arranging component processes determines the total cycle time. In addition, automation, simplification and consolidation of processes could also reduce total cycle time. The latter often results in transaction cost reduction as well. Among these usual strategies, automation is the one commonly associated with ROI — the tangible benefits in the form of cost reduction due to reduction in cycle time (and transaction cost).

In contrast, the general concept of *transaction cost* appears to be intangible at first glance, since organizational tasks and processes outside shop floors tend to be non-definitive or even random. This non-definitiveness is reminiscent of service cocreation. However, transaction cost is indeed measurable even in the general sense without invoking the IT-based information systems. Albeit not as concrete as time and money, transaction cost is firmly related at least to utility functions and overall performance, in terms of which the cost can be represented. Often, it may even be measured directly through the evaluation of workload and workflow involved in their performance. For example, how much does using paper currency save over bartering for trade? This is societal transaction cost, a level as general as it can get. One could answer this broad question by asking specific personal level questions such as the ones concerning collecting deposits on bottles. How much does it cost one to return the bottles and collect the refund at a supermarket; or how much would these deposits be credited by the proprietor if one barters them for groceries at a corner store? The cost is real and concrete, and can be accumulated (scaling up) for society in a definitive way (e.g., estimating the population and the number of such transactions).

In general, the transaction cost of a particular job to the person performing it can be assessed by how much the person is willing to pay others to do it for her/him — such as hiring an agent or a broker. This is a utility function for the person. The value of the Internet can be substantiated on this basis. For instance, how much time (effort) it takes high school seniors to collect information about the colleges that they wish to apply to without using the Internet? In this case, the total sales of all college data books prior to the Internet indicates an upper bound of the fungible value of the Internet on the reduction of the transaction cost for doing the job. All these transaction costs can be assessed case by case in a similar way for all applications of the Internet. We do not have to do this, we are not doing this, and doing this is not easy. But the point is that this is do-able. Transaction cost is measurable. Generally speaking, the so-called "red tape" is precisely transaction cost, which can be so high in particular cases as to become an inhibitor for undertaking an enterprise. As an illustration, if certain tax breaks were required to attract a direct foreign investment, then the value of the breaks could reflect the cost of red tape perceived. Finally, to show one more illustration, an organization could quantify the minimum value of a global database query system by compiling the time its employees spend on the phone and at meetings that could have been saved by the system. In one word, "convenience" succinctly describes the nature of transaction cost. Clearly, *transaction cost and cycle time together determine productivity*. The above discussion explains the core value proposition of the DCS model as stated in Chapter 3.

The DCS model promotes service scaling based on this premise: the principle of reduction of transaction cost and cycle time applies universally to persons, organizations, and society; and it can be related directly to their life cycle tasks as guidelines for developing value propositions for them. Furthermore, the above analysis shows that these concepts are applicable and helpful for assessing and identifying particular value propositions for service systems, as proposed in the DCS model. The traditional ROI could be incorporated in this new, extended measure to assist in the design of cocreation enterprise information systems, and thereby connect the DCS model to traditional results.

Concurrent Service Cocreation

The DCS model calls for concurrent applications and concurrent service cocreation (in particular, the second and third theorems). They are based on the general concept of concurrent processing with specific orientations. The general concept is well-known in the field. However, for the DCS model, we wish to point out that if connection *per se* achieves reduction of transaction cost, then concurrent processing using the connection is the next level that achieves (further) reduction of cycle time. That is, concurrent processing is a principle for engineering the arrangement of processes that determines their total cycle time. Service cocreation relates to processes in the way that processes give rise to service systems, and applications relate via the value propositions of the service cocreation. With respect to cocreation enterprise information systems, both are some aggregate views of the underlying enterprise processes that realize themselves on the information systems — or some users of the systems. The aggregate views manifest particular virtual configurations (paths of usage) of certain elements of the information systems involved. The DCS model suggests that *these elements should be shared by as many processes as possible*.

Therefore, the general concept of concurrent processing is now reduced to a concrete practice of sharing information elements which are defined in the next section. The goal here is to make all processes from all cocreation applications concurrent, constrained only by the physical capacity of concurrent virtual configuration and processing. A reference point to this concept is enterprise databases. The same database infrastructure drives all virtual configurations of the data resources (e.g., views) to allow all users running their processes (e.g., global queries and applications) against it concurrently. The cocreation enterprise information system can perform in the same manner, comparably supporting concurrent service cocreation. The modelbase concept of Chapter 4 reflects this concurrent philosophy as well.

A humble illustration below will quickly show the core logic of concurrent processing: its cycle time reduction nature. If, for example, a job requires 1000 man-hours to complete, then it takes only one hour to finish if 1000 men work on it simultaneously. The sophistication comes when one considers the reality of how to make all 1000 men work at the same time on the same job. Resources availability could be a bottleneck and sequencing of work processes could be another. Also, there is the need for coordination and synchronization. The situation is prototypical of virtually all production systems, cocreation or not, since the core logic is true everywhere. The reality is a struggle between the ideal and the ability to realize it. From this angle, a new service science may be interpreted as one that resolves the limitations of concurrent cocreation and maximizes the concurrent cocreation. Computer science offers some results at the algorithmic level for concurrent processing, and human ingenuity provides many intriguing ideas for concurrent cocreation in various domains (such as the distributed data processing design of the SETI@home project).

The field of manufacturing also contributes some of the most rigorous results for enterprise engineering which the design of co-creation enterprise information systems can employ. These results include technologies to allow for parallel manufacturing control, distributed engineering design, and simultaneous execution of product life cycle tasks. They also include the paradigm of virtual teams for concurrently undertaking multiple enterprise processes. For example, the simultaneous engineering models, referred to as Design-for-X, with X being anything ranging from manufacturability to serviceability, connect product development life cycle tasks and processes to transform them from sequential to concurrent (the later stages of a life cycle are made parallel to or overlapping with the earlier ones). *Virtual teams* are formed from all stages of the life cycle tasks (e.g., marketing, engineering, and manufacturing professionals) to help execute these tasks concurrently. These teams configure persons and resources from different stages without having to physically collocate them. They interweave the detailed steps and tasks of each process with those of others to turn sequential processing concurrent on a common enterprise information system. This precedence is illustrative of concurrent service cocreation.

A cocreation enterprise information system will *extend the concept of virtual teams into one that includes the customers and other external constituencies along the supply chain and the demand chain, or any other life cycle tasks* identified in the value propositions for the service system. Teams could readily implement cocreation for any virtual configurations without changing fundamentally the internal elements involved. Therefore, an application service provider or on-demand business provider could run millions of service cocreation on its common systems, with all processes of the cocreation sharing the common elements. This is a basic form of benefits of the scale, measurable in terms of the *average* transaction cost and cycle time for the provider. The accumulated values to the customer due to the accumulated cocreation are another basic form of benefits, of course. Both are formulated in the DCS model and both are made available by concurrent service cocreation.

Gaining Embedded Assistance, Openness, and Scalability Through Societal Cyber-Infrastructure — An Application of the Population Orientation

Embedded assistance has become commonplace in software design. Examples include the spelling and grammar assistance embedded in word processors. However, the concept is only now being recognized for IS designs. We further generalize it to service scaling design. As stated before, service scaling requires openness and scalability of the underlying service cocreation enterprise information systems. In addition, the person-centered concept also requires that both *the customer and the knowledge worker of value cocreation should enjoy pervasive and ubiquitous assistance from the systems,* such as tapping into the knowledge and other information resources accumulated at the organization and/or on the Web. Therefore, the openness and scalability extend to these resources for embedded assistance as well. Previous results in the field tend to focus the issues on technology — i.e., the implementation building blocks of a system. They endeavor to achieve open source software, application ontology, inter-operation protocols, and industrial standards, to name just the more representative. All these are important. We merely stress that the design paradigms and models using these building blocks are important, too. The open source community has offered many such examples, ranging from the industrial philosophy that OMG (Object Management Group) and STEP communities promote to the emerging Web science. The CED paradigm and the modelbase model are two more examples that we add.

Finally, we also stress that the Web itself represents the most comprehensive and most important accumulation of information resources to date, including immediately usable and quickly inferable knowledge which are open, scalable, and being constantly updated. The Web must be embedded into any cocreation enterprise information system. Integrating all the above sources, and more, into one all-encompassing concept, we term it the *societal cyber-infrastructure or the DCS foundation.* This concept is broad: it includes the usual notion of cyber-infrastructure (the Internet, telecommunications, etc.), the Web (including all homepages, files, and literature, and accumulated data about its operation), the open source technology, and the public domain practices. We now have a general but concrete way to define system openness, scalability, and embedded assistance in terms of the system's capacity for connection to and operation on the societal cyber-infrastructure (see the lemmas of the second theorem of DCS). This definition is reducible to practice and can be verified (predictable), albeit also broad. *The focus on societal cyber-infrastructure is a form of the population orientation* discussed in Chapter 4. Needless to say, this paradigm supports the notion of gaining openness and scalability through immersing the cocreation enterprise IS into the societal cyber-infrastructure — as a basic means to build and reach the population, as well as for prudent cost considerations. The details of the immersing are delineated below in the next section.

We wish to point out that an enterprise cannot confine itself to proprietary technologies in the knowledge economy in any case. It has to open to what the majority in society is using in order to, at least, easily work with its external constituencies. From a cost angle, one physical societal cyber-infrastructure can support many different uses and even be made to appear differently to different users, if necessary. An enterprise has little reason to not explore the possibility of tapping into this societal investment. The concept of virtual teams and virtual configurations describes the virtual nature of societal cyber-infrastructure. On the requirements side, an enterprise has to be able to continuously expand its systems, without requiring reconstruction or causing major disruption. Such a requirement could arise easily from innovations in a firm's business vision. Next, an enterprise has to provide smooth re-configuration and restructuring of its systems and their physical elements, in order to adapt to their changing usage patterns by the virtual configurations. The adjustment optimizes the overall performance of the enterprise system. Finally, an enterprise needs to be prepared to connect with any part of society and deal with perpetuating transient states of their business. All these generic characteristics of modern enterprises also point to gaining embedded assistance, openness, and scalability through societal cyber-infrastructure.

Enterprise information systems possess information resources as well as process them, thus they are capable of providing assistance to the user (customer and knowledge worker) in a responsive or even proactive way. This capacity should be exploited for service cocreation. In a broader sense, the history of the man-machine system evolution is one of "downloading" the burden of mundane operations and analytics, along with their attendant data tasks (gathering, storage, and processing), from man to machine. Examples include CATSCAN, computer-aided engineering, computer-aided manufacturing, computer-based information system, and other models of the application of computers to human jobs. This potential of down-loading defines one more fundamental reason why DCS brings about reduction of transaction cost and cycle time, to make embedding the cocreation enterprise information systems into the societal cyber-infrastructure profitable. (Otherwise, why bother?)

The downloading also explains the person-centered concept which in turn is central to any design of embedded assistance. In fact, as the notion of machine scales up from computer to societal cyber-infrastructure and that of man to (extended) enterprise, man seems to have humbled himself in the alliance and forgot that the former is meant to be an active servant not only to the enterprise but also to the person. Now, the DCS model recognizes the promises of societal cyber-infrastructure and defines them to be working in the background providing person-centered embedded assistance through the cocreation enterprise information system. For example, the cocreation enterprise information system can provide related experience, benchmarks, or facts assembled from the Web to customers and knowledge workers on demand, as well as affording enterprise processes with automatic sensing, monitoring, and adaptive control, real-time and online. Therefore, embedded assistance may be compared to the notion of digital nervous system by MicroSoft. Technically, cocreation enterprise information systems are a step beyond traditional enterprise information systems in the sense that they require person-centered embedded assistance and automatic re-configuration of systems. Their design methodology should focus on these requirements.

6.2 Elements-Oriented Methodology for DCS Design: Embedding Cocreation Enterprise Information Systems into Societal Cyber-Infrastructure

There are two basic concepts invoked by the above title: elements-oriented and embedding into societal cyber-infrastructure. We discuss them here. Briefly, basic information system (IS) elements substantiate a cocreation enterprise IS, a physical service system, and digital connections in actuality. They define a system from start to end, and technical building blocks merely implement them. The DCS model recognizes five basic (types of) *elements*: user, process, information (data and knowledge) resources, computing, and (networking) infrastructure. All DCS designs can be reduced to (a configuration of) these elements and all development and operation efforts based on them. It follows that they should be the focus of any DCS design. This is *elements orientation* which leads naturally to a simple design methodology concerning especially cocreation enterprise IS: *digitizing the basic elements, configuring them into cocreation enterprise IS, and linking them across the extended enterprise to configure cocreation extended enterprise IS*. The elements orientation is compatible with object orientation of (software) system design in that they can be represented and implemented as objects. Therefore, they define the general concepts of virtual configuration and re-configuration discussed above and reduces them to software design as well. In this sense, the elements orientation is consistent with the philosophy of component engineering that drives many design methods, including the CBM approach from IBM (see Chapter 4).

The second concept, *embedding into societal infra-structure*, is a little anti-intuitive. The usual notion of leveraging cyber-infrastructure would be to incorporate it into enterprise IS — i.e., embedding social infrastructure into enterprise IS, not the other way round. However, this is precisely the point: cocreation is not batch production. The usual notion is a system-centered methodology which works best for batch users and batch processing on the basis of batch resources. Cocreation, on the other hand, implies ideally one of a kind IS for one of a kind value proposition. At the limit of this ideal one would expect numerous concurrent IS operating for numerous simultaneous life cycle tasks. This impractical vision serves, nevertheless, as a thought model indicating the direction of evolution for cocreation enterprise IS. For the DCS model, the largest common denominator of all cocreation IS can only be the societal cyber-infrastructure; and all the rest (i.e., the system-specific IS elements, including user interface, processes, information resources, computing, and infrastructure) are essentially the overheads incurred by customization for enterprises. Therefore, the gravity of the collective overheads and the logic of minimization converge to point to the collapse of all concurrent IS onto the societal cyber-infrastructure itself. The Web including its wireless versions, for example, is expected to be the interface of these IS. From a theoretic perspective, this embedding concept implements the population orientation: the cocreation IS uses the population and constitutes a part of the population.

Although embedding an IS into societal cyber-infrastructure is a new concept that we present here, the practices of embedding are not. A straightforward example is the embedded checks on spelling and wording that word processing software offers. Embedded B2C (see Chapter 5) also offers many design ideas and techniques showing how an enterprise may incorporate its business processes (in the form of Web functions and activities) into the standard operations of other websites. Cell phone's and cell phone camera's readable extended barcodes (e.g., the so-called two-dimensional code widely used in Japan) represent yet another example of embedding websites into pervasive and ubiquitous user interface available today. Finally, embedding tools and "hooks" are available, too. Many open source technology sites and even business websites provide user tools to query the established information resources, create new pieces, and interexchange them for processing, either for specific use on their own sites or for general use on the Web. In addition, many business sites also open some of their enterprise processes to customers for the latter's tracking — e.g., tracking the movement of parcels on logistics carriers' websites. As an example of possible design, an ordering-receiving process of enterprise supply chain IS can embed its supplier information into the suppliers' appropriate processes on their websites (or, at the least, embedding their public websites and functions into the IS), and embed its shipping tracking processes into the carriers' tracking processes. Open source technology exists that allows these connections to happen without requiring proprietary agreements. A ubiquitous and pervasive IS will result in the process, from just taking advantage of what the societal cyber-infrastructure has to offer it. These ideas are generalized for the design methodology.

Combining the elements orientation with the embedding concept, we arrive naturally at a design approach.

The Elements-Oriented Embedding Design Approach:

This is embedding IS elements into societal cyber-infrastructure, to the extent that is practical. *A service cocreation enterprise IS provides the particular design of employment and deployment for these elements plus any additional proprietary elements* — or their configuration. The configuration should support person-centered concurrent virtual configurations for particular value propositions, (automatic) system reconfiguration, and, ultimately, service scaling. The embedment has a pivotal, signature aspect which differentiates this approach from any other that also incorporates the Web: this approach employs the whole Web and allows for all the usual activities on the Web (e.g., the use of search engines and websites) to be a part of the system. We recognize it as a particularization of the population orientation paradigm for cocreation enterprise IS. The other particularization, CED of Chapter 4, provides complementary results to work with this elements-oriented embedding design.

We now elaborate on the above approach to arrive at a more complete design methodology. For this purpose, three models are presented next to formalize the core concepts and suggest some generic strategies for design. These results are major extensions of some earlier work by the author (see Hsu, 2007; Hsu and Spohrer, 2008).

Model of Digitization: Digitizing IS Elements and Embedding them into Social Cyber-Infrastructure (basis for DCS)

Digitally connected service starts with digitization of elements, including both the *representation* of elements (e.g., persons and physical production factors) and the elements themselves (e.g., shared information resources, IT, and institutions). The scope of digitization

extends to the digital requirements of service systems in their configuration of user, provider, and resources in accordance with particular
value propositions. This is a basic premise of the DCS model and
hence of the design of service cocreation enterprise IS. We define the
five basic types of IS elements recognized above from the perspective
of system development. However, they also characterize digital connections and service systems in the context of DCS. The Web, for
instance also contains these five types of elements. The following definition applies uniformly to both service enterprises and the Web, to
allow for a methodology calling for *element-to-element connection
within the same type or between types across both domains* — i.e., the
elements orientation of the DCS design methodology.

Person: customers and knowledge workers at either side of service
cocreation; including both the physical entities and their digital representation in the IS, complete with security, interface, and embedded
tools for interaction with each other as well as with other IS elements;
collectively, they are the human users of the IS.

Process: software enterprise process resources; including tools,
process libraries and application software for or of the digital representation, storage, and processing of service resources (production
factors), the embodiment/implementation of the process of cocreation, and the interaction of the persons (customers and knowledge workers) with the processes of security control; collectively, they
are the process users of the IS.

Information: sharable information resources; including repositories
of data and knowledge, digital representation of persons and physical
production factors, and the standards and protocols that define them
(e.g., ontology and embedded intelligence, business component
models, and modelbase).

Computing: digital hardware resources; including the physical IT components of the computing capacity of cyberspace for the processing and
storage of software resources and information resources, and connection of persons to the infrastructure e.g., personal digital connection

(server) devices, computer, collaborating computation platform, and shared facilities providing utilities of computing.

Infrastructure: digital connecting resources; including networks (private or public) of all levels, telecommunications (wired or wireless), and built-in protocols and network management systems that connect computing elements and administer the infrastructure; collectively, they include the usual public cyber-infrastructure and proprietary enterprise cyber-infrastructure.

A metamodel may be designed to represent these IS elements and facilitate the DCS design — perhaps in the spirit of the modelbased discussed in Chapter 4. These elements should be shared and reused for as many cocreation enterprise IS as possible. In any case, when the scope of design includes only proprietary elements, then the resultant IS will be completely proprietary, too, and suffers presumably in its openness and scalability. On the other hand, a completed embedded IS may use only the elements taken or constructed from the elements available in the societal cyber-infrastructure. Any combination in the middle is evidently possible and the combination will also be characterized in terms of the configuration of elements within and/or between types, within and/or between the enterprise domain and the public domain. *The first step will always be the recognition and digitization of these IS elements,* in DCS design.

The Roadmap of DCS for Cocreation Enterprise Information Systems

Overarching Objective: apply DCS to IS elements across the customers, providers, and resources of the service enterprise, both within each category (i.e., customer-customer, provider-provider, and resource-resource) and across categories (user-provider-resource), for maximum sharing among them to support concurrent service cocreation and reduce transaction cost and cycle time. In addition, when appropriate, seek maximum embedment of the IS into societal cyber-infrastructure to achieve maximum embedded assistance, openness, and scalability. This objective guides all ensuing models below.

Digitization: recognize *paper trails* (paper workflows and workflows that require paper documents), *file trails* (workflows that require multiple isolated, perhaps even duplicated files), and *decision trails* (workflows that require multiple, perhaps even overlapped chains of decision makers); identify barriers to the connection of business processes for new and old value propositions; and build/expand IS elements to simplify the trails and remove the barriers by digital connections — e.g., convert paper-based data resources and manual processes into (stand-alone) digital enterprise systems, using application-level (dedicated and proprietary) models, designs, and technology.

Intra-Enterprise Scaling (Transformation): apply the DCS model to the whole service enterprise but focusing on IS elements — i.e., connect and configure these elements to accumulate them as service resources and share them for (concurrent) service cocreation to reduce cocreation transaction time and cycle time using (proprietary) models, designs, and technology as well as societal cyber-infrastructure.

Inter-Enterprise Scaling (Collaboration): apply the DCS model across collaborating enterprises (the extended enterprise) — i.e., connect the corresponding IS elements throughout the extended enterprise value chains (e.g., supply chain and demand chain), and configure them to accumulate resources for sharing in (concurrent) service cocreation to reduce transaction cost and cycle time; using primarily societal cyber-infrastructure to achieve the collaboration in an embedded manner.

The next two models elaborate the last two steps from the perspective of IS development. They also refer to new business designs on the Web (Chapter 5) and propositions in the DCS model (Chapter 3).

Model of Enterprise Transformation: Connecting IS Elements Across the Enterprise

This model applies DCS to an enterprise to transfer or enhance it into a cocreation enterprise. In particular, it develops a service cocreation enterprise IS according to the methodology discussed above. In this sense, it is an elaboration of the methodology with a scope limited to the service enterprise itself.

- **The Objective:** reduce the transaction cost and the cycle time of service cocreation — for the whole service enterprise, for the customers and knowledge workers performing their cocreation jobs, and for their collaboration in new and old value propositions.

- **The Means/Decision Variables:** digitization and application of the DCS propositions, especially the accumulation and sharing of resources, to pursue concurrent service cocreation with a methodology of embedding the cocreation IS into societal cyber-infrastructure. In addition, new designs on the Web may serve as thought models to assist the design.

- **IS Design Principles (enterprise engineering):**
  - Implement the digitization model (see above).
  - Identify limitations of the digitization, e.g., exposing current and potential paper trails, file trails, and decision trails by *experimenting with new value propositions for life cycle tasks* and new cocreation processes performing these tasks.
  - Apply the DCS propositions to guide for removal of the above limitations and search for further innovations, and reduce these ideas to configurations of IS elements.
  - Accumulate (homogeneous) IS elements by digital connections of like-types, to allow them to be used as common service resources (e.g., customer pools, knowledge worker teams, and information repositories) in different service cocreation.
  - Develop embedded or automated capabilities in real-time analytics and data processing to enhance the performance of persons and machines in the enterprise, using societal cyber-infrastructure as much as possible.
  - Develop either global or peer-to-peer administration capability to enable the cocreation enterprise IS to support sharing of digital resources among distributed persons and machines.

— Simplify enterprise processes by using the cocreation IS (through sharing resources and consolidating sub-tasks and/or sharing results).

— Convert sequential enterprise processes into concurrent processes by using the cocreation IS (through sharing resources and interweaving sub-tasks and/or sharing resources).

— Employ the concepts of teams and virtual organizations, flexible machinery, and automated control systems to make the cocreation enterprise and its facilities agile.

— Use new business designs on the Web as possible thought models to seek out new paradigms of conducting cocreation and formulating the cocreation enterprise IS. For example, the B2E/B2M enterprise portal and Internet enterprise models may be employed as the analogy and guide the innovation of the IS design.

— Seek out the possibility of *using social networking as a collaboration tool* to facilitate service cocreation for both customers and knowledge workers.

— Maximize the use of societal cyber-infrastructure throughout the cocreation IS.

• **Constraints:** availability of the open, scalable, and re-configurable technologies; industrial standards for inter-operation; and costs.

A simple industrial case depicted in Figure 6.1 will help illuminate the model and its application for enterprise engineering. The basic story is straightforward: a commercial bank tries to streamline its commercial loan approval process and reduce the cycle time from an average of a week to within a few hours. The "as is" system involves five isolated "islands of automation", from the formulation of the proposals to their final decision, each of which is in and of itself an IS while also being a part of the overall workflow system. Such a situation is commonplace in many enterprises, service or not. The workflow may reflect a paper trail which is not the case with the bank, or it may reflect a file trail and/or a decision trail — as is the case here. The bank has performed the digitization stage according

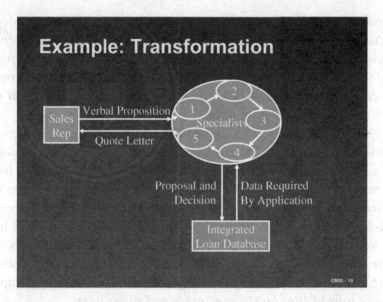

Figure 6.1: Enterprise transformation: the first example of DCS design.

to the DCS roadmap, and the new objective amounts to enterprise transformation.

We now apply the model. A straightforward innovation would be to improve each process and its island system. However, the model calls for more. Thus, a thorough review would reveal that the information resources of these IS could be integrated into an enterprise database with all processes re-engineered to be applications of the database. This design provides concurrent processing of different proposals. There are two ways to implement it: retooling the previous process-specific specialists into generalists conducting all processes, or supporting these specialists to continue doing their previous jobs on the new database. The second way is permitted by the virtual configuration capability of modern database technology, such as defining views to support application software reminiscent of the previous process-oriented IS. Figure 6.1 depicts both approaches, with the large circle representing the generalist solution. Previous results favored the first way since it is obvious; however, retooling is costly, too. The model reveals the second way and puts it in context for proper evaluation. Finally, the societal cyber-infrastructure concept should expose one more class of innovation: putting the loan approval process on the Web to involve directly the customers, and hence really turn the process into a service cocreation enterprise. At the minimum, the customer can apply online, track the application online, and get notification of the decision online.

Further, she/he may get embedded assistance through embedded or on-demand analytics to help her/him choose among loan products and formulate the final application. Naturally, the bank can learn from the many practices of the B2C business design on the Web and inspire its own cocreation design. Immersing the loan process into the Web leads ultimately to embedding the cocreation enterprise IS into the Web. Value propositions of the embedding may include better cocreation — and hence better service and better value to all involved, more pervasive access to (potential) customers, and more comprehensive information on the customers and the market.

Many banks have already developed automated decision regimes and embedded them into their processes. A consumer loan application may get preliminary approval during the online application right on the spot. This is a major step toward making embedded assistance a common practice. However, we expect to see the practice to gain even more value not only by propagating to all applications, but also by embracing the person-centered view of the assistance. An automated analytic can be a mere automated process — a self-contained robot replacing persons, or be a decision support tool to persons (customers and knowledge workers) — a robotic protégé. Both may have similar technical rendition in themselves, but they will see differentiation in the design of their employment and deployment — their roles in the cocreation enterprise IS.

The next model, enterprise collaboration, applies the above model to extended enterprises along its supply/demand chain. These two models share a common logic, except that the collaboration design itself is envisioned to rely on societal cyber-infrastructure, and all collaborating enterprises are expected to have embraced digitization as the roadmap provides.

Model of Enterprise Collaboration: Connecting DCS Elements Across Enterprises

One could argue that the fundamental difference between an enterprise and an extended enterprise — and by extension between transformation and collaboration — is proprietary control. Without considering this point, the model of enterprise collaboration can be reframed as the transformation of extended enterprises. Collaboration has many forms, and some of the common ones are revealed in the new business designs on the Web that Chapter 5 reviewed. However, for supply chains and demand chains, collaboration may also include some proprietary control such as in the case of a prime provider/manufacturer actually controlling its suppliers, through stock-holding or some other long-term bonding arrangements. The model covers this wide range of possibilities. Some of its principles may correspond more to transformation than to loose collaboration.

- **The Objective:** reduce the transaction cost and the cycle time of service cocreation — for the whole community of collaborating service enterprises, for the customers and knowledge workers performing their cocreation jobs for the extended enterprise, and for their collaboration in new and old value propositions in the community.

- **The Means/Decision Variables:** digitization and application of the DCS propositions, especially the accumulation and sharing of resources, to the whole community in pursuit of concurrent service cocreation for the extended enterprise. The collaboration part of the cocreation IS should be built primarily on and embedded largely into societal cyber-infrastructure. In addition, new designs on the Web may serve as thought models to assist the design. The design should deal with the mechanism and boundaries of collaboration and provide connection methods, including the additional IS elements and their configuration in the resultant federation.

- **IS Design Principles (enterprise engineering):**
  - Implement the digitization model for all participating enterprises, and implement the transformation model as much as possible to make participant IS consistent with the requirements of cocreation.
  - Identify limitations of the digitization and transformation with respect to collaboration, e.g., exposing current and potential paper trails, file trails, and decision trails by *experimenting with new value propositions for life cycle tasks* and new cocreation processes performing these tasks within the community.
  - Apply the DCS propositions to guide for removal of the above limitations and search for further innovations, and reduce these ideas to configurations of IS elements across the entire community of collaboration.
  - Accumulate (homogeneous) IS elements for the whole community by *digital connections of like-types across collaborating enterprises*, to allow them to be used as common service resources (e.g., customer pools, knowledge worker teams, and information repositories) in different service cocreation of the collaboration.
  - Make digitized information resources (data and knowledge), communication channels (persons and machines), and process resources (control and workflow) compatible for collaboration among participants, either directly or through some intermediary design (e.g., middle-ware). This may not be required if societal cyber-infrastructure covers the whole community.
  - Create an inter-operable proxy for each cocreation enterprise IS, for connection with other *enterprise proxies*, and thereby construct a virtual community cocreation IS for the collaborating extended enterprise. The ideal is to make the virtual community IS completely compatible or even based on societal cyber-infrastructure.
  - Develop embedded or automated capabilities in real-time analytics and data processing for the collaboration processes, to enhance the performance of persons and machines in the collaboration, using societal cyber-infrastructure as much as possible.

— Develop either global or peer-to-peer administration capability to enable the virtual configuration of the community cyber-infrastructure and support sharing of digital resources among distributed persons and machines of the community.

— Simplify extended enterprise processes of collaboration by using the new virtual community cocreation IS (through sharing resources and consolidating sub-tasks and/or sharing results, along the supply chain).

— Convert sequential extended enterprise processes of collaboration into concurrent processes, by using the new virtual community cocreation IS (through sharing resources and interweaving sub-tasks and/or sharing resources).

— Employ the concepts of teams and virtual organizations, flexible machinery, and automated control systems along the demand chain and supply chain to make the community and its facilities agile.

— Use new business designs on the Web as possible thought models to seek out new paradigms of conducting community cocreation and formulating the virtual community cocreation IS. For example, the Internet utilities and industrial exchange models may be employed as the analogy and guide the innovation of the IS design.

— Seek out the possibility of *using social networking as a collaboration tool* to facilitate service cocreation for both customers and knowledge workers of the extended enterprise and develop new possible value propositions for the community.

— Maximize the use of societal cyber-infrastructure throughout the virtual community cocreation IS.

• **Constraints:** business designs; availability of open, scalable, and reconfigurable technologies; industrial standards for inter-operation; and costs.

Enterprise value chains can serve as guidance for identifying the candidates for process-level collaboration for the extended enterprise. The collaboration model is more involved than the transformational model because it requires inter-enterprise operations, or inter-operation of independent enterprise IS and databases. The model also makes reference to such concepts as enterprise proxy and virtual configuration, which require explanation. Chapter 8 will serve this purpose. Related results by the author are also found in Hsu *et al.* (2006) and Hsu *et al.* (2007).

The following industrial example illustrates the collaboration model. The case involves a global retailing chain and its major suppliers (manufacturers). The collaboration seeks to achieve a high end integration of a supply chain — i.e., connecting life cycle tasks of the chain (the extended enterprise) at the level of enterprise processes to reduce transaction cost and cycle time for all, in the magnitude of over 80 percent in each case. The particular retailing life cycle here is concerned with the forecasting, replenishing (ordering), order processing, and manufacturing of certain products at the retailing chain. The first two processes pertain to the retailer while the last two, the manufacturer. When both enterprises of the collaboration are digitized, their respective enterprise IS can connect to allow the forecasting process of the retailer to feed directly into the manufacturing process of the supplier, as if they were one enterprise, and, also, as it would have no doubt been done if these two enterprises were indeed one. Figure 6.2 shows the "as is" workflow in solid lines and the "to be" collaboration in the dashes. The saving is obvious, in terms of both transaction cost and cycle time.

The collaboration described above can be accomplished by a number of ways, and the enterprise collaboration model here may be deemed as an overkill if only these two enterprises are collaborating. However, the idea may scale up to include other products, other suppliers, and other retailers; it may even be cascaded through the entire supply chain (suppliers' suppliers). In this vision, some sharable community resources are clearly required. For example, the integrated extended enterprise needs to "drill through" the databases pertaining to the life cycle tasks for every participant to gain the total picture; and participants can use some process libraries to help them join and play in the community. Needless to say, the collaboration is in fact a cocreation between the constituencies. Therefore, the enterprise

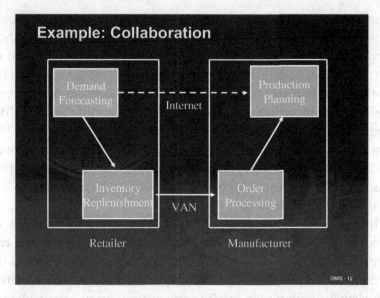

Figure 6.2: Enterprise collaboration: the second example of DCS design.

collaboration model of cocreation enterprise IS design applies fully here, and may even be required to develop and implement the full visions promised. Embedding the IS into the societal cyber-infrastructure may be the only way to scale up its performance for the population of the (immediate) global supply chain, let alone applying the DCS model to expand to other related spaces.

Is it feasible to "manipulate" and reuse societal cyber-infrastructure the way the design methodology envisions? We now attempt to address some hard issues associated with the (otherwise seemingly naïve) notion of societal cyber-infrastructure and zoom in on possible innovations.

6.3 Embedding into the Societal Cyber-Infrastructure

The Web is a global cooperative IS. In this sense, a website is both a part of the Web and an enterprise IS embedded into the Web. This observation may be construed to imply a riveting claim that embedding service cocreation enterprise IS into societal cyber-infrastructure is to follow Web-based IS design. The situation is a little more complicated than this. To begin with, the Web is not necessarily the whole societal cyber-infrastructure. Moreover, even when we concentrate on the Web *per se*, embedding here requires both employment and deployment: using Web technology to develop the cocreation enterprise IS elements, incorporating the Web into the IS (drawing Web resources into IS elements), and incorporating the IS into the Web (distributing IS elements throughout the Web). Finally, the embedded IS operates with a population orientation, as the DCS propositions require. The usual Web-based IS design focuses on the first: employing Web technology.

Implementing this ideal may require new results to assist the employment and deployment of Web resources. For example, each cocreation may have its own view of the Web resources required that correspond to a particular virtual configuration of the Web resources. Each virtual configuration may in turn correspond to a particular way of assembling these Web resources involved. Therefore, for the service enterprise as a whole, the employment and deployment may incur a considerable amount of overheads which should be streamlined and minimized. In other words, it may require some common facility to reduce the transaction cost and cycle time of embedding the cocreation enterprise IS into societal cyber-infrastructure. This facility may take the form of a common Web front end with built-in utilities of searching, connection, and inter-operation. The accumulation and sharing of these utilities may be proprietary. At the other end of sophistication, the facility may also take the form of some open source technology for sharing societal cyber-infrastructure for all systems. The actual practices may require both types of facilities and efforts.

We envision a core open source facility to be a repository of sharable IS elements on the Web — either in the form of metadata referencing to the real resources, or in these resources themselves, or both; and the modelbase of Chapter 4 provides a particular example of such an idea. Similar repositories may also be developed for open embedding software and solutions. In addition, the facility may include industrial protocols and standards to regulate and implement the connections required in the embedding and sharing. Finally, it may also require some ontology for defining IS elements out of the sharable resources on the societal cyber-infrastructure.

Now, we contemplate a general model to describe such a common open source facility for sharing societal cyber-infrastructure. First, we recognize some commonplace IS elements available from the societal cyber-infrastructure. Then, we propose a model of sharing in the spirit of the three-schema database model.

Additional Societal Cyber-Infrastructure Elements for IS

User: Embedded/ubiquitous personal tools, systems, and information for access and interaction, e.g., cell phones, RFID/ubiquitous coding, personal digital devices, and embedded bio-chips.

Process/software resources: Open source technology and tools/functions/processes on websites, e.g., search engines, B2C/B2B functions and activities, public business process libraries (XQUERY and ebXML), open standards and protocols.

Information/data and knowledge resources: Internet information utilities and homepages (including files and databases embedded in the homepages), e.g., information portals, metamodels, and modelbase.

Computing: Internet computing utilities, e.g., storage networks, public platforms, and Internet transaction portals.

Infrastructure: The usual cyber-infrastructure; e.g., the Internet, telecommunications, and built-in network management.

Sharing societal cyber-infrastructure for cocreation enterprise IS is sharing these additional IS elements among enterprises for service cocreation. As long as the sharing is expected to be commonplace and the design concept of embedding common, an open facility to support the sharing will be beneficial. We propose below a three-schema conceptual model to technically define the requirements of such a facility. This thought model is referred to as the *Web resources application system* (*WRAS*): a management system for the sharing of societal cyber-infrastructure by service cocreation enterprise IS. A key concept here is the formulation of a service systems as the collection of service cocreation each of which — be it a consulting, a process, or an enterprise job — is, in turn, a concurrent user of the societal cyber-infrastructure (e.g., running a client company's payroll processes). Therefore, the service cocreation (or, the digital connections involved) is a session (e.g., running payrolls) of the sharing of the societal cyber-infrastructure, rather than being a dedicated physical structure on it (e.g., a dedicated payroll EDI/network). Each service cocreation can be unique, in terms of the processes involved and the (virtual) configuration of resources required, but they will be supported by the societal cyber-infrastructure as sessions. The processes involved and production factors used in the service system do not have to be repetitive, nor standardized. The economy of scale comes from the concurrent service systems performed on the same societal cyber-infrastructure — or, simply, the sharing of digital resources. The economy will come primarily in the form of transaction cost and cycle time reduction to the entire population of the service enterprise concerned.

This thought model actually describes many e-commerce enterprises. For example, the models of ISP, ICP, and portal (see Chapter 5), along with search engines, have thrived on sharing their digital resources among customers each of whom may customize on their respective uses — or, concurrent service cocreation using the same societal cyber-infrastructure. Although their type of service cocreation is simple, which does not involve enterprise processes, professional consulting, and any other complicated tasks, they still help illustrate the virtual configuration concept.

Figure 6.3 depicts the WRAS model and further substantiates it in terms of a three-schema design. The high-level WRAS design envisions a common facility to manage (employing and deploying) the common Web resources of societal cyber-infrastructure for creating virtual configurations and supporting application sessions. As stated above, the resources include the Web itself, and common reference

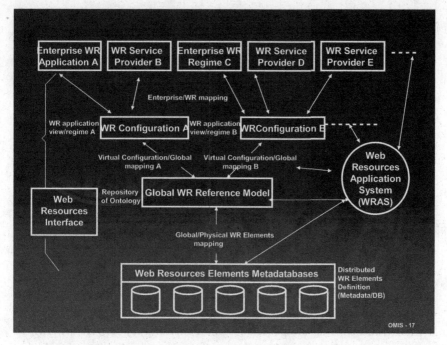

Figure 6.3:   Web resources application system: a three-schema model.

models, open standards, and embedded intelligence including ontology and analytics available in the open source community. The WRAS results may be Web resources in and of themselves, too.

Implementing the WRAS model as an open source facility clearly requires collaborative effort of the field. However, employing the concept to help embed cocreation enterprise IS may not. The methodology will first be premised on acquiring an open, scalable, and re-configurable enterprise cyber-infrastructure for the service enterprise. On this basis, it will endeavor to design the cocreation enterprise IS with a goal of immersing it into societal cyber-infrastructure, by perhaps considering the models of this chapter. Common Web resources for the IS will then be recognized from the design. Similarly, requirements such as person-centered "control levers" for customers and knowledge workers to perform virtual configurations of the

Web resources for individual cocreation, will also be determined. These levers will ideally be augmented with embedded assistance from the societal cyber-infrastructure itself.

For instance, the IS should be able to customize its jobs (e.g., helpdesk processes, customer relations processes, and payrolls) for the particular cocreation sessions on the users' command, in a manner in which the IS appears to be custom-designed just for the particular cocreation job at hand. This way, the processes of cocreation can afford to be one of a kind since they are realized in the on-demand employment of the societal cyber-infrastructure, or, the virtual configurations commanded. Once these requirements are on hand, the methodology will call for the obvious step: designing the implementation so that the IS leverages the common Web resources toward satisfying the requirements.

In conclusion, we submit that the DCS model contributes to the design of service cocreation enterprise IS — the backbone of service systems. It adds new concepts to the previous results and leads to a methodology that helps *reduce the challenge of service scaling to service system design*, rather than to the standardization of service resources, especially the processes and the knowledge workers involved. The former can draw from the vast results in the fields of science, engineering, and management; while the latter may be both intractable and inappropriate. The methodology presented is another leg supporting the DCS model.

The next chapter develops an application of the DCS model, especially the vision of instrumentation of the environment and the first theorem. The application domain is intelligent network flows using infrastructure for Smart highways. It is based on an actual work performed for New York State, USA.

Chapter 7

Instrumentation of the Environment: A Design for Connecting Cyberspace with Physical Infrastructure for Intelligent Network Flows

How to unite cyberspace with physical space? The answer begs two additional questions: what physical space and why? At an empirical level, many industrial applications have touched on both questions many times over, with mounting digital devices and systems on factory equipment, constructions, and vehicles, vessels, and aircraft to achieve computerized control. Scientific research has also routinely used digital devices for monitoring of the environment, animals, tsunamis and earthquakes. The military offers perhaps the most comprehensive case for such unification. However, how and why have not been comprehensively answered for the Web, in particular, and for service scaling and transformation, in general. For example, does unification mean the potential expansion of digitally connected service to manufacturing, energy, agriculture and other traditionally non-service sectors? A small piece of the puzzle is attempted here: instrumentation of the infrastructure, as a focus of the what question. In particular, the first theorem of DCS is applied here to *explore unification designs that support a person's and an organization's life cycle tasks that involve highways*. These tasks may customarily be referred to as global logistics, intelligent transportation, and tourism. For the how question, a *subject-environment-enterprise interaction* model is presented which integrates *multi-modal data* (data from RFID, wireless sensor networks, and enterprise databases) for task-centered use. For the why question, particular value propositions are formulated and discussed in detail.

7.1 The Subject-Environment-Enterprise Interaction Model: An Instrumentation Design for Infrastructure

The overarching technical problem is how to include infrastructure in population-oriented cocreation? That is, how to apply DCS to infrastructure, to include the (real-time) information about infrastructure and the activities performed on infrastructure in the population of value cocreation? The implication is broad. All economic activities of our society are arguably a form of interaction with the environment surrounding us. That is, the physical environment is always a dimension of the activities. However, the activities may or may not care to recognize the interaction in its design and operation, depending largely on how directly and significantly they are affected by the environment. However, more frequently than not, economic activities ignore the environment — i.e., leave it to chance because they lack the ability to incorporate the environment into their planning and control and do anything about it. Industrial network flows are cases in point. Transportation systems, for one, require real-time control based on the real-time (traffic) conditions on streets and highways (e.g., see Demers *et al.*, 2006). Tolls represent another typical real-time system (e.g., McKinnon, 2006). Logistics in global supply chains also requires real-time control to reflect the real-time (availability) conditions manifested in the ongoing freights in transit — this is the real-time supply and demand on the move (e.g., see Gourdin, 2006; and Mentzer *et al.*, 2006). Tourism, in a similar way, requires real-time conditions of the environment. They also tend to involve multi-modal data — i.e., different data sources using different scales and data models (e.g., as in Grasman, 2006).

In the past, before the age of digital connections, all such network flows tended to ignore the environment dimension — or, more precisely, they contented themselves with relying on additional resources (e.g., inventories or backups) to cope with deviations from the environmental conditions they presumed should have occurred. With digital connections, using for, example, sensors and RFID (radio frequency identification), the environment becomes measurable and can be monitored, on a real-time and online basis. Hence, it is increasingly being incorporated and accounted for in the network flows, such as intelligent transportation systems (e.g., Smart buses, toll collections, fast lane controls). Network flows, in turn, can be incorporated into the scope of sully chain management (e.g., see Hugo, 2006). The question is that how much farther we can continue to expand the applications and extend the reach of unification with the environment dimension for all genres of economic activities? Can we expect the environment dimension to be a common factor in any mathematical formula of microeconomic production functions?

From the perspective of the service scaling and transformation theory, the question is one of *general expansion of digital connections to include the physical environment, and the general application of the DCS model to this expanded population which unifies the physical environment with cyberspace.* We use the term *instrumentation of the environment* to refer to the addition of digital devices and systems to the environment for its monitoring, and the unification of these devices and systems to the other digital connections of the world. We also refer to the instrumentation as creating a *DCS layer for the environment.* How can service scaling benefit from an instrumented environment? How can the DCS layer be employed to create additional value propositions? They are the overarching quest of this chapter. To help substantiate the concept, we focus on a specific application domain: *life cycle tasks of persons and organizations that are performed on or involving highways and related infrastructure,* such as logistics in global supply chains, intelligent transportation systems, and tourism. For simplicity of reference, we collectively term the domain *service scaling of intelligent network flows* (perhaps it can also be coined as intelligent network flows as a service). The chapter develops an instrumentation design for this domain, and analyzes for new value propositions using the instrumentation, according to the new theory of the book: its DCS model and population orientation paradigm.

The instrumentation involves three dimensions: infrastructure, individual subjects of movement, and planning and control of the movement. These traditionally isolated dimensions can be digitally connected to enhance their performance. Digitization of the infrastructure with a DCS layer provides real-time data to facilitate its operation (new value propositions), while digitally connecting the subjects to the infrastructure allows for tailored services and support to particular subjects (new value propositions). Connection of both to the enterprise information systems enables adaptive control for the application (e.g., logistics) at a global optimization level (e.g., see Lei *et al.*, 2006 for an example of global optimization of production, inventory, and logistics) — which also represents new value propositions. Previous results in the field provide planning/routing, real-time monitoring, and trip support, but the chapter focuses on their integration. A metaphor for the integration is an adaptive control panel administering an automated material handling system. In this metaphor, the service cocreation enterprise information system (IS) (see Chapter 6) for the (extended) enterprise of intelligent network flows will serve as the person-centered or task-centered control panel, with the global infrastructure becoming "controllable" in a way comparable to factory conveyors and automated guided vehicles. The population orientation of cocreation enterprise IS implies that the virtual "control panel" is open, scalable, and embedded in societal cyber-infrastructure, too.

The following statement consolidates the concepts discussed above:

Subject-Environment-Enterprise (SEE) Interaction Model

General: *build a DCS layer for the environment, develop a service cocreation enterprise IS for the persons and organizations involved in the service system intended using the results of Chapter 6, and extend the cocreation IS to incorporate the environment DCS layer into it to achieve new value propositions enabled by the extension.*

Intelligent Network Flows: *use mobile system-on-a-chip devices (e.g., RFID), stationary systems (e.g., wireless sensor network), and multimodal data fusion to build the instrumentation for infrastructure, and incorporate the resultant DCS layer into the cocreation IS of intelligent network flows for scaling network flow services.*

We now consider the details of the model as it applies to service scaling of intelligent network flows. First, on the digitization front, two particular technologies stand out: wireless sensor networks and RFID systems. Both have been widely employed for environment monitoring (e.g., seismic study, animal habitats, and military applications), intelligent transportation systems (e.g., vehicle tags, rider Smart cards, and rush-hour traffic control), and inventory management (e.g., item tags) — e.g., see Akyildiz *et al.*, 2002, and Koh *et al.*, 2006. They have been proven to be capable of serving as real-time data collectors, processors, and even dispatchers for enterprise information systems. As the technology continues to improve, we expect each RFID tag and wireless sensor node to continue shrinking in size while expanding on computing power to become a PC on a chip, with adequate energy supply.

Next, concerning new value propositions: We can recognize the benefits and opportunities of service scaling from observing the limitations of previous applications. For example, just-in-time (JIT) production systems tend to have a weak link in freights on highways, which can be monitored by using a GPS or global positioning system, but cannot be rerouted automatically according to the real-time conditions on the roads. Previous results tend to therefore focus on the planning of delivery (i.e., routing, scheduling, and supply chain integration) and intra-factory level monitoring and adjustment (e.g., see Moin and Salhi, 2006). In general, if intra-factory material handling systems are a benchmark of performance, then inter-factory network flows fail to provide similar control since they lack reliable information on the real-time conditions of the highways, lack sufficient journey support for the individual subjects on the move (e.g., drivers, vehicles, and cargos), and lack integration of these real-time data with enterprise information systems (e.g., logistics, production and inventory, and infrastructure operation). These limitations all represent opportunities for improvement, as values to the organizations.

The SEE interaction model, when implemented, promises to facilitate the operation of the infrastructure (e.g., using, global or fleet data) and provision of customized journey support to the users of the infrastructure (e.g., through, access to individual need and history). When it is connected to enterprises databases along the global supply chain, this new capacity further becomes an enabler for adaptive control of network flows at a global level.

As stated above, the baggage handling systems at some airports (e.g., the Hong Kong Airport and the I-Chon Airport of Korea) offer a metaphoric reference point: They attach an RFID label to every piece of luggage and move them through material handling systems equipped with networks of sensors interacting with the RFID labels. A control panel displays the status of the system, down to the level of individual pieces of luggage, and directs their individual movement on the conveyers to different dispatching points. Infrastructure can be compared to conveyors in the example and the subjects to baggage, with the network flow cocreation IS performing the control: dispatching operational decisions back to the subjects and the infrastructure, if necessary, for taking new actions.

In this context, the notion of environment is reduced to the usual physical *infrastructure* including highways, bridges, airports, seaports, and other physical civil foundations of society. Implementing the model entails (1) adding a digital layer to the infrastructure and the users (or, the subjects); (2) determining the information requirements for adaptive control of the subjects (e.g., safety and journey decision support), infrastructure (e.g., operation), and enterprise processes (routing, scheduling, and production and inventory planning); and (3) implementing the control through information integration over the extended enterprise of global logistics. At present, adaptive control is feasible for air cargos and maritime shipping. However, land-based infrastructure remains a blind spot since it cannot be globally monitored and operated. Without digital connections to the infrastructure, the network flow enterprises cannot perform globally synchronized adaptive routing, scheduling, and journey assistance by using only connections to the subjects alone via GPS.

The technical elements required of the implementation are available today, except for the common standards of inter-operation among wireless sensor networks, RFID systems, and enterprise databases. Of them, the central concern is the subjects that move globally, e.g., the RFID bearers, which provide a center of global inter-operation under the SEE model (i.e., person-centered and task-centered). Thus, the lack of international standard for RFID systems is a major inhibitor to the global implementation of the SEE model. At present, a number of national authorities exert considerable influence on the regulation and standard development for RFID. They include USA/FCC; Canada/DOC; EU/ERO, CEPT, ETSI, etc.; Japan/MPHPT; China/MII; Australia/AUMA; and Singapore/IDA. International standard groups are also being organized under the auspices of the ISO and United Nations, in addition to industrial consortia (e.g., EPCglobe). For the purpose of the book, we consider the standards belonging to future research of the SEE model, and we focus here only on its generic design that can be implemented by using common technologies, and that promises to remain valid under future standards.

The conceptual design has to be based on the requirements of the model, which are the flip side of value propositions. Therefore, analyzing the SEE vision to suggest new value propositions and requirements is a major task of the design. The remaining design is concerned primarily with information integration: connection of wireless sensor networks with the existing operation processes of the infrastructure, the interaction of RFID systems with the sensors, and the fusion of sensor data with enterprise databases. The information integration is a major part of the SEE service cocreation enterprise IS. Existing cyber-infrastructure is capable of transferring data between wireless sensor networks and enterprise databases, and it is ready for extension to RFID with appropriate standards. It follows that the integration design is essentially a methodology for data fusion among these multiple sources. The rest of the chapter presents both the analysis for value propositions and requirements, and a methodology for information integration. The discussion is based on the author's prior work (Hsu and Wallace, 2007).

7.2 Conceptual Design of the SEE Interaction Model for Highways

7.2.1 *Digitization of Highways: A New Public Asset*

This is a direct application of the first theorem of DCS to infrastructure. Enhancing infrastructure, a public asset, with a DCS layer has to be considered as a public policy and justified as such. An example is a recent I-87 multi-modal study (Parsons, 2003) conducted for New York State with US Federal funding. The study proposed a Smart highways vision from the perspective of intelligent transportation. We use this vision to explore how the SEE model can further expand it to support persons' and organizations' life cycle tasks performed via the Smart highways. As shown in Figure 7.1, a layer of digitization is added to the highway, using RFID and wireless sensor networks. The new digital abilities were originally envisioned to facilitate the highway authority's operations and transportation control, the highway users' trips, and regional economic growth. However, the SEE model considers the same abilities also facilitating other tasks. As an example, enterprises can collaborate with highway authorities to use the public data for their own logistics control. This way, each enterprise's logistics control becomes a (concurrent) user of the digitization layer. Figure 7.2 depicts the synergism among these general tasks using the common DCS layer.

Figure 7.1 shows the basic system components of the DCS layer envisioned here in the chapter. As a public asset, the layer is envisioned to be integrated with the existing cyber-infrastructure, including among other things, the backbone networks and telecommunications systems. Therefore, the wireless sensor networks will include the usual sensor nodes and central nodes, plus special nodes for transceivers (RFID readers) and gateway nodes for connection with the cyber-infrastructure. In the particular case of the New York State's Smart

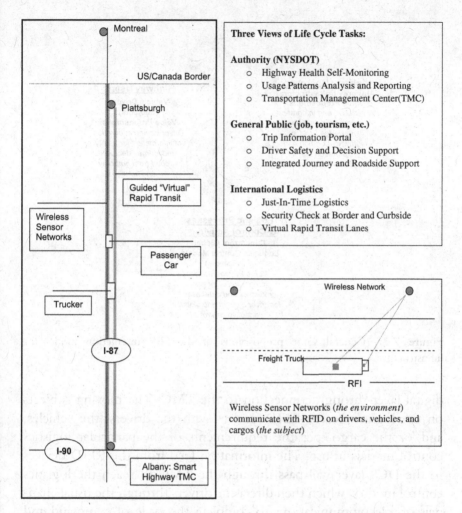

Three Views of Life Cycle Tasks:

Authority (NYSDOT)
- o Highway Health Self-Monitoring
- o Usage Patterns Analysis and Reporting
- o Transportation Management Center(TMC)

General Public (job, tourism, etc.)
- o Trip Information Portal
- o Driver Safety and Decision Support
- o Integrated Journey and Roadside Support

International Logistics
- o Just-In-Time Logistics
- o Security Check at Border and Curbside
- o Virtual Rapid Transit Lanes

Wireless Sensor Networks (*the environment*) communicate with RFID on drivers, vehicles, and cargos (*the subject*)

Figure 7.1: A DCS layer for the infrastructure of the SEE interaction model.

highway, the connection will be achieved through the State's backbone system and tier 1 providers of mobile telecommunications. A public sector transportation management center (TMC) is envisioned as the nervous center for the combined facility of the new digital layer and the previous intelligent transportation systems. In the logistics example, the enterprises will gain access to the logistics data from the

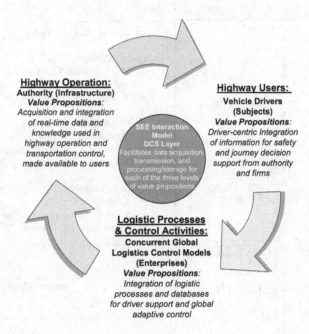

Figure 7.2: General value propositions of the SEE interaction model for infrastructure.

digital layer through connection to the TMC. The moving subjects on the highway carry RFID devices with the drivers, the vehicles, and/or the cargo, per the requirements of the particular logistics control models in use. The information feed from the RFID devices to the DCS layer will pass through the TMC to reach the logistics control models, which then direct the drivers through the usual channels of telecommunications to complete the cycle of command and control. Drivers also gain journey support as the users of the highway from the TMC and even directly from the DCS layer. In the latter scenario, the wireless sensor networks could trigger commands directed at the appropriate RFID devices, TMC signs, or driver support portals.

As shown in Figure 7.2, the DCS layer enables service scaling of intelligent network flow across different categories. Although the figure depicts only three main categories, others can also be envisioned and supported by the same common facility. We now turn to the basic value propositions and requirements that the SEE model predicts.

7.2.2 *Value Propositions and Requirements Analysis: The Roles of the DCS Layer*

The DCS model seeks values to persons, organizations, and society. We apply the first theorem of DCS to formulate three progressive and integrative levels of life cycle tasks from the SEE model for service scaling of intelligent network flows: the *infrastructure life cycle tasks* from the authority's perspective (i.e., infrastructure project initiation and planning, engineering design, construction, on demand and scheduled maintenance, transportation management, inspection, and renovation); the *highway journey life cycle tasks* from the subjects'/ users' perspective (e.g., the scheduling, routing, moving, monitoring, and receiving of cargo for the class of freight users; other life cycles for other classes of users); and the *logistics control process life cycle tasks* (e.g., the demand, supply, monitoring, adaptive control, and integration of logistics for enterprise processes at both ends of the journey). These life cycle tasks define the basic classes of value propositions which then determine the requirements of the capacity of the DCS layer. The technical requirements are similarly analyzed based on the capacity envisioned. In particular, we recognize the DCS layer as the core of a cocreation enterprise information system (a digital nervous system) for the infrastructure, and employ its design principles (see Chapter 6) to develop these classes of technical capabilities: *message generation and acquisition, transmission, and processing/storage.*

- **Value Propositions and Requirements for Infrastructure Operations:** acquisition and integration of data and knowledge used in the authority (e.g., New York State Department of Transportation) to better develop the Smart highways and better run the transportation management centers.

The DCS layer should help the infrastructure monitor its own health and usage, and thereby acquire automatically important data to streamline the authority's operation. Possibilities include environment assessment data and usage patterns by location for project initiation and planning; usage and maintenance data for engineering design; 24/7 real-time and historic traffic data for construction and work zone management; road conditions' surveillance and reports for on demand and regular maintenance; non-destructing, non-intrusive data collection and evaluation for inspection; work zone monitoring, 24/7 traffic surveillance, incident reports, and computer sign/signal systems for project control and transportation management centers; and integration of these data for renovation of the Smart highways. In a sense, the DCS layer should facilitate its own planning, design, construction, maintenance, inspection, control, and renovation to help the authority's mission. The digital layer could be likened to a map that "talks"; in the sense that each ever-refining spot or locality on the map demands data and knowledge for its development and functioning, while it also feeds back data and knowledge of some kind to its owner to operate it. Therefore, the locality-identified messages become an agent of integration for the whole life cycle of operation since tasks are traceable to these localities. At present, data collection and tasks integration are difficult to achieve, and this problem results in high transaction cost and long cycle time for infrastructure maintenance and development.

For instance, the New York State Department of Transportation uses different information systems to maintain environmental impact assessments, geographical data (land, bodies of water, etc.), initiation plans, design files, construction contracts, maintenance reports, inspection records, and other mandated data for the operation of its projects. In addition, TMC operations add their own computerized signs, signals, video cameras, and even Web-based systems. The DCS layer could provide location-based message feedings on a 24/7 basis to facilitate or supplement these systems. It could add real-time road conditions for maintenance and traffic data for control; even the vehicles on the highways could, when equipped with proper sensors on board, serves as probes for the Smart highways to automatically generate these location-based data. Locations, then, could provide a link to all groups within the Department, tying together different time frames, too. In addition, an integrated life-cycle operation promises to be easier to provide seamless support to users. Transportation management centers would become an immediate beneficiary of the new capability, since they could use the integrated, 24/7 messages to better coordinate with emergency services, schedule routine maintenance, and help direct trucks and other rapid response systems.

- **Value Propositions and Requirements for Infrastructure Users:** integration of journey information and driver decision support to achieve Smart/safe driver and Smart public transportation, as well as Smart freight, for the general public.

The highway users include local commuters, tourists, and truckers doing transshipments. These users are all drivers and hence have similar driver requirements: information and assistance to enable them to achieve zero-accident safety in all weather conditions, one-call/stop assistance to personal needs of the passengers and crews, and 24/7 decision support throughout the journey. The safety requirements and personal assistance are generic to all; however, the decision support requirements for conducting the tasks of the journey are different, and need to be fleshed out from the perspective of the life cycle of these tasks for each genre of users.

Safety is the first concern for all users. Safety is determined by the road conditions, the interaction of the vehicle and the road, and the user's ability to negotiate the road and the traffic. The DCS layer should help in providing the users with real-time information about the road and making the delivery, assimilation, and implementation of such information automatic. That is, the digitized infrastructure allows for direct digital connections with the vehicles and the users, through information integration of global positioning systems, driver information support systems (such as On-Star), and user's hand-held wireless devices. When vehicles are equipped with on-board computers, they can interact directly with the road sensors and other DCS layer devices/systems; or even for the vehicles to function as mobile sensors to feed road conditions to the DCS layer. The interaction may go into the rapid response teams and help trucks on the provider side, or into the control and maneuvering of the vehicles themselves on the user side (trip guidance of the vehicles). When the infrastructure design dictates, the DCS layer can also complement highways that embed guiding cables, magnetic strips, or other systems to help control the vehicle and help manage the traffic on demand.

Personal assistance extends the concerns for safety and includes all the services that a user requires. The very nature of the assistance can be described as an e-commerce or e-business portal coupled with a number of one-stop stations for service-telecommunication-computing along the highways. The information-transaction portals connect the users to all kinds of service providers including hospital, lodging, and local attractions that the extended cyber-infrastructure serves. Service-telecommunications-computing stations, on the other hand, are physical facilities and can be compared to an extended service station equipped with computing and telecommunicating supports and gateways to local service providers. The service cocreation enterprise IS will use these personal assistance facilities as a supplement to the usual control measures to enhance their ability to direct the subjects and freight on a real-time and adaptive basis.

The notion of **24/7 decision support for the journey** goes beyond personal assistance and into business assistance, whose nature depends on why the user makes a journey on the highways, or the genre of the user. The life cycle of a journey starts with its planning for the journey, followed by executing the journey, adopting the journey as required, and completing the journey. A common theme is to avoid traffic jams and find optimal routes to the destination. In general, the DCS layer should help bring the journey planning decision support capabilities found in the home and office to the vehicle for the user, by digitally connecting the user to similar capabilities that s/he uses in the home or office. For industrial truckers of freight, the unique tasks are characterized by business communications and monitoring associated with the freight. Similar to the notion of the general public's home and office on the move, the additional value propositions and requirements for intelligent network flows are to enable the notion of a **warehouse and inventory on the move**. The warehouse here is, of course, the vehicle, and the inventory: the cargo on board. The user here needs ubiquitous and pervasive connection to his/her business or company networks not satisfied by GPS and cell phone alone; and require more heightened decision support through the digital layer of the infrastructure. One example is the handling of hazardous materials. A trucker needs accurate, comprehensive, and on demand information on the life cycle of the journey for situation monitoring, exceptions handling, and, most acutely, damage control after a problem occurs. The digital layer has to support these needs.

- **Value Propositions and Requirements for Logistic Processes and Control Activities:** integration of logistic processes and enterprise databases to achieve adaptive control of optimal routing and scheduling, just-in-time supply, and reduction of logistics cost and cycle time.

The notion of "a warehouse and inventory on the move" is discussed above from the truckers' perspective (the subjects). It is raised here to the level of the extended enterprise of global logistics (the enterprises). To understand this enterprise perspective, one could compare the infrastructure to the linkage of distributed production. The factory uses automated guided vehicles or other material handling systems to connect physically the various workshops and workstations within it. The JIT model of manufacturing conceptualizes highways and railroads as the material handling systems among factories and enterprises. This model actually accomplishes an "internalization" of public infrastructure as a part of extended enterprise processes — i.e., enterprises rely on the public infrastructure to deliver JIT for their processes as if it were their private material handling systems connecting the supply chain. Thus, the life cycle of logistics from this extended enterprise view consists of the planning/initiation for the freight between the processes that receive it (demand) and those originating (supply), the supervised and monitored movement of the freight (transportation), the adaptive control of the freight on the journey (change execution), and the incorporation of the cargos on the freight into the receiver's processes. As with the case of manufacturing, processes at both ends require 24/7 informational connection to the status of the freight throughout the life cycle, and respond to any changes accordingly. The previous intelligent transportation systems did not focus on this level of service and have in fact missed out this enterprise perspective.

A service cocreation enterprise IS will achieve the different levels of integration envisioned in the above analysis. Clearly, the common core is the DCS layer of infrastructure which facilitates the enterprises involved to logically internalize the infrastructure as their own *extended, controlled material handling systems*. That is, the DCS layer provides messages, transmits messages, and processes and stores messages to connect the "warehouse and inventory on the move" at all time with the suppliers and the demanders of the cargos and with the enterprise processes slated to use the cargos. The DCS layer is a common asset to all so enterprises could build their own custom processes over it, and thereby achieve global supply chain integration at the weak link that has been previously recognized for JIT: the open highways.

The messages pertaining to logistics control include, in general, all data and knowledge about the freight, the movement of the freight, and the use of the freight, with respect to the supplier's processes the customer's processes, and the transshipping or logistics provider's processes that are related to the freight. The specific requirements imposed on the DCS layer are both physical (technology) and logical (information). The physical side, such as the message generation and acquisition capability of the infrastructure, is further discussed in the next section. The logical side is primarily the design and the repository of data and knowledge on the physical systems. The core challenges are concerned with information integration at a potentially massive scale such as the inter-operation and collaboration of massively distributed and heterogeneous databases on a 24/7 basis. At the high end of enterprise integration, the tasks could include the real-time monitoring and processing of the freight information to feed the enterprise resources planning systems, production and inventory control systems, shop floor level manufacturing execution systems, and warehousing and delivery scheduling throughout the supply chain. The database industry has yet to provide a standard, turnkey technology to achieve this goal, and it may never will since the integration is, by nature, highly dependent on the particular domains and requirements of the user industry (such as data semantics and business rules). Therefore, the solutions may have to be developed on a custom-design, improvising basis by enterprises.

However, for particular applications of intelligent network flows, such as logistics control *per se*, the development of custom solutions should be much less involved. Information models could be determined for interpreting the raw data from wireless sensor networks based on the information feed into the standard databases that drive existing application systems. Then, some inter-operation protocols, including parsers, could complete the cycle of information feed in both ways, using the information models. This information model-centric solution approach is outlined next.

7.2.3 *SEE Information Integration: A Methodology Using a Metadatabase*

The Methodology

1. Identify the information requirements of the intelligent network flow application systems concerned, including the databases in use and their information models.
2. Determine the data transfer regime and choice of technology for the interaction of RFID devices and wireless sensor networks, by using the sensor nodes as the RFID transceivers, and incorporating RFID readers into the purview of central nodes.
3. Identify the possible information feed from the DCS layer of the infrastructure (through possibly the TMC and/or other authorities) into the databases.
4. Develop information models to describe the semantics of the data feeds and the feeds from the databases into the freight driver/controller, for logistics control applications and control measures.

5. Develop protocols, procedures, and/or parsers to translate and transcribe the data feeds into the logistics databases. Tools such as XML may be used to interact with the authority that provides data from the digital layer.
6. Calibrate and store all information models, including those for the RFID (subjects), those for the data feed (infrastructure), and those for the databases (enterprises), into a common schema for semantic synthesis and logical integration.

Data fusion of the SEE model is achieved through, first, the inter-action between RFID and wireless sensor networks, and second, the feeding of DCS layer data into the logistic databases. The common schema achieves integration for common information. The proposed methodology is straightforward except for the common schema. Theoretically speaking, the notion of a common schema is a generalization of the well-known three-schema database model from dealing with a single database to dealing with a large collection of databases. The task has been proven to be daunting. A common schema needs some ontology to provide it with structural stability and a definitive scope of contents. Chapter 4 presented a metadatabase model as the metadata representation method for the modelbase. This model is also a common schema design suitable for the above methodology. Thus, it at least establishes the conceptual feasibility of developing an information integration scheme for the multi-modal data that the SEE model requires.

As reviewed in Chapter 4, the metadatabase uses an ontology that comes directly from a class of generic information modeling concepts that the field uses to design databases. Therefore, the ontology does not presume a comprehensive linguistics on one hand, nor a universal set of meta-knowledge about all applications on the other; both of which are hard to acquire and hard to maintain. The field has been using a number of generic modeling concepts, including entity-relationship-attribute and object-classification; and the metadatabase includes them. To the extent that these concepts are applicable to all participants and that a general methodology exists to reverse-engineer the participants' proprietary data models into these concepts, a set of common TYPES of metadata is readily at hand. This set is open and scalable as long as these conditions hold, and it is as simple as the concepts themselves. Figure 4.1 shows the logical structure of the metadatabase model. We enhance the discussion in Chapter 4 a little to shed further light on its application here for the SEE model as follows.

Steps 4 and 6, in particular, require a common schema. In the case of using a metadatabase, an enterprise application (participant) information model would be represented (reverse-engineered) in terms of the generic concepts, and be saved in the metadatabase as entries to the metatables. Thus, a local model would have a scalar number of entries in the metadatabase, and the average of these numbers for all models is a known constant. When a new participant (e.g., gate nodes of wireless sensor networks and enterprise databases) is added to the community, a new proxy database server will be fine-tuned for the participant to create a new local site. The local site will register itself and create a TSER representation of its export database(s) as new metadata entries to the metadatabase. This process is amenable to using a CASE tool. The metadatabase does not need to shut down at any time during the update, since only ordinary database operations are involved; and hence the whole community will not be disrupted either. Ongoing update to existing local models uses a similar process. In this sense, the common schema is open and scalable, as required by the on demand information exchange for enterprises collaboration.

A minimum metadatabase design is attainable from Figure 4.1, to facilitate efficient computing on sensors and RFID chips. That is, depending on the specific technology used for the sensor nodes, the transceivers, and the transponders, the global equivalent metatable can be used as the core of a minimum metadatabase which can be implemented on any participating enterprise to facilitate data transfer between them. It is also possible to decompose the software and hardware resources metatables and include them in the local metadatabase to support the onboard analytics and light databases on sensors and RFID chips. The actual design has to be based on the implementation technology and be fine-tuned to save computing energy. Chapter 8 provides more discussion on the topic, addressing on demand collaboration of massive independent enterprise databases.

7.3 Multi-Modal Data Fusion: Message Generation, Transmission, and Processing and Storage for the DCS Layer

The above conceptual design provides a guideline for assessing the technology available today for the SEE model. Since the DCS layer is conceptually comparable to a nervous system for the infrastructure, we can analyze its technical needs from the perspective of generating (acquiring) messages, transmitting messages, and processing and storing messages. The analysis looks beyond the existing cyber-infrastructure such as wired or wireless telecommunications, GPS and other satellite-based technology, and Internet services, and focuses on new chip-based technology and systems. The goal is to garner the future promises for seamlessly inter-operation among components of the DCS layer, the enterprise databases, and intelligent network flow application systems. (See our earlier works for more technical details of multi-modal data fusion across RFID, wireless sensor networks, and enterprise databases e.g., Hsu–Levermore–Carothers-Babin, 2007).

- **Message Generation/Acquisition: Wireless Sensor Networks and Beyond**

At the core of data acquisition technology — and hence the message generation technology — is chip-based wireless sensor networks. This class of technology and systems has been proven in numerous science and military applications. Their application to infrastructure, however, is still novel. A wireless sensor network typically consists of a central node with significant computing capacity and a large number of sensor nodes whose computing power tends to be limited by the capacity of its battery. The chip on a sensor node performs data collection, on board storage, and wireless transmission to the central node, which could be further connected to enterprise information systems. The contents of the chip are programmable and can be updated from commands issued at the central node. Sensor nodes are rapidly becoming full-fledged processors as the industry moves to realize the vision of a PC on a chip, and the power supply enhanced by solar technology. It is entirely likely that sensor networks in the near future will have a database and an operating system on board to function as a self-contained autonomous information system capable of activating RFID devices and collaborating directly with enterprise databases.

A large number of wireless sensor networks can be deployed along major highways and their significant limbs. Their purposes (and hence their control logic and configuration) are simply to *monitor the environment*, including road conditions, and to *monitor and interact with the users and user activities*. While the former can be performed by the sensor networks alone, the latter could be enhanced by *collaborating with appropriate RFID devices* as well. The collaboration is the innovation brought about by the SEE model. With the interaction with RFID devices, the digitized infrastructure promises to not only monitor and direct the general traffic, but also interact with the particular freight, vehicle, and cargo. The interaction could then extend from there to enterprise databases supporting intelligent network flows. The specific design of the complete system is a function of the requirements determined, as discussed above.

- **Message Transmission and Inter-Operation: Chip-Based RFID**

At present, infrastructure users already use any of the numerous available mobile technologies to communicate with rest of the world. However, the SEE model incorporates the entire infrastructure into the purview of intelligent network flows. From the perspective of the subjects, automatic and non-intrusive interaction with the infrastructure for their particular need during a particular journey is the object. Therefore, the subjects need to be "digitized" beyond the usual means of radio, GPS, and Internet services, which are non-ubiquitous and/or non-integrative with the infrastructure. The paradigm of active RFID serves this purpose. It calls for the users and user activities to constantly and proactively *report themselves* to the infrastructure.

The current RFID specification is primarily a traditional bar code on a chip embodied in a tiny, inexpensive (a few cents a piece), label-like transponder that transmits the identifier on activation through radio to a remote transceiver. However, chip-based RFID does not have to limit the information contents to bar code only and could store an entire Smart card, for example, on a chip and transmit it over radio frequency. In a broad sense, RFID devices also include technologies that pre-code information on a chip embedded in some end user items (engines, vehicles, packages, containers, parts, etc.). For example, utilities companies apply RFID to their meters to allow remote meter-reading. Similarly, intelligent transportation systems also use RFID, such as the pass to rapid transits and toll roads.

As the chip technology continues to progress rapidly, an RFID is expected to be able to store and transmit an array of data about, for instance, the whole history of a cargo, a truck, and a driver while it continues to miniaturize. Compared to wireless sensor networks, an RFID device does not generate (new) data, only transmits pre-loaded data upon activation by a reader. Technically, the only thing that separates these two classes of technology is really the operating system on board the chip — the sensors need one while the RFID does not. Therefore, inter-operating and even integrating these systems could be accomplished by designing a special reader class of sensor node to accommodate RFID devices. The design would depend on the standards used for RFID. The authorities of infrastructure might actually become promoters of standards if they implement a DCS layer along the infrastructure that accommodates certain RFID standards.

- **Message Processing/Storage: Data Fusion of Messages and Enterprise Databases**

The vision of a warehouse and inventory on the move involves data fusion at the wireless sensor networks and RFID level as well as the enterprise databases level. Section 2.3 discussed a framework that serves these purposes. To be more specific, consider the needs of an international logistics company. The global logistics control certainly involves databases at vastly distributed localities, and it also needs to connect to their vastly distributed and heterogeneous client databases, in order to facilitate coordination of the supply chain for the extended enterprise. The newness of the SEE model is the further connection with the infrastructure: the data acquired by the wireless sensor networks from the environment and by the RFID from the users and user activities. The generic problem of databases collaboration is best handled by the industry, and there have been increasingly powerful solutions developed by vendors. The specific data fusion issues of the sensor networks and RFID, and their inter-operation with enterprise databases could be addressed in the following manner.

The minimum requirement for data fusion is only to exchange messages obtained from sensor networks and RFID, with data originated from enterprise databases. The methodology of Section 2.3 provides an approach for custom design without any common protocols. However, some general protocols would help. A core element of the protocol is expected to be common metadata that all sources subscribe to for the processing of messages and enterprise data. The definition, structuring, and implementation of such metadata would help define a common industry information model, which in turn would represent a major milestone for realizing the vision of the SEE model. From the information integration perspective, a most interesting development would be the integration of the usual database collaboration technology with that of sensor networks and RFID, where an appropriate metadatabase (populated with sufficient metadata about the global environment) would be stored on board a sensor node and a transponder. With this capacity, the DCS layer can inter-operate seamlessly with the users' own enterprise databases and information systems elsewhere, and enable a service cocreation enterprise IS satisfying all three levels of requirements: operation, user, and logistics. Service scaling will be enabled as well.

To conclude, we assume two classes of technology for the moving subjects of the SEE model: regular (current) RFID chips and full PC-capable RFID nodes. In either case, the RFID systems possess their own data capability at the system (e.g., transceiver) level. Subjects connect themselves to the enterprise databases through digitized infrastructure (e.g., wireless sensor networks), and all three — subjects, infrastructure, and enterprise databases — are represented in a common schema which may be distributed. The cocreation enterprise IS provides overall administration to the processing and integration of the network flow information. All components — i.e., the IS elements — use the common societal cyber-infrastructure for data communication and, as available, embedded analytics support. The above assessment is supported by some empirical experiments which verify the feasibility of data transmission and processing envisioned. Details are provided in Hsu and Wallace (2007).

The whole environment may be developed in phases by following a **progressive strategy**. We discuss the strategy below.

Strategy I (Conservative): Assume that the central nodes and gateways of sensor networks and the transceivers of the RFID systems possess PC-class computing capability or more, and can be connected to the networks on which regular enterprise databases reside. This assumption allows for regular subjects (RFID only) shown in Figure 4.1. In this case, the implementation strategy considers each (complete) sensor network and each (complete) RFID system as an enterprise data source, and a common local site architecture will be implemented at the central sites of these networks and systems. In fact, most sensor networks and RFID systems already manage their data resources as databases; it is just that they need a new model such as the information model based on the common schema (see Figure 4.1 and Section 2.3) to treat them as enterprise-level data sources and integrate them with the traditional enterprise databases. Strategy I can be implemented today to facilitate the feeding of real-time enterprise data into enterprise databases from these real-time data sources.

Strategy II (Moderate): Assume that sensor nodes and transceivers are widely distributed, and each could possess light databases, such as the TinyDB technology for sensor nodes and the transceiver nodes at the toll booths of the EZ-PASS technology. The full vision of subjects (RFID + DB) may be supported. The implementation strategy is two-fold. First, we still implement the local site at the central sites and consider each complete network or system as an enterprise data source; but second, we also represent the data models of the sensor nodes and the distributed transceivers into a local metadatabase. That is, these data models, which would most likely be homogeneous within each network or system, along with their on-board instructions that use these local data will be represented as metadata and processed as such. This way, the central nodes can perform queries against the distributed light databases, and to possibly update their data-triggered rules and instructions there.

Strategy III (Aggressive): Assume that the capability of "system-on-chip" exists for sensor nodes, distributed transceivers, and RFID chips. We further assume that their system design will embrace a PC-class database component on the chip, along with its communication capabilities. Finally, we assume that an industrial standard exists to allow the RFID chips to function as mobile sensor nodes, and the sensor nodes transceivers. Therefore, the class of full subjects (RFID+DB) is fully supported. As such, we will have the flexibility to consider each sensor node, each distributed transceiver, and even each RFID chip as an independent enterprise data source and apply the local site architecture to it. A combination of this strategy and the above two will become desirable when the number and heterogeneity of the myriad sensor networks and RFID systems involved increases. This combination helps assure scalability.

These strategies are in essence phases of implementation. Their main difference is one of practicality versus functionality. Strategy I requires only the common RFID and wireless sensor network technology, but it does not support full digital connection for individual subjects with two-way interaction capabilities. Strategy III requires new results, but offers full digital connection at the individual level. Strategy II is at the middle of the above two, and its actual results will depend largely on the particular design of the whole system and the particular technology used. Phased implementation accompanies phased application to gain benefits. We review this aspect next.

7.4 Progressive Applications and Benefits: A Public Domain Perspective

We consider a few possible phased applications of the DCS layer. They illustrate the potential benefits to the public, and hence provide some generic value propositions for developing such a DCS layer as a public asset. Some benefits have been discussed before, but are nonetheless summarized here in the context of a phased application.

- **Benefits to the Operations of the Infrastructure**

The layer of wireless sensor networks *per se* can provide **stored sensor data** to facilitate the infrastructure operation life cycle tasks at the highway authorities. The benefits are primarily the reduction of transaction cost and cycle time for certain data acquisition tasks. When the digital layer connects to transportation information systems, then it could provide **real-time sensor data feeds** to such applications as real-time driver guidance to improve safety. New variable programmable text signs could be added to each ramp, on each bridge, and at all locations of high risks of incidents to feed on these sensor data. Further connection with GPS and geographic information systems promises to proactively assist drivers and manage traffic in all weather, all road conditions all year round. The connections also promise to support on demand maintenance and other infrastructure operations by the authorities.

- **Benefits to Infrastructure Users: Integrated Freight Services and Hazardous Material Monitoring**

When subjects of the SEE model are digitized as well, with RFID and vehicle-embedded wireless computing devices, they can interact with the DCS layer of the infrastructure. Sensor nodes could serve as transceivers to bring about direct, ubiquitous support to the users. Consider, in particular, **customized roadside services**. Current public systems (e.g., 911) do not have data concerning the particular vehicles, drivers, and cargos that they try to assist or handle, while private services (e.g., On-Star) do not connect to real-time conditions on the road and traffic. Moreover, all such systems require the users to call to activate the services, and yet radio communications may not work in all areas under all weather conditions. Therefore, an RFID system that stores the owner/driver information and the cargo/vehicle information for activation by sensor networks which provide real-time conditions will fill in the gaps. In some extreme cases, emergency services may proactively reach out to the driver if the sensor networks detect incidents. Value-added service centers can be developed for users and firms, including logistics providers.

The same technology and systems can monitor *freight* for *hazardous materials monitoring*. From the public safety perspective, RFID may be required of cargos as well as vehicles. In the event of incidents, the response teams can act quickly on the data about the hazardous materials, the vehicles, and the origins and destinations, as well as the precise locations of the incidents.

- **Benefits to Logistics: Adaptive Global Routing, Supply Chain Scheduling, and Fast Public Security Checking**

When the sensor network data and RFID information are fused with enterprise information systems, the infrastructure would become a controller of the network flow model, as discussed in Section 1 for the concept of a "control panel". Previous measures of logistics control rely on GPS and radio communications to adjust routing, which lack reliable information about the choices, such as the conditions of all alternate routes at the time, to really make optimal decision even just locally. The SEE model avails infrastructure information for conducting adaptive logistics control at a global optimization level. Besides, the model also makes it possible to connect logistics to production planning and control (i.e., the "warehouse-inventory on the move" notion) across the supply chain, and thereby reduce the transaction cost and cycle time of the whole extended enterprise. This is the purpose of connecting the infrastructure, the subjects of shipment, and the enterprise information systems.

The digital connections can be further extended to include such public sector databases as transportation management, national security control, and law enforcement to reap additional benefits for both the public and the logistics industry. In particular, the SEE model promises to facilitate *security check* at the roadside and border crossings by providing real-time comprehensive information on the *drivers/passengers, the vehicles, and the cargos*. The federally mandated commercial vehicle information systems and networks (CVISN) program in the USA represents a harbinger.

- **Benefits to Intelligent Transportation**

An interesting class of future possibilities is the connection of the DCS layer with emerging automatic vehicle guidance technology. The vehicle guidance systems can be some embedded guidance cables in the designated lanes of highways using on board sensing and computing systems to interact with the digitized infrastructure to adapt, movements by human drivers or by the on-board control systems. The added capability allows virtual configuration of highway traffic, such as separating the fast lanes designated for freight from regular uses. The designation of the fast lanes could be adaptive and on demand, and constitute a virtual rapid transit on the highway, as illustrated in Figure 7.1.

The SEE Interaction model helps substantiate some general concepts of service scaling. First, it shows how the DCS model and the population orientation may guide the development of new visions for instrumentation of the environment. Second, it expands the scope of the population for scaling, at least in the case of intelligent network flows. Third, it formulates specific value propositions, along with their implementation strategies for a broad class of applications. In addition, it provides some implementation design for the SEE model, which complements the design methodology of Chapter 6 for service cocreation enterprise information systems. That is, the SEE model substantiates additional information resources (e.g., RFID and wireless sensor networks) for the information type of IS elements, and provides a particular application for the cocreation enterprise IS. On the note of IS elements, the SEE model works with the market-based methods in the next chapter, Chapter 8, to offer a complete multimodal data fusion design, scalable to a large population of service cocreation. The combined design serves to facilitate applying the second theorem of the DCS model.

We now turn to the market-based methods for collaboration of massively distributed independent information resources in the next chapter. They help implement the DCS propositions concerning accumulation and sharing of knowledge.

Chapter 8

Collaboration of Independent Massively Distributed Information Resources: A Market Paradigm

Is it feasible to connect independent information resources everywhere? Take the global supply chain as an example: drilling information throughout the chain is an ideal that has long evaded the field. The struggle is about reconciling two fundamentally contradicting needs of collaboration: allowing participants to control their (peer-to-peer, on demand) cooperation; and providing a common regime to assure consistency and integrity of the information. The situation is not too different from international diplomacy. With this metaphor, the field knows how to reconcile conflicts of multiple databases within the purview of an enterprise in a way similar to modern sovereign democracies handling internal frictions. However, just like the state of world affairs, these results are insufficient for collaborating databases across enterprises, to garner value from joining knowledge from anyone for everyone. In this context, the population is the union of pertinent information resources across all concerned enterprises, and DCS is the on-demand sharing of them. The second theorem of DCS pertains to this goal. This chapter summarizes results by the author and his colleagues in their quest. The core of the effort is an *information matching paradigm* that embraces a *market orientation* for connecting and sharing information resources. The full market design employs a price mechanism, but less purist versions allow for collaboration under any command mechanism. A *two-stage design* integrates information matching with local query processing to complete the collaboration.

8.1 Market Orientation for Connecting and Sharing Information Resources

The overarching technical problem is how to collaborate information resources for population-oriented cocreation? The key word here is of course population. It implies that the scope of collaboration is not only inter-organizational, but also may involve vastly different databases in vast number. Therefore, the design task here is concerned with *collaboration of massively distributed independent databases* across potentially heterogeneous enterprises (persons and organizations).

In relation to the previous chapters, the new design methods here follow the design methodology for service cocreation enterprise information systems. It implements some of the requirements there, i.e., connecting information resources, and supports the second theorem of DCS for accumulation and sharing of knowledge. In terms of the knowledge pyramid of Figure 2.1, the effort in the chapter contributes to the service scaling and transformation theory as new results of information and database systems. Therefore, we define the concept of collaboration of massively distributed independent databases from this perspective. In the phrase, the term "massive" refers mainly to their number, although it can also mean size; "independent" is primarily in the sense of proprietary ownership, design, and control; and "database" includes the usual enterprise databases but also extends to personal and light databases (e.g., on board of RFID and sensor nodes). All three concepts are broader than the usual meaning of autonomous, distributed, and heterogeneous databases which tend to apply to enterprise databases within an organization; but they are consistent with the SEE model of Chapter 7, and hence support DCS for service scaling.

Next, we recognize the scope of collaboration of massive independent databases. The DCS model envisions collaboration of customers and providers throughout the population of their service cocreation (e.g., the space of the business applications). It follows immediately that the scope of independent databases involved in the collaboration is the population, and the nature of collaboration is on demand (for cocreation). We submit that, therefore, the best descriptor for such scope and nature is none other than the historical principle of *market*: On-demand collaboration of massive independent databasess is actually a market, commanded by price or whatever other mechanism for value that the information users (customers and knowledge workers) envision. The DCS model can create such a market for the population, and the market can become a ubiquitous mechanism for participants to directly realize the DCS effects and value propositions, as well as indirectly help by supporting the service cocreation. For example, with a price mechanism or fungible credits of some form, owners of information resources may actual generate tangible benefits from the market by providing (selling) or requesting (buying) the information. Without such mechanisms, the market will still be a tool by which collaborators can account for goodwill and performance, as well as allocate resources in the community (e.g., see Clearwater, 1996).

The application context of such a market can be social networking. However, independent databases are usually concerned with organizations rather than individuals. Therefore, we concentrate our discussion below on communities of globally integrated enterprises such as global supply chains. The rest of the chapter synthesizes our previous works on the topic: Hsu–Carothers–Levermore, 2006; Hsu–Levermore–Carothers–Babin, 2007; and Levermore and Hsu, 2006. Technical details (e.g., system architecture, matching language, and collaboration algorithms) are omitted here since they are provided fully in these publications. We establish below the basic concepts in the context of globally integrated enterprises, so we can proceed to develop the market model and its attendant two-stage collaboration method.

Sharing information resources in a DCS manner has precedence to an extent. Previous practices are found in B2B-style supply chains, application service providers (ASP), and industrial exchanges; all of which are analyzed in Chapter 5. These models tend to impose "hard-coded" regimes of interoperation to connect independent enterprise databases because the field does not fully support any other ways (e.g., Litwin *et al.*, 1990; Sheth and Larson, 1990; Kim, 1995; Stonebraker *et al.*, 1996; Braumandl *et al.*, 2001; and Halevy *et al.*, 2004). The hard-coded nature makes the collaboration difficult to change and thereby limit the flexibility for enterprise databases to participate in multiple, dynamic business relations ("federations" of databases) using different data standards and information contents. For example, a company may supply to both Wal-Mart and Cisco, and hence would have to abide by each customer's prime requirements for data interchange. However, these two sets of requirements may not be compatible with each other, and both may be in conflict with the company's own needs of proprietary control.

Consider a supply chain consisting of a sequence of B2B pairs: The sequence defines the federation and the B2B pairs the inter-operation. In this example, the transaction phase of supply chain integration requires, ideally, the independent databases in the extended enterprise (e.g., those of retailing forecasting, retail inventory, suppliers' ordering, suppliers' production, suppliers' delivering, and other life cycle tasks) to work together as if they were pertaining to one organization using one data management regime (e.g., drilling through these databases for information required by global scheduling). The ideal is not reality yet, of course. In practice, the independent databases, which tend to use their own proprietary designs under their own proprietary control, would limit their collaboration to relying on using some fixed protocols (or, "work-around") to enable inter-operation for a particular supply chain (e.g., Wal-Mart or Cisco). Different protocols will have to be developed for different chains. This approach allows for on-demand retrieval of random information from the databases, but the protocols could be intrusive and costly to change. Open technologies such as XML, ebXML, and UDDI can facilitate the problem, but their effectiveness is generally dependent on how standardized these independent databases are in their design and semantics. Often, only basic file transfer (e.g., using, fixed format) is available between databases even when they use the open technology when data semantics are at issue, e.g., the XQuery technology.

The industrial exchange model further develops the dynamics of B2B pairing relations into common and scalable marketplaces for all buyers and sellers to meet and transact, and thereby gain economies of scale. A supply chain is formed by linking all buyer-seller relations, but the linking is virtual in the sense that the pairing is tenuous and on demand, and each pair is essentially a bubble floating potentially among many virtual chains. An exchange, as explained in Chapter 5, can either be public, in the style of the New York Stock Exchange, or private, led by some prime companies of certain supply chains such as automotive in a particular space. The model entails a technical "federation" design linking the global market servers and the massively distributed information systems of the participating enterprises. All B2B transactions are consolidated at the global server to, again, gain benefits of scale: the accumulated and shared (IT and information) resources. To support on-demand pairing, the model promotes new information system design paradigms that employ software agents to process transactions (e.g., Swaminathan, 1998) at the global server, and proxy sites to facilitate the inter-operation of enterprises with the global market sites (e.g., Glushko *et al.*, 1998). However, there is no comparable provision for inter-operation of the databases at the enterprise sites beyond file transfer. For instance, buyers and sellers at an exchange do not have the ability to query each other's databases to establish the requirements of collaboration or coordinate the production and shipping schedules throughout a (virtual) supply chain. The ASP model, on the other hand, turns a software vendor to an online processor for the clients. Therefore, its information system designs require shared data and transactions management under proprietary purview, featuring client-side computing as well as strong sever capabilities (e.g., Tao, 2001). The regime of inter-operation of databases is hard-coded by definition.

Better designs are needed. Enterprises in a supply chain should be able to tap into each other's databases to facilitate their respective transactions, while maintaining independence to operate concurrently in many other supply chains and business collaboration designs. Enterprise databases should be able to simultaneously join many supply chains, and switch easily among them, coupled with the ability of offering/selling as well as requesting/buying random information from all participants. More generally, the collaboration should allow enterprises to dynamically determine when and what data resources to offer, to whom, on what conditions, and thereby further reap the value of their information resources in the databases. This is beneficial to all parties in the supply chain — and indeed for all parties in the general economy concerning the economic efficiency of information. It is a basic premise of the DCS model. The objective here in the chapter is to afford the DCS model a new design of connecting and sharing independent databases for service scaling.

Market-Oriented Approach to Databases Collaboration:

Develop market-style models (e.g., exchanges and auctioning portals) to provide more flexible collaboration of federated independent databases by combining results of matchmaking with global database query.

For service scaling: the results should be implemented as a service cocreation enterprise information system and be embedded into the societal cyber-infrastructure (Chapter 6);

For general theory: the results should improve on autonomy, heterogeneity, openness, and scalability over the traditional federated databases.

Such ability promises to be a milestone in the collaboration of extended enterprises. More specifically, it is also another step for the design methodology of service cocreation enterprise information systems (IS) discussed in Chapter 6. That is, *for cocreation IS design*, the new results contribute directly to the information category of IS elements and help connect databases across the population of service scaling. Through the cocreation IS, users are connected with databases everywhere in the "federation" of collaboration, which could be an exchange, a supply chain, and a social networking user community; where the users and databases can both give and take information on demand. In this sense, the new design is a way to implement the second theorem of DCS, accumulating and sharing information resources throughout the population concerned.

The technical core of the new design is *information matching*, which, in a nutshell, extends the previous scope of distributed databases to independent databases. This concept may be best illustrated by a thought model which we call "an eBay for information resources". In this vision, a large number of information users are matched with a large number of information providers on a concurrent and continuous (24/7) basis as an *information market*. Unlike eBay, however, the "information eBay" has a number of important unique properties, stemming from the unique properties of information. They include the fact that information can be presented in many different ways from the same physical data (the notion of "views" of data); that information can be used, re-used, and shared by many without diminishing its value (i.e., not physically "consumed"); and that any participant could possess information resources that others want at any time (i.e., little separation of buyers from sellers). A participant can post ad hoc requirements to look for suppliers in particular tasks, as a buyer, and simultaneously offer multiple views of its databases for use by prospective suppliers, as a seller. The actual sharing of information will take place as database executions after the match is made. The market becomes the mechanism for reaching the population by DCS.

Parallel supply chains are the norm at an exchange. Therefore, parallel *information supply chains* are also expected to be the norm at the information market. A virtual information supply chain is formed when B2B pairs which comprise the supply chain are identified and connected at the market. Information matching establishes the relationships of a supply chain; i.e., posting requests (for buyers or sellers) — or issuing "global queries", as in database terminology, to find the partners who fit. However, it also executes the queries for the transaction phase of a supply chain. The execution supports sequential information flow by following some ordered list of transactions (e.g., forecasting, tier 1 supplier production, tier 2 supplier inventory, and so on); but its unique property is concurrent processing since all pairs are connected at the market in parallel. A participant can therefore connect to different pairs pertaining to many parallel virtual supply chains. When additional managerial controls are added, such as certification of suppliers for particular prime companies, a virtual supply chain can become as binding as any practice desires. These managerial regimes are beyond the scope of the book.

The purest form of the matching model will allow for any number of providers from any type of information repositories, anywhere in the digitally connected community — the theoretical population. A far more modest model will assume a pre-defined community capable of regulating the participants and imposing certain (open technology) protocols to make the model practical — the practical population. In any case, the practicality consideration should not under-achieve the functionality of global supply chain integration in actuality, nor over-achieve the requirements in the field. Information customers (buyers) are comparable to traditional global database queries, called here as the subscribing query; which will be satisfied either by using single individual information providers or by joining such multiple providers on an as-needed basis. Information providers (sellers/publishers) are, on the other hand, a new type of query called publishing, representing the proactive and dynamic provision of ad hoc data resources which will be satisfied by single or multiple customers. The matching also involves satisfying rule-based negotiation and other matching conditions from each type of query. Three technical properties are essential to information matching: both the information customers and providers search for their counterparts on demand, the matching is automated and can prolong for a period per demand, and the matched queries are executed automatically to complete the transaction according to the demand.

The new information matching model, similar to the previous results of distributed databases, assumes that the global community requires a registration process and some global protocols through which the participating databases join the community. However, unlike the previous results, the model uniquely allows for any number of databases subscribing **and** publishing with any degree of flexibility (contents, rules, and proprietary control), within a community ("federation") of collaboration. The new model is integrated with the previously established metadatabase (e.g., see Hsu *et al.*, 1991; Babin and Hsu, 1996; Cheung and Hsu, 1996; and Bouziane and Hsu, 1997) to execute the actual information retrieval (the database queries) after the match is made. Again, the metadatabase is reviewed in Chapter 4.

To be more precise, the model employs the metadatabase representation method to develop a new query language (for processing both publishing and subscribing queries) and a new repository structure of all queries (for managing queries at a global Blackboard of matching), and unify them with the previous global query processing methods of the metadatabase through the common representation method. The design simplifies the whole life cycle transactions of information exchange, and thereby gives the new model computational efficiency and makes it feasible. Other matching methods in the field do not unify the representation of bids with their processing; and previous global database query results do not support publishing queries and their proactive matching with subscribing queries.

The information matching model is tested and documented in Levermore and Hsu (2006). It supports two theoretical designs for connecting and sharing massively distributed information resources: the information resources market (IRM), and the two-stage collaboration model (TSCM). The term "information" was originally replaced by "enterprise" (and hence ERM, rather than IRM) in Hsu *et al.* (2006). Although "enterprise" in ERM refers to any endeavor ranging from an organization to an extended enterprise — and in the context of databases collaboration, to the enterprise of collaboration, replacing it with "information" still makes the term more straightforward. The IRM model is general in concept — e.g., it considers all classes of information and IT resources (e.g., databases, computing and network resources, and documented human expertise) and proposes an agent-based general system design. It also considers explicitly a market valuation mechanism in its design. In contrast, the TSCM is a particular design reduced from the general IRM model for expressly the collaboration of massively distributed databases, including, however, personal databases and light databases on board of RFID and sensor nodes of wireless sensor networks. It implements the general IRM concept using the information matching model and without requiring a market valuation scheme. These models provide an additional new design science for service scaling, by virtue of enhancing the connection of the information category of IS elements throughout the population of service cocreation.

Define: **Information Resources Market** is a set *IRM(A, M, B, S, P)*, where

A: a structure and algorithm of software agent representing an information-requesting task and/or information provision task at an originating site (user and/or database), and being executable by the Blackboard and by the proxy server at the database;

M: a structure and algorithm of enterprise metadata, e.g., a metadatabase, sufficient for integrating data semantics at the performance level required by the applications and for inter-operating with agents;

B: a structure and algorithm of market administration, called the Blackboard, capable of executing the first stage and the second stage solutions defined below;

S: a structure and algorithm operating at the local site as an added shell to the database, called a proxy server, responsible for inter-operating with the Blackboard with the database and managing the agents and metadata for the database; and

P: a structure and algorithm, called the price and performance model by which the market valuates the resources and information exchange and sharing, and measure the overall performance of the system.

From the IRM definition we derive a particular model for databases collaboration. The databases concerned are primarily enterprise class, but the logic extends to personal databases and light databases as well. That is, the TSCM design supports multi-modal data fusion discussed in the SEE model of Chapter 7.

Two-Stage Collaboration Model (TSCM)

Definition of Collaboration:

Participant: a single or a cluster of data sources that controls its own participation in the community and the information contents with which it participates; responsible for its own data models; and can independently issue information requests and/or information offers. (This definition is stronger than the usual notion of autonomy in the distributed databases literature.)

Community: a collection of participants which joins through a community-sanctioned registration process and subscribes to a community-sanctioned protocol of collaboration.

On Demand: The self-controlled initiation of a request and/or an offer (the publication and subscription for information exchange) by a participant; which can start at any time, last for any duration, and change at any time.

Collaborators: the matched information requests and information offers (or the participants who initiated these matched requests/offers).

Basic logic of the TSCM:

The *objective function*: the maximization of collaboration.
The *decision variables*: information offers and information requests.
The *constraints*: the transaction requirements and data semantics of tasks.
A *feasible solution*: a match of information offers with requests.
The *solution*: The execution of the matched offers and requests for the collaborators.

Stage 1: match requests with offers to find the right information collaborators; i.e., determine the optimal alignment of participants for a global query-processing task.

Stage 2: execute the global query task; i.e., distribute the task to participants and process it at the local sites, and then assemble the query results for the user.

The above definition allows for peer-to-peer collaboration as well as using a global administrator. Nonetheless, a minimum (passive) global site that implements a registration process is required. We now turn to the logical details of these two designs.

8.2 Information Resources Market

The IRM model also features the same basic two-stage collaboration logic as the TSCM design. The only difference is that global query processing of TSCM is generalized to be (information or IT) resources allocation. In other words, the first stage is the same for both models, but the second is broader in the case of IRM. We defer to the next section to elaborate on the design of TSCM; here we focus on the general logic of the agent-based market design for IRM.

Overall Logic and the Agent Model

The general process is the following: Customers and providers of information and IT resources initiate their offers and requests through custom-created *task agents*. They log on (remotely) to the *agent-base* at the market site (the IRM server) and instruct it to create a task agent for their offers or requests; and get the software agents uploaded to their respective local sites after creation. They use the same mechanism to update or delete their agents. The participants can now initiate a task by launching the agent created to the *Blackboard* at the market site. The agent posts its information content at the Blackboard, with possible subsequent modifications. The Blackboard uses this information to conduct matching, negotiation-auction, and assignment.

Now, we elaborate on this general idea. First, the agent:
Define agent (communicator, information content, rule-base).

The *communicator* includes a header (e.g., ID or IP address, XML-SQL or inter-operation protocols) and other metadata and routines required for agent processing. The field offers many good practices which can be tailored to design the communicator for the user community according to the operating policies of the enterprise. The *information content* describes the conditions and semantics of the task according to certain representation methods acceptable to the enterprise. In any design, the conditions specify the price that the provider demands or the customer offers, the deadline, and processing requirements; while the semantics use either the enterprise's common schema or a common dictionary of keywords to communicate to other agents the information nature of the task. The processing requirements include the type of resource offered or requested, job constraints, and task status if the task belongs to an automated work-flow (series of single tasks) or complex task. A complex task will be processed as a sequence of single tasks according to processing or workflow rules.

The *rule-base* contains operating knowledge for conducting automatic negotiation, auction, and other similar behaviors such as choices of pre-determined negotiation schemes. It also contains workflow rules and other logic for the processing of complex tasks. Its representation follows directly the design established in Bouziane and Hsu (1997). All agents follow a unified protocol regulated by the agent-base which consists of a repository of agents and a shell operating on top of the agent repository and another repository of enterprise metadata (e.g., participant data models and semantic constraints) and other knowledge, to create and manage agents for the market.

The **metadatabase** model is a candidate for the repository of enterprise metadata and other knowledge — e.g., enterprise global query policies pertaining to the information market (such as rules about particular user-application families, entities, and relationships). The metadatabase can also be a depot of reusable objects or common software resources (communication software, information content, and rules) from which the agent-base builds task agents. In fact, the metadatabase amounts to a version of the common communal schema for the collaboration enterprise. It, along with the proxy server (see below), constitutes the connector through which a participating system plugs into the overall information market. While the proxy server provides physical connection in an API manner, the metadatabase offers logical integration for the enterprise.

The task agent can use the syntax of the metadatabase to express its three elements. The additional elements of the IC that the previous metadatabase query language (MQL) does not support will become extensions of the MQL. Basically, the syntax will take a declarative form and provide pointers to the software objects contained in the rule-base. The following example illustrates a possible syntax:

EX1: *Get* customer *where* make = 'Ford' and product = 'mustang' and date ≥ 07/01/2008 *using match* "2" *auction* "3" *with price* = "30" *and deadline* = "1 hr".

The user posts an interest to purchase information about Ford Mustang customers. The expression specifies the matching rule to be within 2 per cent of the price and auction being the 3rd regime, as provided in the extended MQL. The query part of the IC, i.e., the Get and Where clauses, can also be expressed in a free text natural language form:

EX2: "Show me who have bought Ford Mustangs in the past month."

The expression can also include designated commands such as "*Provide*" and "*Have*". The properties and limitations of the metadata-based natural language query are available from the literature — e.g., see Boonjing and Hsu (2006). In any case, the templates or canned methods used by matching, auction, and complex tasks can be included as enterprise metadata in the metadatabase and be copied into the rule-base of the agent. This way, agents can become more self-reliant in their processing in a distributed computing regime at local databases.

The **agent-base** is primarily a method to mass-customize a large amount of agents at run time. Since the agents could number in thousands or even millions at any one time, and be custom built, the new model needs an efficient way to create and manage these agents online and on demand. The metadatabase provides community resources required by mass production, while the agent-base customizes the configuration of these resources for particular tasks. It will also support the owners of the agents to add information (e.g., specific data values of some entities, relationships, or attributes, and operating rules) and route them to the metadatabase for possible inclusion into its content. Another aspect is the ability to automatically update the contents of agents when these metadata are changed at the metadatabase. This capability is very important for maintaining the logical consistency across agents, or the integrity of the agent community. The third aspect is a log of the task agents currently active at the Blackboard. This design allows the software agent to be a persistent surrogate (24/7) at the market for conducting asynchronous negotiation, among other things. Thus, agent-base is both a management shell and a gathering of active agents.

The Blackboard: Match, Auction-Negotiation, and Assignment

The Blackboard serves the agents and conducts match, auction-negotiation, and assignment during matching and assignment. It then administers the global query algorithm during the execution of the assignment. This engine maintains a list of all tasks published by agents, including their information contents, and consults with the metadatabase for the latest enterprise policies to avoid chaos at the information market. One of these responsibilities is to break ties and ascertain that all (worthy) tasks find a match before their deadlines.

The basic logic of match goes in this manner. For a given task, it first satisfies the semantic constraints by looking for counterparts possessing the same information content. The match can either be exact or partial, depending on the rules specified in the information content of the software agent. When semantic constraints are met, the matching proceeds to check conditions. If a single perfect match exists, then the Blackboard will assign the task to the resources matched. If multiple perfect matches are found, then a round of auction among them will decide the final assignment. If only partial matches are found, then the task enters negotiation. The negotiation could be automated where the agents at the agent-base use their rules to find an optimal match and break ties by auction; or the agents can inform the task initiators to modify the original conditions — i.e., human-intervened negotiation.

On the other hand, if no match, perfect or partial, is found, then the agent and/or the initiator could update the task information content depending on whether the difficulty is caused by semantics or by conditions. The Blackboard will post current market conditions — e.g., statistics of bids, usage patterns of keywords, and status of hot issues — to facilitate the modification and negotiation. The initiators can also proactively update the task agents stored at the local site and re-launch it to replace the old one. Certain conditions, especially those related to workload at local resources, will be suitable for automatic update from the participant sites. The Blackboard intervenes only on an as-needed, exceptional basis to break ties and enforce enterprise policies. For example, it may check on certain types of requesting tasks that have no match and increase their offering prices on a loan basis to find them a match on or near the deadline.

The assignment phase is essentially a connection (notification) between the seeking tasks and their satisfying resources. It entails an update of the communicator of the resident agent by the agent-base, if necessary, to prepare it to communicate with the proxy server at the destination site. The updated agent will then be uploaded to the task initiating site and initiate a peer-to-peer transaction from there. Now, the task agent is ready to commit to the resources; namely, connect to their system. This commitment triggers the execution of the assign-ment. The Blackboard at the new stage interprets the global job requested by the task agents and reduces (if necessary) and translates it into local bound (sub-) jobs in the local language (SQL) according to the metadata about the local sites maintained in the metadatabase (software resources and data-entity-relationship mappings). These local bound (sub-) jobs are then transmitted to the local proxy servers for distributed execution. Results are sent back and assembled at the Blackboard, which in turn returns them to the requesting sites and updates or removes the task agents for both the demand side and the supply side upon completion of the job.

The two-stage solution logic of IRM has a complexity dominated by the first stage of the assignment whose analytic nature is schedul-ing. It is well-known that the computational complexity of traditional scheduling algorithms is NP-hard; but the complexity of sorting (according to price) is $O(N\log N)$ with N being the number of tasks. Thus, the self-scheduling nature of the IRM assures an efficient regime of computation with complexity in linear to low order of polynomial (including negotiation and feedback), and makes the solution exponentially scalable in theory.

The Proxy Server: Peer-to-Peer Transaction and Systems Inter-operation

The proxy server is a software system that the information market places at the local site. It accomplishes two basic jobs towards connecting the IRM side with the participant side: systems inter-operation and peer-to-peer transaction. The server interacts with the market site and collaborates with the agent-base to store, maintain, and process (launch) the software agents owned by its local site, as well as to respond (execute) to the call of task agents from other sites. In this capacity, it functions as the server of the local site for all task agents initiated at the site but processed elsewhere at the Blackboard or other local sites. Thus, it executes the workflow logic for its complex tasks to, sequentially launch the component single tasks and maintain the overall task status. The server offers a data standard for the task agents to communicate among themselves. The standard is maintained together with the communicator design of the agent. The exact standard will depend on the enterprise requirements; but a good standing design is to use XML-SQL, coupled with the MQL.

That is, the proxy server has a metadata processing shell and a standard protocol to receive and process task agents for information transfer. Part of the protocol is a standard schema for view tables contained in the shell that the proxy server maintains for interfacing with the (operating systems of the) local information resources at the site. It works two ways. First, the local information resources publish the select content that it slates to share with the artificial market as view tables at the proxy server, using the format provided by the latter. The information requesting task agents that the Blackboard sent to the (operating systems of the) local information resources can then query the view tables to retrieve or transfer the selected content in the following manner: The agent transmits the query to the shell, which posts the query against the view tables for the host site to execute.

Second, if the proxy server's own task agents transfer in content from other resource sites, then the input is stored as view tables for the database to acquire under its own management. In either case, the shell enables the mobile agents (the ones being sent by the Blackboard) to interoperate with local information resources without breaching the local sites. The queue discipline at the proxy server is self-scheduling based on prices. However, if the requesting task from outside is to use the computing facility for data processing, as opposed to information retrieval, then the proxy server passes it as a regular job to the local systems and follows the local queue discipline. In a similar way, it monitors the work load, task status, and other relevant data of the host server to update its task agents at the agent-base and elsewhere in the system.

The proxy server also controls peer-to-peer negotiation, including matching and auction, as described below, if the local site has sufficient computing power to invoke this option. In this capacity, the proxy server launches its task agents to visit task agents published on proxy servers at other local sites, as well as prepares them for negotiation with visiting agents from other participants. The proxy server from which the task agent first (time stamp) initiates a peer-to-peer negotiation in the community will function as a *mini-Blackboard* during the life of the negotiation. The basic logic of the Blackboard applies here, except that the initiating task agents call on other sites rather than other agents posting onto the initiating proxy servers. As such, a proxy server may control a number of concurrent auctions involving different tasks at different sites, and the community may have numerous such auctions controlled by different proxy servers at numerous local sites at the same time; all are autonomous to the global Blackboard at the market site. In this mode, a proxy server will maintain a list of visiting task agents and matches its own task agents against them.

Proxy servers allow for peer-to-peer transaction and hence secure the assurance of the computational efficiency promised by the price-based Blackboard. Peer-to-peer transaction is advantageous to the environment for these basic reasons: (1) it allows for the participants' direct control of all tasks originating at their sites as well as tasks being

processed there, and hence simplifies the global control requirements
and work load; (2) it supports distributed updates and processing of
agents based on local conditions; and (3) it provides a backup to the
Blackboard. Furthermore, it also contributes an open and scalable
way to connect any number of local information resources into the
IRM without interrupting the operation of the market. Along with
the metadatabase, which offers an open and scalable way to incorporate any number of information models into the market during the
run time, and the Blackboard, which promises computational scalability, these elements make the proposed IRM design uniquely open
and scalable.

Peer-to-Peer Negotiation: Virtual and Distributed Mini-Blackboards

Peer-to-peer computing has a general complexity of $O(N^2)$ which
hinders scaling up the collaboration. We develop a new basic logical
structure, the *virtual match circle*, to help reduce the complexity.
The basic logic is a hybrid design combining global server computing
and peer-to-peer computing: the global community is self-divided
into a number of match circles each of which employs the global
server model within its circle, but conducts peer-to-peer among circles.
The circle is defined by tasks — i.e., a circle is a group of nodes (local
sites) whose tasks match. Pair-wise computing is unnecessary within a
match circle since it has a node serving as its *mini-Blackboard*. A local
site can have a number of simultaneous tasks alive in the community
and hence can belong to a number of simultaneous match circles.
Therefore, both the circles and the mini-Blackboards are virtual and
task-based. The overall complexity of the peer-to-peer computing is
primarily $C*O(N)$, where C ($\ll$ N when N is large) is the number of
such virtual circles and $O(N)$ is the complexity of distributed computing within a circle.

The agent-base maintains a global protocol for determining time
stamps for all task agents initiating a negotiation, which starts with a
search for matches at other local sites and finishes when an assignment
is finalized after, if necessary, auctioning among multiple matches. It is
worthwhile to note that negotiation is concerned with task constraints,

but auctioning is about the objective function. The initiating task agent, the one with the earliest time stamp among all agents that match, has the control of the negotiation and its proxy server becomes the mini-Blackboard.

It first launches a round of search where the task agent visits and looks for matches at (all) other local sites in the community. If a single perfect match is found within a pre-determined time period, then the proxy server acts according to the nature of the task: for requesting task, it obtains necessary inter-operation parameters or routines from the agent-base for the task agent and sends it to queue at the matching site through the proxy server at that site; and for offering task, it informs the proxy server of the match task to launch the requesting agent. Optionally, the proxy server can also contain a reduced copy of the metadatabase to allow it to augment its task agents with the inter-operation data. If multiple matches exist, then the proxy server conducts an auction among the matches where it singly controls the auction session. The result will either be a single meeting of the best price — in which case the proxy server assigns the task as mentioned above, or a declaration of failure of the auction which results in a deletion of the current task. The participant in the latter case can opt to re-initiate the task or re-create a new task agent.

If no perfect match is found when the time expires, then the initiating task agent starts a round of lock-step negotiation with its host agents everywhere, respectively. Each pair of negotiation is independent of all other pairs under the initiating task agent's autonomous control and uses the same negotiating regime. The regime could be rule-based, staged modules, or any appropriate design, as long as it follows a definitive procedure to define and control the give and take, with each step associated with a certain time window. Thus, all simultaneous negotiations at all local sites proceed in the same step by step manner at all times. Each step modifies certain constraints in a certain manner within each window, and the proxy server terminates the negotiation at the first moment when a perfect match or matches are found. At the conclusion of each step of the modification on constraints, the task agent returns the matches (when achieved) with an indicator of the step during which they are obtained, along with the identification of the local proxy servers of the matched task agents. The initiating proxy server can use the indicator to prioritize the matches, on the assumption that more modifications result in less favorable terms and hence the earlier the matches, the better. This way, if some successful negotiations are reported back late because of their local queuing situations, or for any other reason, they can pre-empt incumbent matches or ongoing auctions when they arrive at the initiating proxy server.

Alternatively, the proxy server can opt to ignore late results. The task agents use time-based progression of negotiation to self-synchronize their autonomous processing. The initiating proxy server, i.e., the mini Blackboard, does not actively control the processing of its task agents at each local site, but only determine the matches from all reported results. When the time expires without any matches found, the task agent ceases to exist and the owner could either revive it or forgo it. The peer-to-peer design allows a proxy server to control the negotiations (matching and auctioning) of its task agents, individually as well as collectively (to manage its own local resources), and thereby promotes distributed computing. There can be many proxy servers controlling many concurrent match circles, each of which represents a virtual mini-market.

8.3 Two-Stage Collaboration Model

The TSCM design reduces the general IRM concept of agent model to the particular method of query database and exMQL, to gain simplicity. Massive concurrent online agents in this design no longer require custom processing, but rather reduce themselves to ordinary, non-hectic concurrent query processing by a DBMS. That is, the task agents of the agent model become the publishing and subscribing queries, with the agent base corresponding to query database. The task agent example included above in Section 8.2 is interpreted as queries according to the exMQL syntax. This simplification is possible because TSCM design assumes databases to be the only kind of information resources shared. In addition, it foregoes the price mechanism and hence removes any negotiation and auction. Accordingly, the agent processing logic is implemented as, of course, exMQL. The rest of the IRM elements such as the Blackboard and the proxy server are respectively implemented in the TSCM design using the query database and exMQL. The processing algorithms required follow directly. We discuss the rationale of this particular design below.

Overall Logic and New Results

Collaboration of massive independent databases has three technical aspects: determining the (task-oriented) collaborators; globally querying the heterogeneous independent data sources; and executing the information exchange tasks on thin platforms (RFID chips and sensor nodes) as well as traditional databases. The first aspect of the problem is characteristic of collaboration. In traditional global query, there is always just one fixed set of participants $(C(n,n))$; while there are many possible sets in collaboration (all combinations of n, n ≥ 2), and each set can contribute different performance (perceived value and technical efficiency) to the overall community. This difference shows the need for a new regime to provide control to the participants, as well as to match them and execute the global query in an information market. A derived requirement of control is to support the participating databases to publish with differential "personalities", in order to fit different collaborations. This aspect characterizes the first stage of TSCM. The information matching model is developed to facilitate the determining-assigning problem and thereby delivers the first stage.

Next, the global query aspect of the problem, which characterizes the second stage of TSCM, entails an open and scalable metadata technology to deal with heterogeneity when participants use different data models. The metadatabase model is proposed for use in this regard. As stated before, openness and scalability are difficult to achieve. Previous results tend to rely on industrial standards and application ontology to facilitate the problems facing the usual methods of common schema and federated registry to reconcile information semantics. Unfortunately, standards tend to be proprietary and numerous, and domain-specific application ontology is hard to develop and evolve. The information matching model, being based on the meta-database model, extends the previous metadatabase-supported global query results to address the extended needs of global query due to the nature of collaboration as analyzed above.

The third aspect, executing on thin platforms, is generic to both stages and is interwoven with the progress of chip technology and energy supply. However, efficient computing results exist (e.g., Carothers *et al.*, 2002) to allow for generic designs with a range of possible function-ality, without predicating on any particular technology. Therefore, thin platforms can be incorporated into the new design to explicitly connect sensors and RFID with traditional databases for collabora-tion. In fact, the view of (light) databases collaboration makes sense for RFID and wireless sensor networks for their own sake. Since computation is, in general, inexpensive relative to communication for this class of technology, it is advantageous to embed some data-base capability into on-board computing for sensor nodes to make them self-sufficient in control. The same can be argued for chip-based RFID; that is, RFID chips could function as mobile data processing and transmitting nodes. The results will be their becom-ing light databases in their own right, amenable to the paradigm of collaboration.

The specific new results of the information matching model includes exMQL (extended metadata query language), query data-base (the repository of publishing and subscribing queries), and exMGQS (extended metadatabase global query system). These par-ticular methods are amenable to coupling with industrial standards such as ebXML and XQuery. The common denominator metadata-base leads to simplified computation because it provides the same exMQL to unify matching and processing of participant offers and requests (queries), while previous results separate them as two unre-lated regimes. In addition, the metadatabase model also provides the basic representation method for the query database used in both stages. As a result, it integrates the query language, query processing, and matching into a simplified regime.

More specifically, information requests and information offers are both formulated in exMQL as database queries and saved in the query database whose schema reflects the basic semantics of the exMQL; as both are based on the metadatabase model. Matching is but a regular database query processing against the query database. After the optimal participants are determined from the matching, the exMGQS also executes the requests represented in the exMQL expressions at the local sites of the matched offers — i.e., global query processing. The query database schema and the exMQL syntax both include rules as well as data, to not only support the data resources in an information offer/request but also observe their constraints. The inclusion of rules is an extension to the previous matching methods and previous query languages. Finally, the design reduces the usually custom-developed matching Blackboard to a standard database management system (DBMS) augmented with certain SQL-based procedures. From the perspective of service scaling, the exMGQS can be an engine for a service cocreation enterprise IS that employs collaboration of massive independent databases.

Architecture: The Global Site and the Participant Site

Basic architecture of the TSCM system includes a global (or market) site networked with participant sites at local independent databases. The global site provides full functionality for global data semantics reconciliation, while the participant sites feature a reduced set functionality to work with the former as well as inter-operating with the participating databases which remain independent, albeit connected, of these sites. Each participant site may become a mini-global site with lesser design if it is to function in a peer-to-peer mode. The choice is a part of the implementation design of TSCM for particular collaboration enterprises.

The global site has three major parts: the Blackboard, the query database, and the metadatabase. The Blackboard performs the matching and global query functions while the metadatabase is essentially the (open and scalable) schema of the collaborating community. The Blackboard is essentially a shell of a collection of processing methods augmented to a usual database management system (DBMS), upon which the exMQL is processed. The shell includes elements for processing the query database, in connection to a message processor, a result integrator, and a network monitor, which inter-operate with the local sites for the execution of the global query. The query database, as described above, also includes a rule-base as the repository of the rules included in the exMQL expressions, which is structured as a database, too. The schema of the rule-base is a subset of that of the query database. The metadatabase supports the query database and the Blackboard with its ability to provide global query processing.

More significant is the role of the metadatabase as the community registry for the information market. A formal registration process with varying degrees of central coordination is required of all participants. In the maximum registration, the metadatabase integrates all *published* local data models; while in a minimum regime, the metadatabase contains only global equivalence information through its "equivalent" sub-model (see Chapter 4). These published local models are designated as the "export databases" and views for participants, respectively; and are reverse-represented as metadata tuples to enter into the metatables of the metadatabase. Metadata entries (data models) are added, deleted, updated, and retrieved as ordinary database operations against the metadatabase without interrupting the continuous operation of the market. Since the metadatabase contains only data models with fixed metatables, its size (number of rows) is a linear function of the number of local sites.

The local sites are responsible for maintaining one or more export database(s) as the proxy database(s) for their actual databases to be used in collaborations on the market. These export databases can just be some database views in the minimum regime. In any case, the participants can opt to register a large, stable data model for the export database within which they publish their smaller ad hoc offerings as often as they wish; or, they could frequently register different, small local data models that represent their published views (export databases) and change them on the fly. The most demanding part of the registration is the establishment of a list of global data items across local sites, and the maintenance of the data equivalence among them. We stress, however, that this is an ongoing research goal in the field, not a problem that the TSCM design uniquely faces.

On this note, we wish to point out that the TSCM design actually facilitates these pervasive problems. The metadatabase method affords a minimum common schema to minimize the demand of registration — a list that is automatically derived from all registrations, which can reveal any peer-to-peer correspondence of local data items. More significantly, *registering a proxy-export database tends to be much easier and more practical to participants than registering an enterprise database*. That is, a company can subject an external-use-oriented proxy (see below) to certain community protocols, which it could not do with a mission-critical production system.

The local sites are connected to the global site and to each other through a proxy database server. A local site is constructed and maintained according to a global design, but is otherwise administered by the participant. The proxy database server in the maximum version replicates the global blackboard, so that it can administer any *peer-to-peer information exchange* when the global site is not involved. In this case, the proxy server has the ability to initiate a virtual circle of matching among peers and serve as the "global" site of the circle during the life of the match — as discussed above for the ERM model. In this way, the global Blackboard coexists with many concurrent, distributed local Blackboards and their virtual sub-communities of collaboration. The peer-to-peer version of the design promises to reduce the computing bottlenecks in the community, enhance overall system reliability (against system or network failures), and support maximum flexibility of the collaboration regime. The proxy server as such serves as the surrogate of the global site, as the agent of the participant, and as the firewall between the global and local sites.

Lesser versions are also possible, which can be reduced from the maximum design. For example, the proxy server may reduce its requirement on a full metadatabase when peer-to-peer metadata interfacing or interchanging is included; and hence becomes a reduced version. Similar to the minimum regime of registration, a minimum set of metadata at proxy servers includes only the list of global data equivalents. A partial metadatabase ranges between the minimum and the maximum contents. The cost for maintaining the distributed copies of global equivalents represents an upper bound to the real-time performance of peer-to-peer collaboration.

Participants formulate their information requests and information offers through the proxy server, which provides user-friendly interface to the query language exMQL. The export (proxy) database is the image of the local enterprise databases that the participant publishes to the collaborating community. The proxy DBMS manages the image as a real database for global query processing. The extent to which the backend enterprise databases are taking part, directly, in the global query can be controlled through the controls of the proxy DBMS.

We wish to note that the TSCM design promises to simplify the complexity of dealing with intricate enterprise systems through the employment of export databases, since multiple enterprise databases can have their views consolidated at the export database. Conversely, a participant can maintain multiple export databases for the same production systems, to subscribe to multiple standards and protocols imposed by, for instance, multiple supply chains. Both make the collaboration model more practical than traditional global database query models. The local site also includes a message processor and a network monitor which are the elements pertaining directly to global query processing and inter-operating with their counter-parts at the global site. These elements at the local sites and their counterparts at the global site constitute a distributed processing environment called ROPE in the metadatabase literature (e.g., Babin and Hsu, 1996). The Rope shell is responsible for deploying the metadatabase for databases inter-operation.

Additional Processing Methods: exMQL, exMGQS, and Efficient Computing

The information matching model extends previous MQL (Cheung and Hsu, 1996) to include rules in a uniform query format for both information publication and subscription — implementing the first stage of TSCM. Each query operation is performed via the extended metadatabase global query system (exMGQS), which is the combination of the global Blackboard and the proxy database servers at local sites — implementing the second stage of TSCM. The exMQL automatically retrieves metadata from the metadatabase (e.g., local data models and their semantic equivalence) to facilitate query formulation, and hence provides certain interesting design features. It supports joints of data from different participants that have different definitions (i.e., differing names, formats, units, and/or value coding), and hence relieves the users of the burden to know such technical details as the physical locations, local names, and implicit joint conditions. Users can use familiar names in queries to qualify data elements in different databases, since the metadatabase utilizes an internal identifier for data item resolution, while associates these with "friendly" user-defined names.

The above-mentioned Rope shell is the distributed core of the extended metadatabase global query system (exMGQS) that interoperates with elements of the Blackboard and the proxy database server for global query processing. The processing is assisted not only by the metadatabase, but also by the new query database. At the second stage of the TSCM, exMGQS converts the matched queries into local-bound sub-queries for the set of participants determined at the first stage, by using the global Blackboard and the metadatabase. The sub-queries are then transmitted to participants and processed by the Rope shells at their proxy database servers, with the results sent back for assembling at the global Blackboard. For peer-to-peer collaboration, the local Blackboard at the proxy database server will play the role of the global Blackboard. The maximum version requires a protocol to maintain the distributed copies of the full metadatabase for the community. It is also possible to devise different processing regimes for different classes of participants, such as RFID versus wireless sensor networks versus enterprise databases versus personal data sources. Furthermore, exMGQS can also use proven methods to optimize the processing for all sites that have homogeneous data semantics, e.g., decoupling queries for each binding supply chain.

Now we consider specifically the collaboration involving RFID and wireless sensor networks, i.e., the need for efficient computing. The full local site design is appropriate for the central nodes of sensor networks and the master nodes of transceivers of the RFID systems. However, we need new designs to accommodate the particular requirements of sensor nodes and RFID chips, if they are to be treated as autonomous enterprise data resources as well. This possibility deserves further explanation.

Service scaling may indeed benefit from including sensor nodes and RFID chips into the population of DCS, for reasons such as those exposed by the SEE model of Chapter 7. In the vision, they can be participants of information integration under the TSCM regime for the service enterprise of intelligent network flows, and be a part of the cocreation enterprise IS. Therefore, they need to be searchable by global queries initiated at other sites; and they need to be the subjects issuing global queries to obtain necessary data from other sites. The second capacity allows sensor networks and RFID chips to update their control regimes and analytics based on conditions published elsewhere, using, e.g., data-triggered control and decision rules. These rules can initiate global queries (publish or subscribe) based on data sensed or received and the time elapsed. The Blackboard, therefore, needs to process at least simple rules and possess minimum Rope functionalities. Not all sensor nodes and RFID chips in the literature possess such computing capacity; but some do. The TSCM requirements will guide the design of efficient computing to implement the vision.

In conclusion, the IRM model proposes an agent-based logic for a general market design to implement DCS on information resources. Its implementation requires major new effort. Thus, we include it here as a thought model for future research. The TSCM design, on the other hand, is more focused and ready to implement. The two-stage collaboration model extends the previous global database query model in two major ways: It allows the participants to offer or request data resources on demand and at will; and it supports not only enterprise database participants, but also wireless sensor networks and RFID systems. The TSCM architecture can be implemented in open source technology and/or standard commercial technology. The feasibility of registration and other related issues could be facilitated by the export database concept and by the minimum metadatabase possibilities, as discussed above. With this new capability, it now becomes possible for an (extended) enterprise to use sensor networks and RFID systems as real-time data sources to feed real-time data to its enterprise databases. These possibilities may enhance the results of Chapters 6 and 7 and contribute to the digitization of persons and non-digital resources, for expanding the population of DCS and facilitating service scaling. For example, they may assist the integration of customer and product information across supply chains and demand chains, as industry promoted by (e.g., FedEX, GE, IBM, and Wal-Mart); and they may simplify transactions at health care systems. For the future, they may help make home-based agriculture and home-based energy that much closer to becoming reality.

The next chapter consolidates results in this chapter with those of the previous chapters, and brings them back to a bird's eye view of the service scaling theory of the book: the perspective of microeconomics. It is also the conclusion of the development of the theory.

Chapter 9

Service-Led Revolution: Empowerment of the Person and Collaboration of the Society

Is a service-led revolution reality or gimmick? We cannot yet answer this question definitively. The world is full of challenges. No one knows what the future holds for humankind. The tea leaves may read as one wishes to read them: clashes of civilizations and worldwide volatility versus global renaissance of rationality and spirituality. Our cherished progress in science and technology also shows its downside: seemingly unsustainable consumption of un-renewable resources. However, we can at least look on the bright side of human history and draw strengths from what humankind has done right — and extrapolate to a more pleasant world. Maybe a digitally connected world does not have to be grim and self-destructive to benign human relationship and trust. Instead, its thermodynamic entropy is meant for removing the barriers to human bonding for the common good. In this sense, maybe we all can help towards answering definitively the above question. The answer naturally also responds to the opening question of the book in Chapter 1. This chapter completes the theory of service scaling and transformation. The core is a conceptual formulation of a new class of microeconomic production functions using DCS, which defines how collaboration and cocreation may be a new basic mode of production for knowledge economy. It helps substantiate the notion of a service-led revolution. At the conclusion of the book, we present a thought model for a person-centered economic view, which then extends to organization-centered and society-centered views. The thought model reflects on the grand research questions that we discussed in Chapter 2.

9.1 New Mode of Production: A Cocreation View of the Knowledge Economy

The book begins with a basic observation that the call for a new service science may reflect some larger possibilities; namely, service may actually be engineering a fundamental transformation, and the knowledge economy may require new, discrete results to explain it and advance it. We contemplated on a notion of service-led revolution and developed a theory of service scaling in the previous chapters in this context. For example, Chapter 1 presented several visions of a transformation led by service for the knowledge economy. They all exhibit a common theme of collaboration and cocreation throughout the population by DCS. Can this theme be the economic nature of the service-led revolution? If so, how does it differ from the past and why it is good? We recognize the microeconomic notion of the basic mode of production to be an anchor for answering these questions. That is, we attempt here to analyze the basic modes of production: prior to the industrial revolution, due to the industrial revolution, and now promised by digitally connected service. Each mode may be characterized by families of particular microeconomic production functions for the economy as a whole as well as for particular industries. In this time-honored tradition, we postulate a general model to describe some possible production functions for the knowledge economy from the perspective of the theory of service scaling and transformation of the book. Our premise is: ***appropriately connecting individual cocreations of value can reap the benefits of both the industrial revolution mode of production and the historical mode prior to it.*** (Earlier and simpler discussion by the author is found in Hsu, 2007; and Hsu and Spohrer, 2008).

What does the concept of digital connections scaling mean in terms of utility theory and production functions of microeconomics (e.g., see Becker, 1971; Friedman, 1976; and Solow, 2000)? Clearly, it has to do with, first, the utility of the product (value) to customers; second, with the utility of making the product (value) to makers/providers; and third, with the role of DCS in the making of the product. We recognize these three basic elements: customer, provider, and production, in the following simple thought model of *microeconomic mode of production*:

$E = O/I$, where E indicates economic efficiency, or the society perspective; O the output, or the customer perspective; and I the input, or the provider perspective. The particular way of yielding the *ratio of output to input (O/I)* represents the production, and its nature as characterized by production functions substantiates the general mode of production to which it subscribes.

Before the industrial revolution, utility to persons was the driving force behind all economical activities that focused on persons; and service and product were unified by utility. That is, cocreation was the norm: a product was custom made according to the utility that it was supposed to deliver to the customer; and the maker provides production as a service. The service of making a product also possessed many other characteristics that we now attribute to service, such as one of a kind and even perishable. We refer to this mode of production as the *Output Pulling Paradigm (O)*. In this O-paradigm, the economical connections in the production were characterized by largely isolated pair-wise relationships, or direct pairing between the provider and the customer. The science was the cocreation on such pairs.

Scientifically speaking, each cocreation has an individual ratio of output to input (O/I), and the performance of the economy under the historical O-paradigm is basically the average of all such individual ratios. It was difficult to scale either input or output in a cocreation, and was near impossibility to connect pairs and scale both in a manner that changes the production function. That is, the pooling of pairs did not change the performance — i.e., did not yield economies of scale. A telling example is cutting hair. Having a thousand barbers concurrently cutting hair for a thousand customers at the same place, rather than at a thousand different places, did not change the economic performance, nor improve the way haircutting was done, a bit. The same was true for block smiths forging swords, and master masons building cathedral steeples. Companies like IBM could not have existed in this paradigm.

Then, modern machinery made the pooling of input possible, and hence came the industrial revolution. The blacksmiths of the O-paradigm could then use large scale foundry and other related equipment to change their production functions and scale up the forging of swords at one place. The pooled production became so significant that the provider side dominated the customer-provider relationship and cocreation ceded. What resulted was a new mode of production that focused on products, and thereby alienated utility (e.g., the 4-inch holes) from the means of providing utility (e.g., the 4-inch drills) — we refer to this mode as the *Input Pushing Paradigm (I)*. Service, which continued to focus on cocreation for utility, was separated from product in this I-paradigm. Production was largely no longer a service. Instead, providing the products' utilities to customers (the owners of the products) became a new major genre of service, such as the economic activities that provide or support the use, operation, and maintenance of aircraft, vessels, and vehicles in the form of transportation, insurance, and gasoline stations.

The I-paradigm featured connection of production factors into a hierarchy of economic entities, which led to the entity firm becoming the core of economic institutions to minimize societal transaction costs. In this paradigm, the science is the science of scaling the input and the product, and thereby the production functions of the ratio (O/I). The end users of products are connected neither with the production, nor with other users. The scaling is also limited in terms of connecting providers. Service by and large remained with the O-paradigm even in the post-industrial revolution economies. So we see barbers working their ancient trade largely in the same ancient way (except for the tools). The master masons offer another story: craft production continues to exist in corners of the economy where scaling the input does not apply. Companies like IBM would have perfected themselves as a manufacturer.

Digital connections opened a completely new world of scaling in which the customer side can be pooled, too. Furthermore, production factors, including knowledge workers, can be connected with customers, and hence the entirety of both sides are amenable to connection. The value cocreation pairs can now be scaled up in any configuration of O, I, and O-I aggregation to change the O/I ratio favorably. In other words, the production functions can now incorporate such digital connections and transform, as they did for machinery in the I-paradigm. With this (possible) basic change in production functions, we are afforded a new mode of production fusing both the O-paradigm and I-paradigm and reaping their benefits: the ***Output-Input Fusion Paradigm (O-I)***. This O-I paradigm is characterized by digital connections scaling and the science is digitization, connection, and scaling for values.

The O-I paradigm scales individual customer-provider pairs of the O-paradigm by connecting customers (output) for the same input, production factors and providers (input) for the same customer, and/or any input and output for any value propositions. Therefore, the basic mode of production in this paradigm is comprehensive cocreation and collaboration, and the production functions feature DCS. Utility could dominate, again, and hence reunite service with product. This is not just renaissance of service, but renaissance of the entire ratio (O/I) for the making of products and services. The barbers (or hairdressers) and master masons may continue their ancient trades in the ancient service (cocreation) way, but they now can enjoy the benefits of population knowledge and reduced learning curves due to DCS, e.g., marketing, professional improvement, and trade promotion. Companies like IBM can excel as population-oriented cocreation providers while practicing this mode of production themselves. Could the O-I paradigm be the defining nature of a service-led revolution?

An industry's ratio (O/I) can be determined by its microeconomic production functions, transformation functions, and taxonomy of economic activities — e.g., see an example of such functions in Betancourt and Gautschi (1998). The field offers numerous such results for the previous O-paradigm and I-paradigm (e.g., Solow, 1999). The O-I paradigm has to be proven on a similar basis, with particular production functions and the empirical substantiation of them; otherwise, it is merely a thought model. We cannot prove the thought at this point, but we can try to propose what the proof may look like. A general model is presented below showing a new class of production functions that feature DCS and characterize the co-creation (collaboration) between the demand chain (customer perspective) and the supply chain (provider perspective). The general model is an embodiment of the service scaling theory to describe the O-I paradigm of production.

The Model of Production by Extended Firms for Collaboration Across Demand Chain and Supply Chain, Using DCS

Objective: maximization of utility and/or minimization of cost (E) across the demand chain and/or supply chain.

Decision Maker: customers and providers of the service cocreation — with the output being either service or product (collaboration through digital connections).

Production Functions: f, g, h, and f^n, where:

$E = f (I, F, S, Z)$ the *total utility or cost function* of production where I: the institution; F: the non-digital, non-person production factors;

$S = g (D, K, P)$, the *scaling function* where D: the digital connections/societal cyber-infrastructure, including the instrumentation of the environment; K: the digital, knowledge production factors; and P: the person customers and knowledge workers;

$Z = h (A, R, M)$ the *exogenous constraining function* where A: the consumption activities; R: the restrictions on the selection of A; and M: the market price for A. (The Z function is modeled after Betancourt and Gautschi, 1998). We further define that the nature of constraints R defines goods versus services.

$$E^n = f^n (I, F, S \mid Z) \qquad \text{if } n = p \text{ (provider) or}$$
$$E^n = f^n (I, S, Z \mid F) \qquad \text{if } n = u \text{ (customer)}.$$

(E^n is *recursively expandable* along the demand chain and the supply chain.)

Two conspicuous elements distinguish the model from previous results in the field: the DCS function S, and the collaboration functions for demand chain and supply chain E^n. A particular production function for a particular industry and/or service enterprise will specify the E function in terms of the definitive mapping forms of f, g, h, and f^n. The forms may be specified at different levels of detail, representing different levels of requirement on the configurations of service systems involved. The configuration will also determine how each of the sub-functions and factors (arguments in the functions) contributes to the object and how they interact amongst them. When sufficient specificity exists, these contributions and interrelationships can be revealed by taking appropriate partial derivatives of these functions, as it has been done customarily in the field. This basic logic is straightforward thus far. However, the complexity of the E function is in its recursive version which defines collaboration among firms — or, the production of the extended firms by *collaboration*. Analyzing the recursive expansion of the E function is mathematically tricky, and requires more assumptions and qualifications.

If the E^n functions are ignored, then the analysis is commonplace. The effects of DCS, for example, can be isolated and recognized from how the S function appears in the mathematical form of the E mapping. In a linear form where S is associated with a coefficient, the DCS model will contribute proportionally to the outcome in a formula weighted by the coefficient (as relative to other terms in E). Therefore, the way to improve the outcome is to scale up, down, or transform the scaling function S. The DCS model, by virtue of its propositions and design methodologies, may help here. If E is non-linear and involves the product of S and other arguments, such as S impacting on I, P, and/or Z, then the contribution can be more pronounced as well as complicated, depending on the specific functional form.

The DCS function, S, embodies the employment and deployment of the DCS model. It may reflect how service scaling and transformation are designed with the incorporation of social networking, how information resources and persons (customers and knowledge workers) are accumulated, connected, and shared in the population of the value cocreation, and how service cocreation enterprise IS is embedded into the societal cyber-infrastructure, to name just a few. As analyzed in Chapter 6, the DCS function may ultimately be evaluated on the basis of transaction cost and cycle time, in addition to the more tangible values. Also as explained before, these intangible values need to explore life cycle tasks that incur transactions in the first place. The DCS propositions help such comprehensive investigation.

With the possibility of establishing the DCS function comes the possibility of establishing the E function — and then comes the possibility of proving the service scaling theory of the book to be correct. Therefore, *the theory of service scaling and transformation of the book is not a faith, but a scientific proposition of design that can be scientifically proven to be right or wrong.* Substantiating the above model is hence a substantiation of the new service science postulated in the book. Such new results may lead to formal analysis of the productivity of digitally connected service. On this basis, we can formally evaluate the design of service systems and the improvement of service quality and value.

We postulated an S-shape growth pattern for the DCS model in Chapter 3 (Figure 3.1) — i.e., the DCS propositions will undergo, generally speaking, three stages of transformation: initiation, general application, and maturing, throughout their acceptance and diffusion of their effects. These stages may be defined in terms of the DCS function and analyzed as such. For example, taking partial derivatives on the particular mathematical forms of the DCS function will determine the growth rate with respect to particular conditions and assumptions. Simulation may also help in formulating the mathematical forms of the S function, as discussed in Chapter 3.

Finally, the recursive application of the E^n function will ultimately lead to persons: the customers and knowledge workers. At this level, the production function will become homogenous in functional arguments with the service cocreation enterprise information systems of Chapter 6, and hence can be substantiated via the latter. Moreover, it will also describe the regimes of **home-based production** (agriculture, energy, service, and manufacturing) that we discussed in Chapter 1. Again, at the level of persons, supported by individual resources, all economic activities, including both service and non-service, can be unified and described by a uniform family of production functions. The view of persons being the center of gravity can then spin off the accompanying organization-centered and society-centered views to complete the synergism of the world of humankind — also demonstrated through the recursion of the E^n function. This is **transformation through service scaling**.

We elaborate below on the last point: three views of the gravitational field of values. If an O-I paradigm is possible for the world, then how will it look like for persons? How does this person-centered view work with organizations and society? How will all three views constitute synergism as Chapter 2 maintains?

9.2 Person-Centered View of Service Scaling

The three worldviews of service — i.e., value to persons, value to organizations, and value to the society, lead to three design perspectives: person-centered, organization-centered, and society-centered. Just like the three worldviews are synergistic, these three design perspectives are also mutually supportive. Their analyses share common logic. We focus the analysis on the person-centered view, and calibrate the other analyses to it.

The person-centered view was first discussed in Hsu and Pant (2000) from the perspective of e-commerce. That is, it postulated that some new business design may thrive by providing the Web in the way required by the person — i.e., a "concierge" portal to personalize the access to resources and services available on the Web. This e-commerce view actually reflects a much deeper conviction that the Web should be personalized as if it were designed and created for each of us expressly; and it is this conviction that we inherit (see Chapter 1) and expand here.

We do away with the notion of a dedicated portal providing the personalization. Instead, we generalize the concept of "embedding cocreation enterprise information systems into the societal cyber-infrastructure" — see Chapter 6, and calls for embedding the provision, or the concierge, into the societal cyber-infrastructure to achieve personalization. We envision the future Web to possess, and provide personalized ubiquitous assistance to allow the user employing and deploying Web resources and activities as she/he wishes in the way she/he wishes. We further envision it to connect all persons, organizations, and even the environment for collaboration of society. This is the *person-centered view of the Web*. Through further generalization, by service scaling and transformation, we also consider it the *person-centered view of the knowledge economy*.

The notion of person here refers to both person customers and knowledge workers, as they appear in the DCS function in the above production model, as they are just different roles of the same persons. This commonality also connects the person-centered view and organization-centered view and puts them not (necessarily) in conflict but (hopefully) in harmony, as discussed in Chapter 2. To the extent that DCS uplifts microeconomic production functions through the O-I paradigm of production, the person-centered view is also a productivity tool. Enterprises use it to achieve economies of scale for services, as well as for personalization of physical products. That is, persons are placed at the center of the economy to perform cocreation with various enterprises in collaboration with various other persons, by virtue of the societal cyber-infrastructure.

Figure 9.1 exhibits such a person-centered view. The so-called personal wizard symbolizes the personalized societal cyber-infrastructure. All business activities are interpreted in terms of their roles in the societal production functions viz., digitization provider, connection provider, utilities provider, applications provider, cocreation provider (products and services), and the like. Different levels of enterprise can also be interpreted from the aggregation of persons, organizations, and resources. For example, meta-enterprises may be defined to represent virtual, extended firms and enterprises that provide collaboration: enable DCS for populations and/or the personal wizard

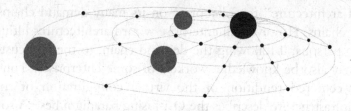

Personal Wizard Architecture

Figure 9.1: A person-centered view of the knowledge economy.

architecture, using societal cyber-infrastructure. The notion of personal wizard is consistent with the Web-based business design that we call transaction portals, as discussed in Chapter 5. The difference is, of course, the scope and general nature that we envision here for the former.

The central node of the personal wizard architecture is the person in command, and all other nodes are enterprises providing services in the O-I fusion sense. We may interpret enterprises on the innermost concentric orbits to be providers of digitization, digital connections, Internet utilities, resources, and personalized societal cyber-infrastructure. Those on the outer orbits may be providers of products, traditional services, and applications. In between we may expect various types of meta-enterprises enabling collaboration, new business designs, and the personal wizard architecture for configuring the other enterprises — such as on-demand business/service. Person-based enterprising may become one of the massive genres of (personal) meta-enterprises. That is, individual professionals, or knowledge workers, may not only work from home, they may proactively franchise themselves as independent consultants to form virtual, extended firms with the support of personal pensions, insurance, infrastructure and other institutions. We have already seen many such practices today.

The person-centered view also describes organizations with largely the same logic. For example, an enterprise may conceive itself at the central node and command through its own virtual "enterprise wizard architecture" to collaborate on its many demand chains and supply chains. However, all enterprise wizard architectures ultimately lead to persons, if following the demand chain, to the end customer who may also be knowledge workers of some enterprises. Thus, the person-centered rendition of the virtual configuration of societal cyber-infrastructure describes the O-I fusing paradigm best. A society-centered view will encompass all these views and consolidate their central nodes. The common denominator is, again, the person. For the sake of brevity, we stop the depiction here. In theory, an economy of the O-I fusion paradigm can feature as many such personal wizard architectures as it has persons; and each is a virtual configuration of the societal cyber-infrastructure. All these configurations may interact and join. Needless to say, these virtual configurations run concurrently on the same cyber-infrastructure and tap (use, not consume) into the same digital resources.

We submit that the person-centered view best describes some emerging trends on the Web, including the convergence of social networking and e-commerce/e-business, and the combination and consolidation of business designs on the Web (see Chapter 5). From the perspective of the book, it actually represents a basic philosophy of the service scaling theory. The cocreation IS design methodology of Chapter 6 is a proof. In fact, for purpose of design, this philosophy can be considered a top-level design principle in the sense that the whole economy is a societal virtual enterprise (or a service system). To the extent that this notion is relevant, a top down recursive application of the philosophy from the whole economy down to industries and enterprises can shed light on design objectives for economic institutions, policies, meta-enterprises, enterprises, and cocreation IS. Conversely, a bottom up pursuit to apply it to enterprise and extended enterprises promises to reveal possible business strategies of collaboration. Although our presentation of the person-centered view may be far-fetched, its empirical evidence is not. All the practices of "my" homepage and iPod reveal a real recognition of the power of personalization. The difference is only that current practices are limited.

9.3 A Look on the Bright Side

The book is about a design science: a new service scaling and transformation theory for the knowledge economy. The overarching concept is simple and its development straightforward: service is defined to be value cocreation between customer and provider in its intellectual nature. From cocreation comes three worldviews: value to persons, value to organizations, and value to society. Scaling cocreation is the means to expand value and cocreation populations are the scope of scaling. Transformation arises from extending cocreation to other sectors of the economy, and results from turning population-oriented cocreation into a common mode of production for economic activities. The design science is then concerned with the systems and methods of population-oriented cocreation. All details follow this simple concept.

The theory may be wrong: it may be wrong in its internal logic and formulation; it may be wrong in its relevance to the knowledge economy; or it may be wrong in its conviction that the knowledge economy is the future. In fact, the knowledge economy may be illusionary for humankind in the longer term. We have worked hard to assure its logical consistency and practical relevancy, so as to establish its internal validity (provability, correctness, and accuracy). We have also worked hard to corroborate the theory with empirical evidence that we have observed over the past decades, to establish its external validity. But we have no way to ascertain whether we are right in terms of humankind, let alone for the future.

Many things can go wrong in our world and in the future. Many factors can make the basic premises of the theory appear naïve and inappropriate. However, if we must speculate, we would rather speculate on the bright side and put faith into human nature. When much of the "dark side" — or the dark energy of the world, is removed from consideration, or at least assumed to succumb to reason, then we have to take the possibility seriously that we may be right. The service scaling and transformation theory does not take away much from the proven results in the field — it only attempts to add to them.

It does not require much artificial sacrifice to make way for its application — it only rides on the waves that are already in motion. Failure may be painful and costly to the beholder, but the failed application of the theory would not cause harm to others — it would mainly only cause disappointment of attempting some good deed that failed.

Consider the cost: Fundamentally, DCS requires materials to build and energy to operate; but it should only be at a level much less than many traditional industries and products. To society, DCS creates small world phenomena, which may imply elitism. However, the (opinion) leaders so emerged are natural and merit-based, and hence may actually conform to the ideal of a more open, liberal, and equitable society. On balance, DCS is a more fluid and level playing field for everyone than most other massive economic platforms. It is also consistent with promoting civil awareness and participation, including helping conservation and direct democracy. Therefore, the service scaling and transformation theory seems benign and promising for supporting sustainability, equitability, and advancement of our global economy. That is, the theory seems to be consistent with the benevolence of humankind. This book humbly presents it with this conclusion.

References

Adams, J. (2000). *Risk*, 2nd Ed. London, UK: Routledge.

Akyildiz, I. F., Su, W., Sankarasubramaniam, Y. and Cayirci, E. (2002). Wireless Sensor Networks: A Survey. *Computer Networks*, Vol. 38, pp. 393–422.

Alter, S. (2006). *The Work System Method: Connecting People, Processes, and IT for Business Results*. Larkspur, CA: Work Systems Press.

Anderson, J. A., Narus, J. A. and van Rossum, W. (2006). Customer Value Propositions in Business Markets. *Harvard Business Review*, March 2006, pp. 91–99.

Argote, L. (2005). *Organizational Learning: Creating, Retaining and Transferring Knowledge*. New York, NY: Springer.

Babin, G. and Hsu, C. (1996). Decomposition of Knowledge for Concurrent Processing. *IEEE Transactions on Knowledge and Data Engineering*, Vol. 8, No. 5, pp. 758–772.

Baker, A. (1998). A Survey of Factory Control Algorithms That Can Be Implemented in a Multi-Agent Hierarchy: Dispatching, Scheduling, and Pull. *Journal of Manufacturing Systems*, Vol. 17, No. 4, pp. 297–320.

Becker, G. S. (1971). *Economic Theory*. New York: Alfred A. Knopf.

Becker, G. S. (1990). *The Economic Approach to Human Behavior*, 2nd Ed. University of Chicago Press. Chicago, IL.

Beinhocker, E. D. (2006). *The Origin of Wealth: Evolution, Complexity, and the Radical Remaking of Economics*. Cambridge, MA: Harvard Business School Press.

Berger, P. L. and Luckmann, T. (1967). *The Social Construction of Reality: A Treatise in the Sociology of Knowledge*. New York, NY: Anchor.

Betancourt, R. and Gautschi, D. A. (1998). Distribution Services and Economic Power in a Channel. *Journal of Retailing*, Vol. 74, No. 1, pp. 37–60.

Bitner, M. and Brown, S. (2006). The Evolution and Discovery of Services Science in Business Schools. *Communications of the ACM*, July 2006, pp. 73–78.

Blass, T. (2004). *The Man Who Shocked the World: The Life and Legacy of Stanley Milgram*. New York: Basic Books.

Boisot, M. H. (2002). *Knowledge Assets: Securing Competitive Advantage in the Information Economy*. Oxford, UK: Oxford University Press.

Bonabeau, E. (2001). Agent-Based Modeling: Methods and Techniques for Simulating Human Systems. *Proceedings of the National Academy of Sciences*, Vol. 99, Spl 3, pp. 7280–7287.

Boonjing, V. and Hsu, C. (2006). A Feasible Approach to Natural Language Database Query. *International Journal of Artificial Intelligence Tools*, Vol. 15, No. 2, pp. 323–330.

Bouziane, M. and Hsu, C. (1997). A Rulebase Management System Using Conceptual Modeling. *J. Artificial Intelligence Tools*, Vol. 6, No. 1, March 1997, pp. 37–61.

Bradley, S. P., Hausman, J. A. and Nolan, R. L. (eds.) (1993). *Globalization, Technology, and Competition: The Fusion of Computers and Telecommunications in the 1990's*. Boston, MA: Harvard Business Press.

Braumandl, R., Keidl, M., Kemper, A., Kossmann, D., Kreutz, A., Seltzsam, S. and Stocker, K. (2001). Object Globe: Ubiquitous Query Processing on the Internet. *The VLDB Journal*, Vol. 10, pp. 48–71.

Buchanan, M. (2007). *The Social Atom: Why the Rich Get Richer, the Cheaters Get Caught, and Your Neighbor Usually Looks Like You*. NY: St. Martin's Press.

Carley, K. (1999). *Organizational Change and the Digital Economy: A Computational Organization Science Perspective*. Cambridge, MA: MIT Press.

Carothers, C. D., Bauer, D. and Pearce, S. (2002). ROSS: A High-Performance, Low Memory, Modular Time Warp System. *Journal of Parallel and Distributed Systems*.

Chan, W. K. V. and Schruben, L. W. Optimization Models of Discrete-Event System Dynamics. To appear in *Operations Research*.

Charnes, A. and Cooper, W. W. (1961). *Management Models and Industrial Applications of Linear Programming*, Vols. 1 and 2. New York: John Wiley and Sons.

Charnes, A., Cooper, W. W., Gorr, W. L., Hsu, C. and von Rabenau, B. (1986). Emergency Government Interventions: Case Study of Natural Gas Shortages. *Management Science*, Vol. 32, No. 10, pp. 1242–1258.

Chase, R. B., Jacobs, F. R. and Aquilano, N. J. (2004). *Operations Management for Competitive Advantage*, Instructor's Ed., 10th Ed. New York, NY: McGraw Hill Irwin.

Checkland, P. and Holwell, S. (2005). *Information, Systems, and Information Systems: Making Sense of the Field*, 2nd Ed. Chichester, UK: Wiley.

Cherbakov, L., Galambos, G., Harishanka, R., Kalyana, S. and Rackham, G. (2005). Impact of Service Orientation at the Business Level. *Special Issue on Service-Oriented Architecture of IBM Systems Journal*, Vol. 44, No. 4, pp. 653–668.

Cheung, W. and Hsu, C. (1996). The Model-Assisted Global Query System for Multiple Databases in Distributed Enterprises. *ACM Transactions on Information Systems*, Vol. 14, No. 4, pp. 421–470.

Chesbrough, H. and Spohrer, J. (2006). A Research Manifesto for Services Science. *Communications of the ACM.*

Clearwater, S. H. (ed.) (1996). *Market-Based Control: A Paradigm for Distributed Resource Allocation*. River Edge, NJ: World Scientific Publishing.

Cohen, L. and Young, A. (2006). *Multisourcing: Moving Beyond Outsourcing to Achieve Growth and Agility*. Boston, MA: Harvard Business School Press.

Dausch, M. and Hsu, C. (2006). Engineering Service Products: The Case of Mass-Customizing Service Agreements for Heavy Equipment Industry. *International Journal of Service Technology and Management*, Vol. 7, No. 1, pp. 32–51.

Davis, M. M. and Heineke, J. (2005). *Operations Management: Integrating Manufacturing and Services*, 5th Ed. Boston, MA: McGraw-Hill Irwin.

Davenport, T. (2005). The Coming Commoditization of Processes. *Harvard Business Review*, June 2005.

Demers, A., List, G. F., Wallace, W. A., Lee, E. and Wojtowicz, J. (2006). Transportation Research Record: Probes as Path Seekers. *Journal of the Transportation Research Board*, No. 1944, pp. 107–114. Washington, DC: TRB, National Research Council.

Dhar, V. and Dundararajan, A. (2007). Information Technology in Business: A Blueprint for Education and Research. *Information Systems Research*, Vol. 18, No. 2, pp. 125–141.

Dietrich, B. and Harrison, T. (2006). Service Science: Serving the Services. *OR/MS Today*, June 2006.

Dixit, A. K. (2004). *Lawlessness and Economics: Alternative Models of Governance*. Princeton, NJ: Princeton University Press.

Erl, T. (2005). *Service-Oriented Architecture: Concepts, Technology, and Design.* Upper Saddle River, NJ: Prentice-Hall.

Fagin, R., Ronald, J., Halpern, Y., Moses, Y. and Vardi, M. Y. (2003). *Reasoning About Knowledge.* Cambridge, MA: MIT Press.

Fitzsimmons, J. A. and Fitzsimmons, M. J. (2007). *Service Management: Operations, Strategy, Information Technology,* 6th Ed. New York, NY: McGraw-Hill Irwin.

Friedman, M. (1976). *Price Theory.* Chicago: Aldine Publishing.

Gandforoush, P., Huang, P. Y. and Moore, L. J. (1992). Multi-project, Multi-criteria Evaluation and Selection Model for R&D Management. In *Management of R&D and Engineering,* D. F. Kocaoglu (ed.), pp. 89–100. Elsevier Science Publishers.

Glushko, R. and McGrath, T. (2005). *Document Engineering: Analyzing and Designing Documents for Business Informatics and Web Services.* Cambridge, MA: MIT Press.

Glushko, R., Tenenbaum, J. and Meltzer, B. (1999). An XML Framework for Agent-Based E-commerce. *Communications of the ACM,* Vol. 42, No. 3, pp. 106–114.

Gotts, N. M., Polhill, J. G. and Law, A. N. R. (2003). Agent-Based Simulation in the Study of Social Dilemmas. *The Artificial Intelligence Review,* Vol. 19, No. 1, p. 3.

Grasman, S. E. (2006). Dynamic Approach to Strategic and Operational Multimodal Routing Decisions. *International Journal of Logistics Systems and Management,* Vol. 2, No. 1, pp. 96–106.

Gourdin, K. N. (2006). *Global Logistics Management: A Competitive Advantage for the 21st Century.* Blackwell Publishing.

Gutek, B. A. (1995). *The Dynamics of Service: Reflections on the Changing Nature of Customer/Provider Interactions.* San Francico, CA: Jossey-Bass Publishers.

Halevy, A. Y., Ives, Z. G., Madhavan, J. and Mork, P. (2004). The Piazza Peer Data Management System. *IEEE Transactions on Knowledge and Data Engineering,* Vol. 16, No. 7, pp. 787–798.

Hsu, C. (1996). *Enterprise Integration and Modeling: The Metadatabase Approach.* Lowell, MA: Kluwer Scientific Publishers.

Hsu, C. (ed.) (2007). Service Enterprise Integration: An Enterprise Engineering Perspective. MA: Springer Scientific Publishers.

Hsu, C., Bouziane, M., Rattner, L. and Yee, L. (1991). Information Resources Management in Heterogeneous Distributed Environments:

A Metadatabase Approach. *IEEE Transactions on Software Engineering*, Vol. 17, No. 6, pp. 604–625.

Hsu, C., Tao, Y., Bouziane, M. and Babin, G. (1993). Paradigm Translations in Integrating Manufacturing Information Using a Meta-Model. *Journal of Information Systems Engineering*, Vol. 1, pp. 325–352.

Hsu, C. and Wallace, W. A. (1993). Model Representation in Information Resources Management. In *Creative and Innovative Approaches to the Science of Management*, Y. Ijiri (ed.), pp. 135–158. Westport: Quorum Books.

Hsu, C. and Wallace, W. A. (2007). An Industrial Network Flow Information Integration Model for Supply Chain Management and Intelligent Transportation. *Enterprise Information Systems*, Vol. 1, No. 3, pp. 327–351.

Hsu, C. and Pant, S. (2000). *Innovative Planning for Electronic Commerce and Internet Enterprises: A Reference Model*. Lowell, MA: Kluwer Academic Publishers.

Hsu, C., Carothers, C. and Levermore, D. (2006). A Market Mechanism for Participatory Global Query: A First Step of Enterprise Resource Allocation. *Information Technology and Management*, Vol. 7, No. 2, pp. 71–89.

Hsu, C., Levermore, D., Carothers, C. and Babin, G. (2007). Enterprises Collaboration: On Demand Information Exchange Using Enterprise Databases, Sensor Networks, and RFID Chips. *IEEE Transactions on Systems, Man, and Cybernetics, Part A*, Vol. 37, No. 4, pp. 519–532.

Hsu, C. (2007). Models of Cyber-Infrastructure-Based Enterprises and Their Engineering. In *Service Enterprise Integration: And Enterprise Engineering Perspective*, C. Hsu (ed.), pp. 209–243. Boston, MA: Springer Scientific Publishers.

Hsu, C. and Spohrer, J. Improving Service Quality and Productivity: Exploring the Digital Connections Scaling Model. To appear in *International Journal of Service Technoogy and Management*.

Hugos, M. H. (2006). *Essentials of Supply Chain Management*. John Wiley and Sons.

Iansiti, M. and Levien, R. (2004). Strategy as Ecology. *Harvard Business Review*, March 2004.

IfM and IBM (2007). *Succeeding through Service Innovation: A Discussion Paper*. Cambridge, United Kingdom: University of Cambridge Institute for Manufacturing.

Kalfoglou, Y. and Schorlemmer, M. (2003). Ontology Mapping: The State of the Art. *The Knowledge Engineering Review*, Vol. 18, No. 1, pp. 1–31.

Kauffman, S. A. (1993). *The Origins of Order: Self-Organization and Selection in Evolution*. Cambridge, UK: Oxford University Press.

Kelton, W. D., Sadowski, R. P. and Sturrock, D. T. (2007). *Simulation with Arena*, 4th Ed. New York, NY: McGraw-Hill.

Kim, W. (ed.) (1995). *Modern Database Systems*. Readings, MA: Addison Wesley.

Koh, C. E., Kim, H. J. and Kim, E. Y. (2006). The Impact of RFID in Retail Industry: Issues and Critical Success Factors. *Journal of Shopping Center Research*, Vol. 25.

Krishnamurthy, A. (2007). From Just in Time Manufacturing to On-Demand Services. In *Service Enterprise Integration: An Enterprise System Engineering Perspective*, C. Hsu (ed.), pp. 1–37. Norwell, MA: Springer Scientific Publishers.

Lei, L., Liu, S. G., Ruszczynski, A. and Park, S. J. (2006). On the Integrated Production, Inventory, and Distribution Routing Problem. *IIE Transactions*, Vol. 38, No. 11, pp. 995–970.

Levermore, D. and Hsu, C. (2006). *Enterprise Collaboration: On-Demand Information Exchange for Extended Enterprises*. Norwell, MA: Springer Scientific Publishers.

Levinson, M. (2006). *The Box: How the Shipping Container Made the World Smaller and the World Economy Bigger*. Princeton, NJ: Princeton University Press.

Litwin, W., Mark, L. and Roussopoulos, N. (1990). Interoperability of Multiple Autonomous Databases. *ACM Computing Survey*, Vol. 22, No. 3, pp. 267–293.

Lovelock, C. (2007). *Services Marketing: People, Technology, Strategy*, 6th Ed. Upper Saddle River, NJ: Prentice Hall.

Lovelock, C. and Gummesson, E. (2004). Whither Service Marketing? In Search of a New Paradigm and Fresh Perspectives. *Journal of Service Research*, Vol. 7, No. 1, pp. 20–41.

Lusch, R. and Vargo, S. (eds.) (2006). *The Service-Dominant Logic of Marketing: Dialog, Debate and Directions*. Armonk, New York: M. E. Sharpe.

Maglio, P. P., Kreulen, J., Srinivasan, S. and Spohrer, J. (2006). Service Systems, Service Scientists, SSME, and Innovation. *Communications of the ACM*, Vol. 49, No. 7, pp. 81–85.

McKenna, C. D. (2006). *The World's Newest Profession: Management Consulting in the Twentieth Century*. In Cambridge Studies in the

Emergence of Global Enterprise Series. Cambridge, UK: Cambridge University Press.

McKinnon, A. C. (2006). A Review of European Truck Tolling Schemes and Assessment of Their Possible Impact on Logistics Systems. *International Journal of Logistics*, Vol. 9, No. 3, pp. 191–205.

Mentzer, J. T., Myers, M. B. and Stank, T. P. (eds.) (2006). *Handbook of Global Logistics and Supply Chain Management*. Sage Publishers.

Miller, J. H. and Page, S. E. (2007). *Complex Adaptive Systems: An Introduction to Computational Models of Social Life*. Princeton, NY: Princeton University Press.

Von Mises, L. (1998). *Human Action: A Treatise on Economics* (Scholars Ed.). Auburn, Alabama: Ludwig Von Mises Institute.

Moin, N. H. and Salhi, S. (2006). Inventory Routing Problems: A Logistical Overview. J. Operational Research Society Advance Online Publication. Available at http://www.palgrave-journals.com

Murphy, W., Pal, N. and Viniotis, I. (2007). Summary of Position Papers. *Conference on Service Sciences, Management, and Engineering*, 5–7 October 2007. Palisades, NY JBM Corp. Available at http://www.rendez.org/ssme-200610-digests/

Nayak, N., Linehan, M., Nigam, A., Marston, D., Wu, F., Boullery, D., White, L., Nandi, P. and Sanz, J. (2007). *Core Business Architecture for a Service-Oriented Enterprise*. Yorktown IBM Corp.

Nigam and Caswell, N. S. (2003). Business Artifacts: An Approach to Operational Specification. *IBM Systems Journal*, Vol. 42, No. 3.

Normann, R. (2001). *Reframing Business: When the Map Changes the Landscape*. New York: John Wiley & Sons.

North, D. C. (2005). *Understanding the Process of Economic Change*. Princeton, NJ: Princeton University Press.

Oral, M., Kettani, O. and Lang, P. (1991). A Methodology for Collective Evaluation and Selection of Industrial R&D Projects. *Management Science*, Vol. 37, No. 7, pp. 971–885.

Palmisano, S. F. (2006). The Globally Integrated Enterprise. *Foreign Affairs*, Vol. 85, No. 3, pp. 127–136.

Parsons, C. H. (2003). *I-87 Multimodal Corridor Study: Long List of Improvement Concepts*. New York: Parsons, Inc.

Prietula, M. J., Carley, K. M. and Gasser, L. G. (1998). *Simulating Organizations: Computational Models of Institutions and Groups*. Menlo Park, CA: AAAI Press/MIT Press.

Roberts, J. (2004). *The Modern Firm: Organizational Design for Performance and Growth*. Oxford, UK: Oxford University Press.

Rust, R., Zeithaml, V. and Lemon, K. (2000). *Driving Customer Equity: How Customer Lifetime Value is Reshaping Corporate Strategy*. Glencoe, Illinois: Free Press.

Sandholm, T. (2003). Making Markets and Democracy Work: A Story of Incentives and Computing. IJCAI-03 Computers and Thought Award Talk Abstract.

Sampson, S. E. (2001). *Understanding Service Businesses: Applying Principles of the Unified Services Theory*, 2nd Ed. Chichester, New Sussex: Wiley.

Sanz, J., Becker, V., Cappi, J., Chandra, A., Kramer, J., Lyman, K., Nayak, N., Pesce, P., Terrizzano, I. and Vergo, J. (2007). Business Services and Business Componentization: New Gaps Between Business and IT. *Proceedings of the IEEE International Conference on Service-Oriented Computing and Applications*.

Schmidt, R. and Freeland, J. (1992). Recent Progress in Modeling R&D Project Selection Processes. *IEEE Transactions on Engineering Management*, Vol. 39, No. 2, pp. 189–201.

Sen, A. (2000). *Development As Freedom*. New York, NY: Anchor/Random House.

SETI@Home, http://setiathome.berkeley.edu.

Sheth, A. P. and Larson, J. A. (1990). Federated Database Systems for Managing Distributed and Autonomous Databases. *ACM Computing Survey*, Vol. 22, No. 3, pp. 183–236.

Shostack, G. L. (1982). How to Design a Service. *European Journal of Marketing*, Vol. 16, No. 1, pp. 49–63.

Simon, H. A. (1997). *Administrative Behavior: A Study of Decision-Making Processes in Administrative Organizations*, 2nd Ed. New York, NY: Free Press.

Solow, R. (2000). *Growth Theory: An Exposition*, 2nd Ed. New York: Oxford University Press.

Sowa, J. F. (1984). *Conceptual Structures: Information Processing in Mind and Machine*. Readings, MA: Addison Wesley.

Spohrer, J., Vargo, S. L., Maglio, P. and Caswell, N. (2008). The Service System is the Basic Abstraction of Service Science. *Proc. Hawaiian International Conference on Systems Sciences*, 2008.

Spohrer, J. and Kwan, S. K. (2007). Service Science, Management, Engineering, and Design: Outline & References. *Proceedings of the IEEE*.

Spohrer, J., Maglio, P. P., Bailey, J. and Gruhl, D. (2007). Towards a Science of Service Systems. *Computer*, Vol. 40, No. 1, pp. 71–77.

Spohrer, J. and Maglio, P. P. (2008). The Emergence of Service Science: Toward Systematic Service Innovations to Accelerate Co-creation of Value. *Production and Operations Management*.

Spohrer, J. and Riecken, D. (eds.) (2006). Special Issue on Service Science, *Communications of the ACM*, Vol. 49, No. 7, July 2006, pp. 30–87.

Spohrer, J., Maglio, P. M., McDavid, D. and Cortada, J. (2006). Convergence and Coevolution: Towards a Services Science. In *Nanotechnology: Societal Implications: Maximising Benefits for Humanity and Nanotechnology and Society*, M. C. Roco and W. S. Bainbridge (eds.). New York, NY: Springer.

Sterman, J. D. (2008). *Business Dynamics: Systems Thinking and Modeling for a Complex World*. Boston, MA: Irwin McGraw-Hill.

Stonebraker, M., Aoki, P., Pfeffer, A., Sah, A., Sidell, J., Staelin C. and Yu, A. (1996). Mariposa: A Wide Area Distributed Database System. *International Journal on Very Large Databases*, Vol. 5, No. 1, pp. 48–63.

Swaminathan, J., Smith S. F. and Sadeh, N. (1998). Modeling Supply Chain Dynamics: A Multi-Agent Approach. *Decision Sciences*, Vol. 29, pp. 607–632.

Tao, L. (2001). Shifting Paradigms with the Application Service Provider Model. *IEEE Computer*, Vol. 34, No. 10, pp. 32–39.

Teboul, J. (2006). *Service Is Front Stage: Positioning Services for Value Advantage*. Palgrave MacMillan: INSEAD Business Press.

Tien, J. and Berg, D. (2006). On Services Research and Education. *Journal of Systems Science and Systems Engineering*, Vol. 15, No. 3, pp. 257–283.

Tien, J. (2007). Services Innovation: Decision Attributes, Innovation Enablers, and Innovation Drivers. In *Service Enterprise Integration: And Enterprise Engineering Perspective*, C. Hsu (ed.), pp. 39–76. Boston, MA: Springer Scientific Publishers.

Tien, J., Krishnamurthy, A. and Yasar, A. (2004). Towards Real-Time Customized Management of Supply and Demand Chains. *Journal of Systems Science and Systems Engineering*, Vol. 13, No. 3, pp. 129–151.

UN/CEFACT (2003). *Core Components Technical Specification*, Version 2.01. New York: United Nations Center for Trade Facilitation and Electronic Business.

Watts, D. J. (2003). *Six Degrees: The Science of a Connected Age*. New York, NY: W.W. Norton & Company.

Watts, D. J. and Strogatz, S. H. (1998). Collective Dynamics of 'Small-World' Networks. *Nature*, Vol. 393, No. 6684, pp. 440–442.

Weinberg, G. M. (2001). *An Introduction to General Systems Thinking*, Silver Anniversary Ed. New York: Dorset House Publishing.

Williamson, O. E. (1985). *The Economic Institutions of Capitalism*. New York: The Free Press.

Williamson, O. E. (1999). *The Mechanisms of Governance*. Oxford, UK: Oxford University Press.

Womack, J. P. and Jones, D. T. (2005). *Lean Solutions: How Companies and Customers Can Create Value and Wealth Together*. New York, NY: Free Press.

Wooldridge, M. (2002). *An Introduction to MultiAgent Systems*. Chichester, UK: Wiley.

Young, H. P. (2001). *Individual Strategy and Social Structure: An Evolutionary Theory of Institutions*, 2nd Ed. Princeton, NJ: Princeton University Press.

Yourdon, E. (1989). *Modern Structured Analysis*. Englewood Cliffs, NJ: Yourdon Press.

Zhao, J. L., Hsu, C., Jain, H. J., Spohrer, J., Taniru, M. and Wang, H. J. (2008). ICIS 2007 Panel Report: Bridging Service Computing and Service Management: How MIS Contributes to Service Orientation? *Communications of the Association for Information Systems*, Vol. 22, pp. 413–428.

Zeithaml, V. A., Bitner, M. J. and Gremler, D. D. (2006). *Services Marketing: Integrating Customer Focus Across the Firm*, 4th Ed. New York, NY: McGraw-Hill Irwin.

Zhang, L. J. (2007). *Modern Technologies in Web Services Research*. Hershey, PA: IGI Publishing.

Index